TEACHINGS OF PRESIDENTS OF THE CHURCH
SPENCER W. KIMBALL

D0181170

Published by
The Church of Jesus Christ of Latter-day Saints
Salt Lake City, Utah

Your comments and suggestions about this book would be appreciated. Please submit them to Curriculum Development, 50 East North Temple Street, Room 2420, Salt Lake City, UT 84150-3220 USA. E-mail: cur-development@ldschurch.org

Please list your name, address, ward, and stake. Be sure to give the title of the book. Then offer your comments and suggestions about the book's strengths and areas of potential improvement.

Contents

Introduction

The First Presidency and the Quorum of the Twelve Apostles have established the *Teachings of Presidents of the Church* series to help you deepen your understanding of the restored gospel and draw closer to the Lord through the teachings of latter-day prophets. As the Church adds volumes to this series, you will build a collection of gospel reference books for your home.

This book features the teachings of President Spencer W. Kimball, who served as President of The Church of Jesus Christ of Latter-day Saints from December 30, 1973, to November 5, 1985.

Personal Study

As you study the teachings of President Kimball, seek the inspiration of the Spirit. Remember Nephi's promise: "He that diligently seeketh shall find; and the mysteries of God shall be unfolded unto them, by the power of the Holy Ghost" (1 Nephi 10:19). Begin your study with prayer, and continue to pray in your heart as you read.

At the end of each chapter, you will find questions and scripture references that will help you understand and apply President Kimball's teachings. Consider reviewing them before you read the chapter.

Also consider the following guidelines:

- Look for key words and phrases. If you find a word you do not understand, use a dictionary or another source to better understand its meaning.

- Think about the meaning of President Kimball's teachings. You may want to mark individual words and sentences that touch your mind and heart.

- Reflect on experiences you have had that relate to President Kimball's teachings.

- Ponder how President Kimball's teachings apply to you. Think about how the teachings relate to concerns or questions you have. Decide what you will do as a result of what you have learned.

Teaching from This Book

This book can be used to teach at home or at church. The following guidelines will help you:

Focus on President Kimball's Words and the Scriptures

The Lord has commanded that we teach "none other things than that which the prophets and apostles have written, and that which is taught [us] by the Comforter through the prayer of faith" (D&C 52:9).

Your assignment is to help others understand and apply the gospel through President Kimball's teachings and the scriptures. Do not set this book aside or prepare lessons from other materials. Dedicate a significant portion of the lesson to reading President Kimball's teachings in this book and discussing their meaning and application.

Encourage participants to study the chapters before Sunday meetings and to bring the book to church. When they do so, they will be better prepared to participate and to edify one another.

Seek the Guidance of the Holy Ghost

As you pray for help and prepare diligently, the Holy Ghost will guide your efforts. He will help you emphasize the portions of each chapter that will encourage others to understand and apply the gospel.

When you teach, pray in your heart that the power of the Spirit will accompany your words and the class discussions. Nephi said, "When a man speaketh by the power of the Holy Ghost the power of the Holy Ghost carrieth it unto the hearts of the children of men" (2 Nephi 33:1; see also D&C 50:13–22).

Prepare to Teach

The chapters in this book have been organized to help you prepare to teach. Also consider the following guidelines:

1. *Study the chapter.* Prayerfully study the chapter to become confident in your understanding of President Kimball's teachings. You will teach with greater sincerity and power when his words have influenced you personally (see D&C 11:21). As you read, keep in mind the needs of those you teach. You may want to mark portions that you feel will help them. Note the chapter's bold subheadings. They outline the main points in the chapter.

2. *Decide which portions to use.* Each chapter contains more than you will be able to teach in one lesson. Rather than try to cover the entire chapter, prayerfully select portions that you feel will be most helpful for those you teach.

3. *Decide how to introduce the lesson.* To spark interest at the beginning of the lesson, you might share a personal experience or ask participants to read a story from the beginning of the chapter or look at a picture in the chapter. Then you could ask, "What does this story (or picture) teach about the topic of the chapter?" Other options for beginning a lesson include reading a scripture or a quotation from the chapter or singing a hymn. Another helpful idea is to let participants know what the main points of the lesson will be.

4. *Decide how to encourage discussion.* This is where you should spend most of the lesson time. Review the suggestions on conducting edifying discussions on pages viii–ix of this book. You might use questions from "Suggestions for Study and Teaching" at the end of the chapter. You may prepare some of your own. Ask questions that help those you are teaching:

   • Look for what is taught. These types of questions help participants find and become familiar with specific information in President Kimball's teachings. For example, after identifying a specific quotation, you could ask, "What are some of the key words or phrases in this quotation?" or "What is the topic of this quotation?"

   • Think about the meaning. These types of questions help participants better understand President Kimball's teachings. For example, "Why do you think this teaching is important?" or "What thoughts or feelings do you have about this quotation?" or "What does this teaching mean to you?"

- Share experiences. These questions encourage participants to relate what President Kimball said to something in their personal lives. For example, "What experiences have you had that relate to what President Kimball said?"

- Apply what is taught. These questions help participants think about ways they can live according to President Kimball's teachings. For example, "What is President Kimball encouraging us to do? In what ways can we apply what he said?"

5. *Decide how to conclude the lesson.* You may choose to quickly summarize the lesson or ask one or two participants to do so. As prompted by the Spirit, testify of the teachings you have discussed. You may also want to invite others to share their testimonies. Encourage those you teach to follow the promptings they have received from the Holy Ghost.

As you prepare to teach, you may want to look for ideas in *Teaching, No Greater Call* (36123), part B, chapters 14, 16, 28, and 29; or in the *Teaching Guidebook* (34595).

Conduct Edifying Discussions

The following guidelines will help you encourage and conduct edifying discussions:

- Seek the guidance of the Holy Ghost. He may prompt you to ask certain questions or to include certain people in the discussion.

- Help participants focus on President Kimball's teachings. Have them read his words to generate discussion and to answer questions. Redirect discussions that begin to stray from the topic or that are speculative or contentious.

- As appropriate, share experiences that relate to the teachings in the chapter.

- Encourage participants to share their thoughts, ask questions, and teach one another (see D&C 88:122). For example, you could ask them to comment on what others have said, or you could direct one question to several participants.

- Do not be afraid of silence after you ask a question. Often those you teach need time to think or to look in their books before they share ideas, testimonies, and experiences.

- Listen sincerely, and seek to understand everyone's comments. Express gratitude for their participation.

- When participants share several ideas, consider listing the ideas on the chalkboard or asking someone else to do so.

- Look for different ways to include participants in the discussion. For example, you might have them discuss questions in small groups or with the person sitting next to them.

- Consider contacting one or two participants in advance. Ask them to come to class ready to answer one of the questions you have prepared.

- Do not end a good discussion just because you want to cover all the material you have prepared. What matters most is that participants feel the influence of the Spirit and grow in their commitment to live the gospel.

Information about the Sources Quoted in This Book

The teachings of President Kimball in this book are direct quotations from a variety of sources. These excerpts have retained the punctuation, spelling, capitalization, and paragraphing of the original sources unless editorial or typographic changes have been necessary to improve readability. For this reason, you may notice minor inconsistencies in the text.

Also, President Kimball often used terms such as *men, man,* or *mankind* to refer to all people, both male and female. He frequently used the pronoun *he* to refer to both genders. This was common in the language of his era. Despite the differences between these language conventions and more current usage, President Kimball's teachings apply to both women and men.

Historical Summary

This book is not a history; rather, it is a compilation of gospel principles as taught by President Spencer W. Kimball. The following chronology provides a brief historical background of his life and a framework for his teachings. It omits many significant events in both Church and secular history. It also omits many important events in President Kimball's personal life, such as the births of his children.

1895, March 28	Spencer Woolley Kimball is born in Salt Lake City, Utah, to Andrew Kimball and Olive Woolley Kimball.
1898, May	Moves with his family to Thatcher, Arizona, where his father presides over the St. Joseph Stake for the next 26 years.
1906, October 18	His mother dies.
1907, June	His father marries Josephine Cluff.
1914, October	Begins service as a full-time missionary in the Central States Mission in the United States. He had been called to the Swiss-German Mission but was unable to go because of World War I.
1916, December	Released from his full-time mission. Soon after, attends the University of Arizona.
1917, November 16	Marries Camilla Eyring.
1918	Called to be stake clerk of the St. Joseph Stake. Enters the banking business as a clerk and teller.
1923	Joins the Rotary Club, a service organization in which he will participate for the

	next 20 years, including as a district governor.
1924, August 31	His father dies. About a week later, as part of the reorganization of the stake presidency, Spencer is called as second counselor. He is ordained a high priest by President Heber J. Grant, the seventh President of the Church.
1927	Becomes president-manager of the Kimball-Greenhalgh Realty and Insurance Company.
1938, February 20	Called as president of the Mount Graham Stake.
1943, October 7	Ordained an Apostle by President Heber J. Grant.
1948	Suffers and recovers from a severe heart ailment.
1950	Loses his voice through a serious throat ailment. His voice is restored following a priesthood blessing.
1957	Undergoes an operation for cancer of the throat; one and one-half vocal cords are removed.
1969	*The Miracle of Forgiveness* is published.
1970	Becomes Acting President of the Quorum of the Twelve Apostles.
1972, April 12	Undergoes open-heart surgery.
1972, July 7	Becomes President of the Quorum of the Twelve Apostles.
1973, December 26	President Harold B. Lee dies.

1973, December 30	Becomes President of The Church of Jesus Christ of Latter-day Saints, with President N. Eldon Tanner as First Counselor and President Marion G. Romney as Second Counselor in the First Presidency.
1974, November 19	Dedicates the Washington D.C. Temple.
1975, October 3	Begins the reconstitution of the First Quorum of the Seventy.
1976	Oversees the addition of two revelations to the Pearl of Great Price. These revelations are later included in the Doctrine and Covenants as sections 137 and 138.
1977, August 24	Dedicates Poland for future Church work—the first visit of a President of the Church behind what was then known as the Iron Curtain.
1978, June 8	With his counselors in the First Presidency, issues a letter announcing a revelation making all the blessings of the priesthood available to all worthy members, without regard for race or color.
1978, October 30	Dedicates the São Paulo Brazil Temple.
1979	Oversees the publication of the LDS edition of the King James Bible.
1979, October 24	Dedicates the Orson Hyde Memorial Garden in Jerusalem.
1980	Oversees the establishment of the consolidated meeting schedule, which places sacrament meeting, ward priesthood meetings, Relief Society meetings, Young Women classes, Sunday School, and Primary in a three-hour block on Sunday rather than scheduled throughout the week.

1980, October 27	Dedicates the Tokyo Japan Temple.
1980, November 17	Dedicates the Seattle Washington Temple.
1981	Oversees the publication of a new edition of the triple combination, with an updated footnote system and index.
1981, July 23	Calls President Gordon B. Hinckley to serve as an additional counselor in the First Presidency.
1981 to 1985	Oversees the dedications of 17 temples.
1982, October 3	A subtitle for the Book of Mormon is announced—"Another Testament of Jesus Christ."
1982, December 2	Reorganizes the First Presidency, with President Marion G. Romney as First Counselor and President Gordon B. Hinckley as Second Counselor.
1984	Area Presidencies are established.
1985, November 5	Dies in Salt Lake City, Utah.

The Life and Ministry of Spencer W. Kimball

During an autumn evening in the early 1900s, Orville Allen stopped by Andrew Kimball's home to deliver some pumpkins. As the two men unloaded the pumpkins, they overheard Andrew's son Spencer in the barn, singing as he milked the cows. Brother Allen remarked to Andrew, "Your boy must be happy." Andrew responded: "Yes, he is always happy. He is a clean and obedient boy and always minds what I ask him to do. I have dedicated him to the Lord and to His service. He will become a mighty man in the Church."[1]

Through years of preparation, Spencer did become a mighty man. The Lord "was not just preparing a businessman, nor a civic leader, nor a speaker, nor a poet, nor a musician, nor a teacher— though he would be all of these. He was preparing a father, a patriarch for his family, an apostle and prophet, and a president for His church."[2]

Heritage

Spencer W. Kimball's family had deep roots in the restored Church. His grandfathers on both sides were prominent in the early history of the latter-day work. Heber C. Kimball was called to the Quorum of the Twelve Apostles when it was organized in 1835. He later served as First Counselor to President Brigham Young for over two decades and was a faithful servant of the Lord throughout his ministry. Edwin D. Woolley, Spencer's grandfather on his mother's side, was a former Pennsylvania Quaker who embraced the gospel in the days of Joseph Smith. He was a respected bishop in the Salt Lake Valley. He also served from time to time as a manager of Brigham Young's personal business affairs. Bishop Woolley's concern for the needy and his unyielding commitment to the gospel were enduring legacies for his descendants.

Spencer's grandmother Ann Alice Gheen Kimball was "a faithful woman, . . . shy in society, tall and plain-faced, with a soft heart for the weak and sick."[3] Andrew Kimball was her third son. Spencer's other grandmother, Mary Ann Olpin Woolley, was from England and became the mother of eleven children, the sixth being named Olive.

Andrew Kimball married Olive Woolley on February 2, 1882, in Salt Lake City, where they made their home. About three years later, Andrew received a call to leave home and serve in the Indian Territory Mission, located in the present-day state of Oklahoma. After serving for two and a half years as a full-time missionary, he was then called to preside over the mission. The new calling allowed him to live at home, however, and so for the next 10 years he resided in Utah with his family while directing the mission through letters and trips to the area.

Andrew's 12 years of service in the Indian Territory Mission were soon followed by another calling, this time to settle in the Gila Valley of south-central Arizona. There he was to preside as stake president over the Latter-day Saint settlements of that region, which were organized as the St. Joseph Stake. In 1898, Andrew and Olive and their six children (including three-year-old Spencer) packed up their household goods and made the move 600 miles south from Salt Lake City.

Youth

Spencer Woolley Kimball was born on March 28, 1895, the sixth of Andrew and Olive Kimball's eleven children.

Recalling the Arizona landscape of his youth, he wrote, "It was an arid country, yet it was fruitful under the hands of determined laborers."[4] He further remembered: "We lived on a small farm on the south edge of Thatcher, Arizona. Our home was on the corner with open farm country south and east. Back from the home were the well, the pump, the windmill, a big wooden tank for our supply of water, the tool building, and a little farther back, a

Andrew and Olive Kimball in 1897 with their children (from left to right):
Ruth, Gordon, Alice, Clare, Spencer (on Andrew's lap), and Delbert.

very large woodpile. Then came the pigpens, corrals, haystacks, and the granary."[5]

Spencer learned important gospel lessons early from his parents. "I remember as a youth," he said, "walking with my mother up the dusty road to the bishop's house in a day when we often paid tithing from our animals and produce. As we walked, I said, 'Why do we take the eggs to the bishop?' She answered, 'Because they are tithing eggs and the bishop receives the tithing for Heavenly Father.' My mother then recounted how each evening when the eggs were brought in, the first one went into a small basket and the next nine went into a large basket."[6]

Andrew Kimball's example of dedicated service had a great influence on Spencer, who later said: "My first impressions of the labor of a stake president came from observing my own father. . . . I believe that father so ministered to his people that he fulfilled a blessing given him by President Joseph F. Smith, who promised that the people of the Gila Valley would 'seek unto him as children to a parent.' Although I am sure I did not then fully appreciate his example, the standard he set was one worthy of any stake president."[7]

The Kimball family lived modestly. "We didn't know we were poor," remembered Spencer. "We thought we were living pretty well."[8] Their clothes were homemade and hand-me-downs. Their meals were basic, consisting of meat and produce raised on their own property.

Spencer assisted with chores around the farm. "I used to pump the water by hand to water the garden," he recalled, "and also I learned to milk the cows, prune the fruit trees, mend the fences, and all the rest. I had two older brothers, who, I was convinced, took all the easy jobs and left me all the hard ones. But I don't complain; it made me strong."[9] Beginning when he was nine years old, Spencer memorized the Articles of Faith, the Ten Commandments, and most of the hymns from the Church hymnal while milking the cows and watering the horses each day.

When Spencer was 11, his mother died. This was one of the great trials of his early years. He wondered how the family could go on. "But I found then," he said, "as I have found out many times since, that one can endure almost anything."[10] In time, Andrew Kimball remarried, and Josephine Cluff became Spencer's stepmother. "Josie," as friends called her, could not fully take the place of Olive in Spencer's life, but her capable and patient ways added stability to the Kimball family.

During his youth, Spencer not only learned basic hard work in a rugged land but also picked up several skills that prepared him to be of greater service later in life. He learned to sing and lead music and was appointed stake chorister at age 15. Although he had fingers that he described as "short and chubby,"[11] he applied himself, learning to read music and play the piano. He improved until he was able to play the hymns and participate in a small orchestra. Years later, he alternated with Elder Harold B. Lee as accompanist for the weekly meetings of the Quorum of the Twelve Apostles.

Spencer started school a little later than most, as related in the following account: "Spencer's mother thought children were not mature enough for school until they were seven, so when

Young Spencer W. Kimball (left) with a boyhood friend, Clarence Naylor.

Spencer started he was a year behind the other children. . . . At noon he usually ran the three blocks from school to home to pump water for the animals, feed the pigs, and eat his lunch. One day his mother said, 'What are you doing home at recess? It's not noon yet.' He ran back to school in a panic and found his classmates already inside from the brief recess. Everyone laughed—except the teacher, who took that occasion to tell the class that Spencer was ahead of all the other students in the second grade and would be moved up to be with the children his own age."[12]

After finishing grade school, Spencer attended the Church-owned Gila Academy. There he earned consistently good grades, participated in sports, and was a school officer.

Spencer also grew in Church experience and had an almost perfect attendance record. Fulfilling priesthood assignments was a priority, as the following account illustrates: "As part of their job, the deacons hitched up horse and buggy each month before fast day and went house-to-house collecting offerings for the poor of the Church. Afterwards they took their gatherings to the bishop—bottles of fruit, flour, squash, honey, occasionally a half-dollar or so in loose change. So eager was Andrew to teach his boy his duty that nothing else interfered with Spencer's collection on that day. The Kimball horse and buggy was never too busy to be used for deacons quorum work. If the other boy assigned to collect with him didn't show up, Spencer went out alone and got the job done."[13]

In addition to his home, school, and Church responsibilities, Spencer worked as a secretary for his father. Andrew wrote many letters, averaging six a day. Spencer took dictation from him and then typed the letters.

These experiences from early in Spencer's life taught him the value of work, a lesson he applied and taught throughout his life. Years later as an Apostle in his 70s, he had occasional days when he felt physically exhausted. Of one such day he wrote: "I started out very miserable and found myself wondering if I could get through the day, but . . . I seemed to become intoxicated with my work and forgot myself and it was a good day."[14]

Missionary Service

In 1914, Spencer graduated from Gila Academy, expecting to enter the University of Arizona in the fall. During the graduation exercises, however, Andrew Kimball announced that Spencer was to be called on a mission.

In preparation for his mission, Spencer went to work in Globe, Arizona, as a dairy hand. This was his first experience living outside the Latter-day Saint settlements of the Gila Valley. He found that, without compromising his own standards, he could adapt to being around people whose standards did not entirely conform to his. He earned the respect of his co-workers. At the end of the summer, his cigar-smoking, non–Latter-day Saint boss threw a farewell party for Spencer and presented him with an engraved gold watch.

From October 1914 to December 1916, Spencer served as a full-time missionary in the Central States Mission, headquartered in Independence, Missouri. This was the same area where his father, his stepmother, and one of his older brothers had served.

Elder Kimball's full-time service in the mission field was a period of growth. He faced physical challenges. His mission president directed the elders to seek food and shelter from those they proselyted. As a result, Elder Kimball spent many uneasy nights in little shacks in the backwoods of Missouri, sharing the bed with fleas or bedbugs while mosquitoes buzzed around. There were many hungry days, and when food was offered, he ate whatever was placed before him.

Door-to-door contacting was hard work, with limited returns. An account is given of an unusual approach Elder Kimball once used:

"While tracting in St. Louis he noticed a piano through the partly opened door, and he said to the woman, who was in the act of shutting the door in his face, 'You have a nice-looking piano.'

"'We just bought it,' said the woman, hesitating.

"'It's a Kimball, isn't it? That's my name, too. I could play a song on it for you that you might like to hear.'

"Surprised, she answered, 'Surely, come in.'

"Sitting on the bench, Spencer played and sang, 'O, My Father.'

"So far as Spencer knew, she never joined the Church, but it was not because he had not tried."[15]

Spencer's mission reinforced what his upbringing in Arizona had already established: faith in the Lord, hard work, dedication, quiet service, and sacrifice.

Marriage and Family

In the summer of 1917, about seven months after Spencer Kimball returned home from his mission, he noticed an announcement in the local newspaper. Camilla Eyring, who had moved to the Gila Valley in 1912 with her family, would be teaching home economics at the Gila Academy. As Spencer read and reread the article, he determined that he would someday marry Camilla Eyring. By "coincidence," he met her waiting at the bus stop near the academy and struck up a conversation. He sat with

Camilla Eyring and Spencer W. Kimball near the time of their wedding.

her on the bus, where they continued to talk, and he received her permission to call on her.

Camilla's mother took a strong liking to the young Spencer Kimball. She invited him to dinner every time he was over to visit Camilla. And Brother Eyring, who was very strict regarding the quality of his daughters' suitors, raised no objection. After 31 days, Spencer had become a fixture at the Eyring household. The couple decided to marry, but their plans were affected by the ongoing World War I. Spencer was obligated to stay in Thatcher, Arizona, to await possible draft into the army, so they would not be able to make the long trip to a temple in Utah. They were married civilly on November 16, 1917, but looked forward to a temple sealing as soon as possible. That goal was realized the following June in the Salt Lake Temple.

Spencer and Camilla eventually had four children: three sons and a daughter (Spencer LeVan, Andrew Eyring, Edward Lawrence, and Olive Beth). As parents they provided an environment in which their children not only felt loved and supported but also entrusted to make individual decisions. One of their sons later recalled:

"When the children performed at school, Church or elsewhere, my parents were in attendance, even at some personal sacrifice. They always showed their interest and pride in us.

"In our family, there was a sense of association, not of ownership. Ultimate responsibility for our acts was on us. Our parents would encourage and guide, but not command."

This same son went on to say of his father:

"I know of no one more generous in spirit than my father. He is kindly and considerate, almost to a fault. Children tend to think of their parents as powerful authority figures, not subject to ordinary needs. But I know how much my father appreciates a sincere compliment or word of appreciation. And no expression of appreciation or affection counts quite as much as from his own family.

"I know there is nothing that gives him more satisfaction—after feeling that the Lord approves of his efforts—than to see his own family following his lead in trying to live righteously.

"If I had a choice by whom to be judged at the last day, there is no human being I would choose before my father."[16]

Professional Life, Church Callings, and Community Service

With Camilla at his side and the responsibilities of a family before him, Spencer began his professional life as a bank clerk. As the years passed, he moved from banking to life insurance and real estate development. The economic upheaval of the Great Depression (1929–39) hit Spencer's business interests hard, but the family was able to weather the adversity.

Spencer's father passed away in 1924, after having served as stake president for nearly three decades. When President Heber J. Grant, seventh President of the Church, subsequently reorganized the stake presidency, 29-year-old Spencer was called to serve as second counselor.

In addition to his family life, professional endeavors, and Church service, Spencer was an active contributor to the community. He helped to found the first local radio station. He was active as a member of the Rotary Club, a service organization, eventually holding the post of district governor.

In 1938 the St. Joseph Stake was divided, and Spencer was called to be the president of the new Mount Graham Stake. Concerned that some over whom he would preside might harbor ill feelings toward him, Spencer and Camilla visited with any who might have such feelings in order to "clear the slate."[17]

In September 1941, during his service as stake president, a major flood hit the community. Continuous rains raised the level of the Gila River until it ran down the streets of some of the settlements. Homes and farms were washed away by the waters. The residents, mostly members of the Church, desperately needed help. Upon hearing of the devastation, Spencer filled his car with food drawn from Church resources and headed for the towns affected by the flooding. He arranged to have dirty clothing cleaned. He helped farmers obtain grain to feed livestock. Soon a truckload of food and clothing arrived. Within a week, those who had suffered the most in the flooding were on the way to recovery. Church members demonstrated unqualified generosity. Spencer directed the assessment of needs and the distribution of resources. In all of this, he stayed in close contact with Elder Harold B. Lee of the Quorum of the Twelve Apostles, whose responsibilities included the welfare program.

The Apostleship

On July 8, 1943, President J. Reuben Clark Jr. of the First Presidency called Spencer at home. He said that Spencer had been called to fill one of the two vacant seats in the Quorum of the Twelve Apostles. To this, Spencer responded: "Oh, Brother Clark! Not me? You don't mean me? There must be some mistake. I surely couldn't have heard you right. . . . It seems so impossible. I am so weak and small and limited and incapable."[18] Spencer assured President Clark that there could be only one response to a call from the Lord, but his willingness to serve did not immediately overcome his feelings of inadequacy and unworthiness.

Those feelings intensified over the next few days, during which Spencer had little or no sleep. While he was in Boulder, Colorado, to visit his son, he went walking in the hills early one morning. As he climbed higher and higher, he reflected on the magnitude of the apostolic office. He was tormented by the thought that he might not measure up, that his calling might have been some mistake. In this frame of mind, he approached the peak of the mountain he was climbing, where he fell in prayer and meditation. "How I prayed!" he recalled. "How I suffered! How I wept! How I struggled!" As he agonized, a dream came to him of his grandfather Heber C. Kimball and "the great work he had done." This awareness calmed Spencer's heart. "A calm feeling of assurance came over me, doubt and questionings subdued. It was as though a great burden had been lifted. I sat in tranquil silence surveying the beautiful valley, thanking the Lord for the satisfaction and the reassuring answer to my prayers."[19] On October 7, 1943, at age 48, Spencer W. Kimball was ordained an Apostle.

Elder Kimball's service in the Quorum of the Twelve spanned three decades. In that time, he traveled extensively, strengthening the members and assisting in the growth of the kingdom. By special assignment from President George Albert Smith, Elder Kimball took a particular interest in descendants of the Book of Mormon prophet Lehi—native peoples of North, Central, and South America. He was an eloquent voice for their interests both in the senior quorums of the Church and among the membership at large. He decried all racial prejudice and oppression of the poor.

In his sermons, Elder Kimball could be both poetic and plain-spoken. He often dealt with sensitive topics of practical concern to the average Church member. In addition to numerous addresses, he authored the book *The Miracle of Forgiveness*. This book arose from Elder Kimball's long experience as an Apostle, counseling those who had yielded to serious transgression. In the book he outlined the Lord's expectations of us, our divine potential, and the pathway we must follow to repent and obtain the assurance of complete divine forgiveness. Elder

The Quorum of the Twelve Apostles in 1958. Standing, left to right: Delbert L. Stapley, Marion G. Romney, LeGrand Richards, Richard L. Evans, George Q. Morris, and Hugh B. Brown. Seated, left to right: Joseph Fielding Smith, Harold B. Lee, Spencer W. Kimball, Ezra Taft Benson, Mark E. Petersen, and Henry D. Moyle.

Kimball bore witness to the reader that the Lord was merciful and would forgive those who sincerely repented.

Health Challenges

Over the course of his life, Spencer W. Kimball suffered various injuries and illnesses. Two significant health challenges figured prominently in his years as an Apostle. The first illness left a lasting mark on Elder Kimball that was apparent whenever he spoke. Late in 1956, he felt a hoarseness in his voice. The diagnosis was cancer of the throat. An operation in July 1957 resulted in the removal of one vocal cord and part of another. In the aftermath, he rested his voice to permit the fullest possible healing. Through sleepless nights, Elder Kimball wondered if he would ever speak again.

Six months after the operation, the doctors declared Elder Kimball's throat healed. Elder Boyd K. Packer of the Quorum of the Twelve Apostles recounted how Elder Kimball used humor to introduce listeners to his new voice:

"Then came the test. Could he speak? Could he preach?

"He went back home [to Arizona] for his maiden speech. . . . There, in a conference of the St. Joseph Stake, . . . he stood at the pulpit.

"'I have come back here,' he said, 'to be among my own people. In this valley I presided as stake president.' Perhaps he thought that should he fail, here he would be among those who loved him most and would understand.

"There was a great outpouring of love. The tension of this dramatic moment was broken when he continued, 'I must tell you what has happened to me. I went away to the East, and while there I fell among cutthroats. . . .' After that it didn't matter what he said. Elder Kimball was back!"[20]

His new voice was soft, deep, and gravelly. It was, in Elder Packer's words, "a quiet, persuasive, mellow voice, an acquired voice, an appealing voice, a voice . . . loved by the Latter-day Saints."[21]

Elder Kimball also experienced serious heart problems. After becoming an Apostle, he suffered a series of heart attacks. In 1972, while serving as Acting President of the Quorum of the Twelve, he underwent a high-risk operation. Dr. Russell M. Nelson was President Kimball's heart surgeon at the time. Later, as a member of the Quorum of the Twelve Apostles, Elder Nelson recounted what happened during the operation: "I shall never forget the feeling I had as his heart resumed beating, leaping with power and vigor. At that very moment, the Spirit made known to me that this special patient would live to become the prophet of God on earth."[22]

President of the Church

The night of December 26, 1973, President Harold B. Lee, the 11th President of the Church, died suddenly. Consistent with the order of apostolic succession in the Church, on December 30, 1973, Spencer W. Kimball, as the senior member of the Quorum of the Twelve, became President of The Church of Jesus Christ of Latter-day Saints.

This came as a surprise to members of the Church—and especially to President Kimball. He had been ordained an Apostle two and a half years after Harold B. Lee. Given that President Kimball was four years older than President Lee and, it appeared, in poorer health, President Kimball fully anticipated that he would not live to be President Lee's successor. As he recounted later: "I felt absolutely certain that I would die, when my time came, as president of the Twelve. . . . I said at President Lee's funeral that no one had prayed harder than Sister Kimball and I for his restoration when he was ill and for his continuation while he was well."[23]

President Kimball was sustained by members of the Church in the April 1974 general conference. He had not aspired to this position, but the Lord had chosen him to be His prophet, seer, and revelator and to lead His Church and kingdom on earth.

In connection with that April general conference, President Kimball gave an address on missionary work at a meeting for Church leaders. Elder William Grant Bangerter, later a member of the Presidency of the Seventy, was a regional representative at the time and was present for the meeting. He later recalled the effect of President Kimball's words:

"We realized that President Kimball was opening spiritual windows and beckoning to us to come and gaze with him on the plans of eternity. It was as if he were drawing back the curtains which covered the purpose of the Almighty and inviting us to view with him the destiny of the gospel and the vision of its ministry.

"I doubt that any person present that day will ever forget the occasion. I, myself, have scarcely reread President Kimball's address since, but the substance of what he said was so vividly impressed upon my mind that I could repeat most of it at this moment from memory.

"The Spirit of the Lord was upon President Kimball and it proceeded from him to us as a tangible presence, which was at once both moving and shocking. He unrolled to our view a glorious vision."[24]

President Spencer W. Kimball, center, with his counselors in the First Presidency from 1973 to 1981: Presidents N. Eldon Tanner (left) and Marion G. Romney (right).

President Kimball's address on that occasion sounded a central theme of his ministry as President of the Church:

"My brethren, I wonder if we are doing all we can. Are we complacent in our approach to teaching all the world? We have been proselyting now 144 years. *Are we prepared to lengthen our stride? To enlarge our vision? . . .*

"I am under no delusion, brethren, to think that this will be an easy matter without strain or that it can be done overnight, but I do have this faith that *we can move forward and expand much faster than we now are. . . .*

". . . I think that if we are all of one mind and one heart and one purpose that we can move forward and change the image which seems to be that 'We are doing pretty well. Let's not "rock the boat." ' "[25]

Thus began a remarkable decade of growth and change. Although missionary work was the initial emphasis, it soon became clear to the membership of the Church that President Kimball was not interested in standing still in any area of righteous endeavor.

Missionary Work

President Kimball sought to open the doors of nations to the preaching of the gospel. The divisions of the so-called "Cold War" between democratic governments and communist governments prevented proselyting in many nations of Europe and Asia. Also, Church policy with respect to ordination to the priesthood limited missionary efforts in Africa, parts of South America, and the Caribbean. President Kimball looked for every opportunity to expand the geographic reach of the Church.

At the same time, he emphasized that greater opportunities to teach the nations depended on Church members' willingness to embrace those opportunities. For those young men worthy and fully prepared, missionary service was not to be viewed as an option but as a divine duty and opportunity. This obligation rested on young men regardless of where they resided. Young women could also serve as missionaries but were not under the same obligation as the young men. In addition, older couples were encouraged to serve in the missionary force. When Spencer W. Kimball began his service as President of the Church, 17,000 full-time missionaries were serving around the world. When he died about 12 years later, that number had increased to nearly 30,000. The increased missionary efforts bore substantial fruit: Church membership rose from 3.3 million to nearly 6 million.

Speaking to a group of young Church members in 1975, President Kimball said: "Do you know what the Lord has done for you young men? You are handsome young fellows. You look strong and well and happy. Who gave you your health? Who gave you your eyes? Who gave you your ears? Who gave you your voice? Did you ever think about that? Somebody must have provided you with these priceless possessions."

He then described his experience of having throat surgery and how it left him with only part of his voice. Continuing, he said: "Let me ask you how many of you would be willing to give up your voice? Did you buy it or trade for it? Did somebody give it to you? Did the Lord give you a voice so that you could express yourself? Then why don't you go out into the world and express the greatest story in the world, and tell the people that the truth has been restored; that the Lord has a continuation of prophets from Adam to now; and that you yourself have the holy priesthood, and you are going to magnify it all the days of your life? Tell the world that! They need it!

"And so I ask you again, who gave you your voice? Why?—just so that you could sing or talk or have fun with people? Or did he give that voice to you so you could teach the gospel? . . .

"Now I think we had better go in the mission field, don't you?—every boy that is worthy."[26]

Temple Work

As President of the Church, Spencer W. Kimball oversaw a significant increase in temple building. At the beginning of his administration, 15 temples were in operation; when he passed away about 12 years later, the number had grown to 36, more than double. President Gordon B. Hinckley, Second Counselor in the First Presidency, testified, "This great impetus in temple building was given by President Kimball under revelation from the Lord."[27]

Regarding temple work, President Kimball said: "The day is coming and not too far ahead of us when all temples on this earth will be going night and day. . . . There will be a corps of workers night and day almost to exhaustion, because of the importance of the work and the great number of people who lie asleep in the eternity and who are craving, needing, the blessings that can come to them."[28]

Church Government

During 1975 and 1976, President Kimball directed a reorganization and expansion of Church government to keep pace with Church growth. As part of the unfolding organization and responsibilities of the General Authorities, the First Quorum of the Seventy was reconstituted and by October 1976 included 39 brethren. "With this move," President Kimball explained, "the three governing quorums of the Church defined by the revelations,—the First Presidency, the Quorum of the Twelve, and the First Quorum of the Seventy,—have been set in their places as revealed by the Lord. This will make it possible to handle efficiently the present heavy workload and to prepare for the increasing expansion and acceleration of the work, anticipating the day when the Lord will return to take direct charge of His church and kingdom."[29] This revelation from the Lord to His prophet has since led to other changes in the government of the Church as required by "the labor in the vineyard" (D&C 107:96).

Scriptures

In 1976, President Kimball directed that two revelations, one to the Prophet Joseph Smith and one to President Joseph F. Smith, be added to the canon of scripture (see D&C 137 and 138). Under President Kimball's direction, an LDS edition of the King James Bible was published in 1979, and a new edition of the triple combination (the Book of Mormon, the Doctrine and Covenants, and the Pearl of Great Price) was published in 1981. Referring to the coming forth of these editions of the standard works, Elder Boyd K. Packer said, "As the generations roll on, this will be regarded, in the perspective of history, as the crowning achievement in the administration of President Spencer W. Kimball."[30]

During President Kimball's tenure, the scriptures also became the basis for the Church's Sunday School curriculum.

Simplification

As the Church's size and sphere of operations extended, President Kimball and other Church leaders recognized the need to simplify the various programs of the Church so that the most essential could be readily available in some form to those in the newest branch as well as those in a long-established ward. President Kimball said:

"The mission of the Church to its members is to make available the principles, programs, and priesthood by which they can prepare themselves for exaltation. Our success, individually and as a Church, will largely be determined by how faithfully we focus on living the gospel in the home. Only as we see clearly the responsibilities of each individual and the role of families and homes can we properly understand that priesthood quorums and auxiliary organizations, even wards and stakes, exist primarily to help members live the gospel in the home. Then we can understand that people are more important than programs, and that Church programs should always support and never detract from gospel-centered family activities. . . .

"Our commitment to home-centered gospel living should become the clear message of every priesthood and auxiliary program, reducing, where necessary, some of the optional activities that may detract from proper focus on the family and the home."[31]

One important change during President Kimball's administration was the introduction of the three-hour block meeting schedule on Sunday. This combined various weekday and Sunday meetings into a simple and more convenient set of meetings on Sunday. The introduction of this consolidated schedule in 1980 greatly reduced the expenditure of time and money by Church members in order that they might participate in the full range of the Lord's program.

Revelation on the Priesthood

One of the most significant changes that came about during the presidency of Spencer W. Kimball was the revelation on the priesthood (see Official Declaration 2 in the Doctrine and Covenants).

On June 1, 1978, President Kimball, with other members of the First Presidency and the Quorum of the Twelve Apostles, met in an upper room in the Salt Lake Temple. President Gordon B. Hinckley, who was present on that occasion as a member of the Quorum of the Twelve Apostles, later reported:

"The question of extending the blessings of the priesthood to blacks had been on the minds of many of the Brethren over a period of years. It had repeatedly been brought up by Presidents of the Church. It had become a matter of particular concern to President Spencer W. Kimball.

"Over a considerable period of time he had prayed concerning this serious and difficult question. He had spent many hours in that upper room in the temple by himself in prayer and meditation.

"On this occasion he raised the question before his Brethren—his Counselors and the Apostles. Following this discussion we joined in prayer in the most sacred of circumstances. President Kimball himself was voice in that prayer. . . . The Spirit of God was there. And by the power of the Holy Ghost there came to that prophet an assurance that the thing for which he prayed was right, that the time had come, and that now the wondrous blessings of the priesthood should be extended to worthy men everywhere regardless of lineage.

"Every man in that circle, by the power of the Holy Ghost, knew the same thing.

"It was a quiet and sublime occasion. . . .

". . . Not one of us who was present on that occasion was ever quite the same after that. Nor has the Church been quite the same."[32]

Announcement of the revelation took the form of a letter dated June 8, 1978, to all general and local priesthood officers in the Church: "Every faithful, worthy man in the Church may receive the holy priesthood, with power to exercise its divine authority, and enjoy with his loved ones every blessing that flows therefrom, including the blessings of the temple" (D&C, Official Declaration 2).

President Hinckley recalled: "The letter was released to the Church and to the world. I need not tell you of the electric effect that was felt both within the Church and without. There was much weeping, with tears of gratitude not only on the part of those who previously had been denied the priesthood and who became the immediate beneficiaries of this announcement, but also by men and women of the Church across the world who had felt as we had felt concerning this matter."[33]

About three months later, President Kimball stated, referring to the revelation: "One of the Brethren said yesterday that now has come one of the greatest changes and blessings that has ever been known. . . . Outside of a few people who always want to be contrary, the people of the world have accepted this change with their gratitude. . . . So we are very, very happy about this, especially for those who had been deprived of these blessings before."[34]

Love for People and for the Work of the Lord

Describing President Kimball, Elder Neal A. Maxwell of the Quorum of the Twelve Apostles said: "There was a pervasive warmth in the ministry of this man. The loving but penetrating look of his eyes, his embrace, his holy kiss, his tenderness—felt by so many—all created a deserved aura about this man, not of unapproachability, but of special warmth. His love was inclusive; no one ever felt left out. Every General Authority could assume that *he* was President Kimball's favorite, for he loved each of us so much! How could one think otherwise?"[35]

President Kimball told the members of the Church, "I would like to be known as one who loves his brothers and sisters."[36] Latter-day Saints felt and expressed love for him in return, for which he was grateful. He said: "I always tell people when they say they love me, 'Well, that's wonderful, because that's what I live on.' And I mean that literally."[37]

In his loving but determined way, President Kimball admonished the Latter-day Saints to stretch themselves further in the service of the Lord, overcoming the complacency, sin, or other problems that kept them from moving forward. In his own life,

*President Kimball said, "I would like to be known
as one who loves his brothers and sisters."*

he served as an example of moving forward in the Lord's service, no matter what the obstacles.

Elder Robert D. Hales, then a member of the First Quorum of the Seventy, said of President Kimball: "He is a man of action, demonstrated by the simple sign on his desk that says, 'Do It.' . . . His example and love motivate those who follow his example to achieve higher goals and lengthen their stride toward perfection."[38]

In an address given at the October 1979 general conference, President Kimball told the Old Testament story of Caleb, who, faced with challenges related to entering the promised land, said, "Give me this mountain" (Joshua 14:12). Referring to these words, President Kimball said:

"This is my feeling for the work at this moment. There are great challenges ahead of us, giant opportunities to be met. I welcome that exciting prospect and feel to say to the Lord, humbly, 'Give me this mountain,' give me these challenges.

"Humbly, I give this pledge to the Lord and to you, my beloved brothers and sisters, fellow workers in this sacred cause of

Christ: I will go forward, with faith in the God of Israel, knowing that he will guide and direct us, and lead us, finally, to the accomplishment of his purposes and to our promised land and our promised blessings. . . .

"Earnestly and fervently I urge that each of you make this same pledge and effort—every priesthood leader, every woman in Israel, each young man, each young woman, every boy and girl."[39]

On November 5, 1985, after nearly 12 years serving as President of the Church, Spencer W. Kimball passed away. At the time of his passing, President Kimball's counselor President Gordon B. Hinckley declared: "It has been my great privilege and opportunity to work at President Kimball's side in the harness of the work of the Lord. On one occasion I tried to slow him down a little, and he said, 'Gordon, my life is like my shoes—to be worn out in service.' He so lived. He so died. He has gone to the company of Him whose servant he was, even the Lord Jesus Christ, of whom he bore witness and testimony."[40]

Notes

1. See Edward L. Kimball and Andrew E. Kimball Jr., *Spencer W. Kimball* (1977), 196.
2. Boyd K. Packer, "President Spencer W. Kimball: No Ordinary Man," *Ensign,* Mar. 1974, 3.
3. *Spencer W. Kimball,* 12.
4. "The False Gods We Worship," *Ensign,* June 1976, 3.
5. "Friend to Friend," *Friend,* Jan. 1971, 34.
6. "He Did It with All His Heart, and Prospered," *Ensign,* Mar. 1981, 4.
7. In Conference Report, Apr. 1979, 140; or *Ensign,* May 1979, 99.
8. In *Spencer W. Kimball,* 23.
9. In Conference Report, Apr. 1979, 140; or *Ensign,* May 1979, 99.
10. In *Spencer W. Kimball,* 46.
11. In *Spencer W. Kimball,* 57.
12. Edward L. Kimball and Andrew E. Kimball Jr., *The Story of Spencer W. Kimball: A Short Man, a Long Stride* (1985), 16–17.
13. *Spencer W. Kimball,* 56.

14. In *Spencer W. Kimball,* 376.
15. *Spencer W. Kimball,* 79–80.
16. Edward L. Kimball, in Gerry Avant, "As Father, Prophet Made Time Count," *Church News,* June 11, 1977, 5.
17. *Spencer W. Kimball,* 171.
18. In *Spencer W. Kimball,* 189.
19. In *Spencer W. Kimball,* 195.
20. *Ensign,* Mar. 1974, 4.
21. *Ensign,* Mar. 1974, 4.
22. "Spencer W. Kimball: Man of Faith," *Ensign,* Dec. 1985, 40.
23. "When the World Will Be Converted," *Ensign,* Oct. 1974, 3.
24. In Conference Report, Oct. 1977, 38; or *Ensign,* Nov. 1977, 26–27.
25. *Ensign,* Oct. 1974, 5, 13, 14; emphasis added.
26. In Conference Report, Buenos Aires Argentina Area Conference 1975, 43–44.
27. In Conference Report, Oct. 1985, 71; or *Ensign,* Nov. 1985, 54.

28. Address given at Priesthood Genealogy Seminar Banquet, Aug. 4, 1977, Archives of The Church of Jesus Christ of Latter-day Saints, 4–5.

29. In Conference Report, Oct. 1976, 10; or *Ensign,* Nov. 1976, 9.

30. In Conference Report, Oct. 1982, 75; or *Ensign,* Nov. 1982, 53.

31. "Living the Gospel in the Home," *Ensign,* May 1978, 101.

32. "Priesthood Restoration," *Ensign,* Oct. 1988, 70.

33. *Ensign,* Oct. 1988, 70.

34. *The Teachings of Spencer W. Kimball,* ed. Edward L. Kimball (1982), 451.

35. "Spencer, the Beloved: Leader-Servant," *Ensign,* Dec. 1985, 12–13.

36. In Conference Report, Oct. 1980, 111; or *Ensign,* Nov. 1980, 77.

37. In "'News' Interviews Prophet," *Church News,* Jan. 6, 1979, 19.

38. In Conference Report, Oct. 1981, 27–28; or *Ensign,* Nov. 1981, 20.

39. In Conference Report, Oct. 1979, 115–16; or *Ensign,* Nov. 1979, 79.

40. "He Is at Peace," *Ensign,* Dec. 1985, 41.

As suggested by President Kimball, the chorus of "I Am a Child of God" ends with the words "Teach me all that I must do to live with him someday."

"To Live with Him Someday"

The only way we can find joy, truth, and fulfillment is to live in harmony with Heavenly Father's plan.

From the Life of Spencer W. Kimball

Church members all over the world love the Primary song "I Am a Child of God," with its simple but profound message of who we are, why we are on the earth, and what the Lord promises us if we are faithful. Sister Naomi W. Randall wrote the text to the song in 1957, when Elder Spencer W. Kimball was a member of the Quorum of the Twelve Apostles. At that time, the song's chorus concluded with the words "Teach me all that I must know to live with him someday."

While visiting a stake conference, Elder Kimball listened to a group of Primary children sing "I Am a Child of God." Soon after that, he commented on the song in a conversation with a member of the Primary General Board. "I love the children's song," he said, "but there is one word that bothers me. Would Sister Randall mind if the word *know* were changed to the word *do?*"[1]

Sister Randall agreed to change the song. Now the chorus ends with the words "Teach me all that I must do to live with him someday."[2] These words reflect a principle that President Kimball emphasized throughout his ministry: "Celestial life may be had by every soul who will fulfil the requirements. To *know* is not enough. One must *do.* Righteousness is vital and ordinances are necessary."[3] He taught that the gospel is "a way of life, the plan of personal salvation, and is based upon personal responsibility. It is developed for man, the offspring of God. Man is a god in embryo and has in him the seeds of godhood, and he can, if he will, rise to great heights."[4]

Teachings of Spencer W. Kimball

In our premortal life, Heavenly Father taught us His plan for our exaltation.

When we were spiritual beings, fully organized and able to think and study and understand with him, our Heavenly Father said to us, in effect: "Now, my beloved children, in your spirit state you have progressed about as far as you can. To continue your development, you need physical bodies. I intend to provide a plan whereby you may continue your growth. As you know, one can grow only by overcoming.

"Now," said the Lord, "we shall take of the elements at hand and organize them into an earth, place thereon vegetation and animal life, and permit you to go down upon it. This will be your proving ground. We shall give you a rich earth, lavishly furnished for your benefit and enjoyment, and we shall see if you will prove true and do the things that are asked of you. I will enter into a contract with you. If you will agree to exercise control over your desires and continue to grow toward perfection and godhood by the plan which I shall provide, I will give to you a physical body of flesh and bones and a rich and productive earth, with sun, water, forests, metals, soils, and all other things necessary to feed and clothe and house you and give to you every enjoyment that is proper and for your good. In addition to this, I will make it possible for you to eventually return to me as you improve your life, overcoming obstacles and approaching perfection."

To the above most generous offer, we as sons and daughters of our Heavenly Father responded with gratitude.[5]

The Lord clearly outlined the plan and its conditions and benefits. . . . Agency would be given man so that he could make his own choices.

Life was to be in three segments or estates: pre-mortal, mortal, and immortal. . . . Performance in one estate would vitally affect the succeeding estate or estates. If a person kept his first estate, he would be permitted the second or the mortal life as a further period of trial and experience. If he magnified his second estate, his earth experience, eternal life would await him.[6]

While we lack recollection of our pre-mortal life, before coming to this earth all of us understood definitely the purpose of our being here. We would be expected to gain knowledge, educate ourselves, train ourselves. We were to control our urges and desires, master and control our passions, and overcome our weaknesses, small and large. We were to eliminate sins of omission and of commission, and to follow the laws and commandments given us by our Father. . . .

We understood also that after a period varying from seconds to decades of mortal life we would die, our bodies would go back to Mother Earth from which they had been created, and our spirits would go to the spirit world, where we would further train for our eternal destiny. After a period, there would be a resurrection or a reunion of the body and the spirit, which would render us immortal and make possible our further climb toward perfection and godhood. This resurrection has been made available to us through the sacrifice of the Lord Jesus Christ, the Creator of this earth, who performed this incomparable service for us—a miracle we could not perform for ourselves. Thus the way was opened for our immortality and—if we prove worthy—eventual exaltation in God's kingdom.[7]

We understood well before we came to this vale of tears that there would be sorrows, disappointments, hard work, blood, sweat, and tears; but in spite of all, we looked down and saw this earth being made ready for us, and we said in effect, "Yes, Father, in spite of all those things I can see great blessings that could come to me as one of thy sons or daughters; in taking a body I can see that I will eventually become immortal like thee, that I might overcome the effects of sin and be perfected, and so I am anxious to go to the earth at the first opportunity." And so we came.[8]

Mortality is the time to prepare to meet God.

We mortals who now live upon this earth are in our *second estate.* Our very presence here in mortal bodies attests the fact that we "kept" our first estate. Our spirit matter was eternal and

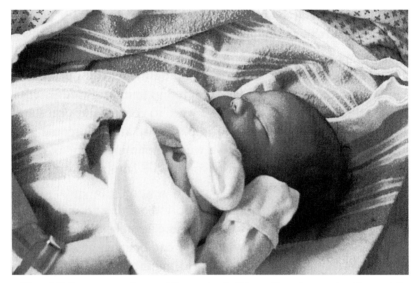

"One definite purpose of our spirits coming to this earth and assuming the mortal state was to obtain a physical body."

co-existent with God, but it was organized into spirit bodies by our Heavenly Father. Our spirit bodies went through a long period of growth and development and training and, having passed the test successfully, were finally admitted to this earth and to mortality.

One definite purpose of our spirits coming to this earth and assuming the mortal state was to obtain a physical body. This body was to be subject to all the weaknesses, temptations, frailties and limitations of mortality, and was to face the challenge to overcome self.[9]

You are sent to this earth not merely to have a good time or to satisfy urges or passions or desires . . . and have what the world calls "fun."

You are sent to this world with a very serious purpose. You are sent to school, for that matter, to begin as a human infant and grow to unbelievable proportions in wisdom, judgment, knowledge, and power.[10]

One of the most serious human defects in all ages is procrastination, an unwillingness to accept personal responsibilities *now*. Men came to earth consciously to obtain their schooling, their training and development, and to perfect themselves, but many have allowed themselves to be diverted and have become . . . addicts to mental and spiritual indolence and to the pursuit of worldly pleasure.[11]

This mortal life is the time to prepare to meet God, which is our first responsibility. Having already obtained our bodies, which become the permanent tabernacle for our spirits through the eternities, now we are to train our bodies, our minds, and our spirits. Pre-eminent, then, is our using this life to perfect ourselves, to subjugate the flesh, subject the body to the spirit, to overcome all weaknesses, to govern self so that one may give leadership to others, and to perform all necessary ordinances.[12]

The gospel of Jesus Christ charts our course back to our Heavenly Father.

To pinpoint a destination not previously visited we usually consult a map. . . . The Lord Jesus Christ, our Redeemer and Savior, has given us our map—a code of laws and commandments whereby we might attain perfection and, eventually, godhood. This set of laws and ordinances is known as the gospel of Jesus Christ, and it is the *only* plan which will exalt mankind. The Church of Jesus Christ of Latter-day Saints is the sole repository of this priceless program in its fulness, which is made available to those who accept it.[13]

The Lord restored his kingdom in these days, with all its gifts and powers and blessings. Any church that you know of may possibly be able to take you for a long ride, and bring you some degree of peace and happiness and blessing, and they can carry you to the veil and there they drop you. The Church of Jesus Christ picks you up on this side of the veil and, if you live its commandments, carries you right through the veil as though it weren't there and on through the eternities to exaltation.[14]

The gospel of Jesus Christ is the eternal plan of salvation. It is the plan devised and announced by God, the Eternal Father, for the salvation of all who will believe and obey.[15]

In order to reach the goal of eternal life and exaltation and godhood, one must be initiated into the kingdom by baptism, properly performed; one must receive the Holy Ghost by the laying on of authoritative hands; a man must be ordained to the priesthood by authorized priesthood holders; one must be endowed and sealed in the house of God by the prophet who holds the keys or by one of those to whom the keys have been delegated; and one must live a life of righteousness, cleanliness, purity and service. None can enter into eternal life other than by the correct door—Jesus Christ and his commandments.[16]

Jesus perfected his life and became our Christ. Priceless blood of a god was shed, and he became our Savior; his perfected life was given, and he became our Redeemer; his atonement for us made possible our return to our Heavenly Father.[17]

The great and wonderful and miraculous benefit of the Savior's atonement cannot have its full saving impact on us unless we repent.[18]

We are so grateful that our Heavenly Father has blessed us with the gospel of repentance. It is central to all that makes up the gospel plan. Repentance is the Lord's law of growth, his principle of development, and his plan for happiness. We are deeply grateful that we have his definite promise that where there has been sin and error, they can be followed by sincere and sufficient repentance that will in turn be rewarded with forgiveness.

"Come unto me, all ye that labor and are heavy laden, and I will give you rest," said the Master. (Matt. 11:28.)

The glorious thing about the whole matter of repentance is that the scriptures are as full of the Lord's assurances that he will forgive as they are full of his commands for us to repent, to change our lives and bring them into full conformity with his wonderful teachings.

God is good. He is eager to forgive. He wants us to perfect ourselves and maintain control of ourselves. He does not want Satan and others to control our lives. We must learn that keeping our Heavenly Father's commandments represents the *only* path to total control of ourselves, the only way to find joy, truth, and fulfillment in this life and in eternity.[19]

The treasure house of happiness is unlocked to those who live the gospel of Jesus Christ in its purity and simplicity. . . . The

"Jesus perfected his life and became our Christ. . . . His atonement for us made possible our return to our Heavenly Father."

assurance of supreme happiness, the certainty of a successful life here and of exaltation and eternal life hereafter, come to those who plan to live their lives in complete harmony with the gospel of Jesus Christ—and then consistently follow the course they have set.[20]

Only the valiant and faithful will be exalted.

If we are true and faithful, we shall rise, not alone in immortality but unto eternal life. Immortality is to live forever in an assigned kingdom. Eternal life is to gain exaltation in the highest heaven and live in the family unit.[21]

One man said the other day, the only thing he didn't like about the Mormon Church was that it claims to be the only one through which a man could be saved. I said, "Oh no, we make no such claim. We say that every good religionist and every good man who is not a religionist will be saved but there are degrees of salvation. . . ."[22]

Those who have lived after the manner of the world shall go to a telestial kingdom whose glory is as the stars.

Those who have been decent and upright and who have lived respectable and good lives will go to a terrestrial kingdom whose glory is as the moon.

Those who have believed in Christ, who have forsaken the world, who have taken the Holy Spirit for their guide and been willing to lay their all on the altar, those who have kept the commandments of God—they shall go to a celestial kingdom whose glory is as the sun.[23]

The road of life is plainly marked according to the divine purpose, the map of the gospel of Jesus Christ is made available to the travelers, the destination of eternal life is clearly established. At that destination our Father waits hopefully, anxious to greet his returning children. Unfortunately, many will not arrive.[24]

Why will only a few reach exaltation in the celestial kingdom? Not because it was not available to them, not because they did not know of its availability, not because the testimony was not given to them, but because they would not put forth the effort to pattern their lives and make them like the Savior's life and establish them so well that there would be no deviation until the end.[25]

There are . . . many members of the Church who are lax and careless and who continually procrastinate. They live the gospel casually but not devoutly. They have complied with some requirements but are not valiant. They do no major crime but merely fail to do the things required—things like paying tithing, living the Word of Wisdom, having family prayers, fasting, attending meetings, serving. . . .

. . . The Lord will not translate one's good hopes and desires and intentions into works. Each of us must do that for himself. . . .

Only the valiant will be exalted and receive the highest degree of glory, hence "many are called, but few are chosen." (D&C 121:40.) As the Savior put it, ". . . strait is the gate, and narrow the way, which leadeth unto life, and few there be that find it." And conversely, ". . . wide is the gate, and broad is the way, that leadeth to destruction, and many there be which go in thereat." (Matt. 7:13, 14.)

It is true that many Latter-day Saints, having been baptized and confirmed members of the Church, and some even having received their endowments and having been married and sealed in the holy temple, have felt that they were thus guaranteed the blessings of exaltation and eternal life. But this is not so. There are two basic requirements every soul must fulfill or he cannot attain to the great blessings offered. He *must* receive the ordinances and he *must* be faithful, overcoming his weaknesses. Hence, not all who claim to be Latter-day Saints will be exalted.

But for those Latter-day Saints who are valiant, who fulfill the requirements faithfully and fully, the promises are glorious beyond description:

"Then shall they be gods, because they have no end; therefore shall they be from everlasting to everlasting, because they continue; then shall they be above all, because all things are subject unto them. Then shall they be gods, because they have all power, and the angels are subject unto them." (D&C 132:20.)[26]

When one realizes the vastness, the richness, the glory of that "all" which the Lord promises to bestow upon his faithful, it is worth all it costs in patience, faith, sacrifice, sweat and tears. The blessings of eternity contemplated in this "all" bring men immortality and everlasting life, eternal growth, divine leadership, eternal increase, perfection, and with it all, godhood.[27]

Suggestions for Study and Teaching

Consider these ideas as you study the chapter or as you prepare to teach. For additional help, see pages v–ix.

- Review the third paragraph on page 2 and the third full paragraph on page 3, in which President Kimball describes our premortal response to Heavenly Father's plan. Why do you think we responded that way?

- Review the second and third full paragraphs on page 4. What do you do to find enjoyment in life without losing sight of your "serious purpose"?

- Study President Kimball's teachings about the purposes of mortality on pages 3–5. In light of these teachings, why do you think procrastination is "one of the most serious human defects"? How can we overcome this tendency?

• President Kimball taught that the gospel of Jesus Christ is like a map that leads us to exaltation (pages 5–7). Ponder where you are on this journey and what you can do to continue to progress.

• What do you think it means to be valiant in the gospel? (For some examples, see pages 7–9 and the story on page 1.) Why is Church membership and knowledge of the gospel not enough to assure exaltation in the celestial kingdom?

Related Scriptures: James 1:22; Alma 34:30–41; 3 Nephi 27:13–22; D&C 76:50–93; Abraham 3:22–26

Notes

1. In Robert D. Hales, "Friend to Friend: I Am a Child of God," *Friend,* Mar. 1978, 9.
2. *Hymns,* no. 301.
3. In Conference Report, Apr. 1964, 94; or *Improvement Era,* June 1964, 496.
4. *The Teachings of Spencer W. Kimball,* ed. Edward L. Kimball (1982), 28.
5. "Absolute Truth," *Ensign,* Sept. 1978, 5.
6. *The Miracle of Forgiveness* (1969), 4.
7. *The Miracle of Forgiveness,* 5–6.
8. *The Teachings of Spencer W. Kimball,* 31.
9. *The Miracle of Forgiveness,* 5.
10. *The Teachings of Spencer W. Kimball,* 31.
11. *The Miracle of Forgiveness,* 7.
12. "Beloved Youth, Study and Learn," in *Life's Directions* (1962), 177–78.
13. *The Miracle of Forgiveness,* 6.
14. *The Teachings of Spencer W. Kimball,* 49–50.
15. In Conference Report, Oct. 1978, 108; or *Ensign,* Nov. 1978, 71.
16. *The Miracle of Forgiveness,* 6.
17. "President Kimball Speaks Out on Profanity," *Ensign,* Feb. 1981, 5.
18. "The Gospel of Repentance," *Ensign,* Oct. 1982, 5.
19. *Ensign,* Oct. 1982, 2.
20. *The Miracle of Forgiveness,* 259.
21. In Conference Report, Oct. 1978, 109; or *Ensign,* Nov. 1978, 72.
22. *The Teachings of Spencer W. Kimball,* 50.
23. In Conference Report, Oct. 1978, 109; or *Ensign,* Nov. 1978, 72.
24. *The Miracle of Forgiveness,* 19.
25. *The Teachings of Spencer W. Kimball,* 51–52.
26. *The Miracle of Forgiveness,* 7–8, 9.
27. *The Miracle of Forgiveness,* 311.

Tragedy or Destiny?

When we face the apparent tragedies of sorrow, suffering, and death, we must put our trust in God.

From the Life of Spencer W. Kimball

Early in his childhood, Spencer W. Kimball suffered the pain that comes with the death of loved ones. When he was eight years old, his sister Mary died shortly after her birth. A month later, Spencer's parents sensed that five-year-old Fannie, who had been suffering for several weeks, would soon pass away. Spencer later told of the day Fannie died: "On my ninth birthday Fannie died in Mother's arms. All of us children were awakened in the early night to be present. I seem to remember the scene in our living room . . . , my beloved mother weeping with her little dying five-year-old child in her arms and all of us crowding around."[1]

Even more difficult for young Spencer was the news he received two years later, when he and his brothers and sisters were called home from school one morning. They ran home and were met by their bishop, who gathered them around him and told them that their mother had died the day before. President Kimball later recalled: "It came as a thunderbolt. I ran from the house out in the backyard to be alone in my deluge of tears. Out of sight and sound, away from everybody, I sobbed and sobbed. Each time I said the word 'Ma' fresh floods of tears gushed forth until I was drained dry. Ma—dead! But she couldn't be! Life couldn't go on for us. . . . My eleven-year-old heart seemed to burst."[2]

Fifty years later, Elder Spencer W. Kimball, then a member of the Quorum of the Twelve Apostles, found himself far away from home, recovering from major surgery. Unable to sleep, he

Spencer W. Kimball and his siblings, about two years before his sister Fannie died.
Standing, left to right: Clare, Ruth, Gordon, and Delbert.
Seated, left to right: Helen, Alice, Fannie, and Spencer.

recalled the day his mother died: "I feel like sobbing again now . . . as my memory takes me over those sad paths."[3]

Facing the deep sadness of such experiences, Spencer W. Kimball always found comfort in prayer and in the principles of the gospel. Even in his childhood, he knew where to turn to receive peace. A family friend wrote of young Spencer's prayers—"how the loss of his mother weighed so heavily upon his little heart and yet how bravely he battled with his grief and sought comfort from the only source."[4]

In his ministry, President Kimball frequently offered words of solace to those who mourned the loss of loved ones. He testified of eternal principles, assuring the Saints that death is not the end of existence. Speaking at a funeral, he once said:

"We are limited in our visions. With our eyes we can see but a few miles. With our ears we can hear but a few years. We are encased, enclosed, as it were, in a room, but when our light goes out of this life, then we see beyond mortal limitations. . . .

"The walls go down, time ends and distance fades and vanishes as we go into eternity . . . and we immediately emerge into a great world in which there are no earthly limitations."[5]

Teachings of Spencer W. Kimball

In His wisdom, God does not always prevent tragedy.

The daily newspaper screamed the headlines: "Plane Crash Kills 43. No Survivors of Mountain Tragedy," and thousands of voices joined in a chorus: "Why did the Lord let this terrible thing happen?"

Two automobiles crashed when one went through a red light, and six people were killed. Why would God not prevent this?

Why should the young mother die of cancer and leave her eight children motherless? Why did not the Lord heal her?

A little child was drowned; another was run over. Why?

A man died one day suddenly of a coronary occlusion as he climbed a stairway. His body was found slumped on the floor. His wife cried out in agony, "Why? Why would the Lord do this to me? Could he not have considered my three little children who still need a father?"

A young man died in the mission field and people critically questioned: "Why did not the Lord protect this youth while he was doing proselyting work?"

I wish I could answer these questions with authority, but I cannot. I am sure that sometime we'll understand and be reconciled. But for the present we must seek understanding as best we can in the gospel principles.

Was it the Lord who directed the plane into the mountain to snuff out the lives of its occupants, or were there mechanical faults or human errors?

Did our Father in heaven cause the collision of the cars that took six people into eternity, or was it the error of the driver who ignored safety rules?

Did God take the life of the young mother or prompt the child to toddle into the canal or guide the other child into the path of the oncoming car?

Did the Lord cause the man to suffer a heart attack? Was the death of the missionary untimely? Answer, if you can. I cannot, for though I know God has a major role in our lives, I do not know how much he causes to happen and how much he merely permits. Whatever the answer to this question, there is another I feel sure about.

Could the Lord have prevented these tragedies? The answer is, Yes. The Lord is omnipotent, with all power to control our lives, save us pain, prevent all accidents, drive all planes and cars, feed us, protect us, save us from labor, effort, sickness, even from death, if he will. But he will not.

We should be able to understand this, because we can realize how unwise it would be for us to shield our children from all effort, from disappointments, temptations, sorrows, and suffering.

The basic gospel law is free agency and eternal development. To force us to be careful or righteous would be to nullify that fundamental law and make growth impossible.[6]

**With an eternal perspective, we understand that adversity
is essential to our eternal progression.**

If we looked at mortality as the whole of existence, then pain,
sorrow, failure, and short life would be calamity. But if we look
upon life as an eternal thing stretching far into the premortal
past and on into the eternal post-death future, then all happenings may be put in proper perspective.

Is there not wisdom in his giving us trials that we might rise
above them, responsibilities that we might achieve, work to
harden our muscles, sorrows to try our souls? Are we not exposed
to temptations to test our strength, sickness that we might learn
patience, death that we might be immortalized and glorified?

If all the sick for whom we pray were healed, if all the righteous were protected and the wicked destroyed, the whole program of the Father would be annulled and the basic principle of
the gospel, free agency, would be ended. No man would have to
live by faith.

If joy and peace and rewards were instantaneously given the
doer of good, there could be no evil—all would do good but not
because of the rightness of doing good. There would be no test
of strength, no development of character, no growth of powers,
no free agency, only satanic controls.

Should all prayers be immediately answered according to our
selfish desires and our limited understanding, then there would
be little or no suffering, sorrow, disappointment, or even death,
and if these were not, there would also be no joy, success, resurrection, nor eternal life and godhood.

"For it must needs be, that there is an opposition in all things
. . . righteousness . . . wickedness . . . holiness . . . misery . . .
good . . . bad. . . ." (2 Nephi 2:11.)

Being human, we would expel from our lives physical pain
and mental anguish and assure ourselves of continual ease and
comfort, but if we were to close the doors upon sorrow and distress, we might be excluding our greatest friends and benefac-
tors. Suffering can make saints of people as they learn patience,
long-suffering, and self-mastery. . . .

15

I love the verse of "How Firm a Foundation"—

> *When through the deep waters I call thee to go,*
> *The rivers of sorrow shall not thee o'erflow*
> *For I will be with thee, thy troubles to bless,*
> *And sanctify to thee thy deepest distress.*
> [See *Hymns,* no. 85]

And Elder James E. Talmage wrote: "No pang that is suffered by man or woman upon the earth will be without its compensating effect . . . if it be met with patience."

On the other hand, these things can crush us with their mighty impact if we yield to weakness, complaining, and criticism.

"No pain that we suffer, no trial that we experience is wasted. It ministers to our education, to the development of such qualities as patience, faith, fortitude and humility. All that we suffer and all that we endure, especially when we endure it patiently, builds up our characters, purifies our hearts, expands our souls, and makes us more tender and charitable, more worthy to be called the children of God . . . and it is through sorrow and suffering, toil and tribulation, that we gain the education that we come here to acquire and which will make us more like our Father and Mother in heaven. . . ." (Orson F. Whitney)

There are people who are bitter as they watch loved ones suffer agonies and interminable pain and physical torture. Some would charge the Lord with unkindness, indifference, and injustice. We are so incompetent to judge! . . .

The power of the priesthood is limitless but God has wisely placed upon each of us certain limitations. I may develop priesthood power as I perfect my life, yet I am grateful that even through the priesthood I cannot heal all the sick. I might heal people who should die. I might relieve people of suffering who should suffer. I fear I would frustrate the purposes of God.

Had I limitless power, and yet limited vision and understanding, I might have saved Abinadi from the flames of fire when he was burned at the stake, and in doing so I might have irreparably damaged him. He died a martyr and went to a martyr's reward—exaltation.

*"Had I limitless power, and yet limited vision and understanding,
I might have saved Abinadi."*

I would likely have protected Paul against his woes if my power were boundless. I would surely have healed his "thorn in the flesh." [2 Corinthians 12:7.] And in doing so I might have foiled the Lord's program. Thrice he offered prayers, asking the Lord to remove the "thorn" from him, but the Lord did not so answer his prayers [see 2 Corinthians 12:7–10]. Paul many times could have lost himself if he had been eloquent, well, handsome, and free from the things that made him humble. . . .

I fear that had I been in Carthage Jail on June 27, 1844, I might have deflected the bullets that pierced the body of the Prophet and the Patriarch. I might have saved them from the sufferings and agony, but lost to them the martyr's death and reward. I am glad I did not have to make that decision.

With such uncontrolled power, I surely would have felt to protect Christ from the agony in Gethsemane, the insults, the thorny crown, the indignities in the court, the physical injuries. I would have administered to his wounds and healed them, giving him cooling water instead of vinegar. I might have saved him from suffering and death, and lost to the world his atoning sacrifice.

I would not dare to take the responsibility of bringing back to life my loved ones. Christ himself acknowledged the difference between his will and the Father's when he prayed that the cup of suffering be taken from him; yet he added, "Nevertheless, not my will but thine be done." [Luke 22:42.][7]

Death can open the door to glorious opportunities.

For the one who dies, life goes on and his free agency continues, and death, which seems to us such a calamity, could be a blessing in disguise. . . .

If we say that early death is a calamity, disaster, or tragedy, would it not be saying that mortality is preferable to earlier entrance into the spirit world and to eventual salvation and exaltation? If mortality be the perfect state, then death would be a frustration, but the gospel teaches us there is no tragedy in death, but only in sin. ". . . blessed are the dead that die in the Lord. . . ." (See D&C 63:49.)

We know so little. Our judgment is so limited. We judge the Lord's ways from our own narrow view.

I spoke at the funeral service of a young Brigham Young University student who died during World War II. There had been hundreds of thousands of young men rushed prematurely into eternity through the ravages of that war, and I made the statement that I believed this righteous youth had been called to the spirit world to preach the gospel to these deprived souls. This may not be true of all who die, but I felt it true of him.

In his vision of "The Redemption of the Dead" President Joseph F. Smith saw this very thing. . . . He writes:

". . . I perceived that the Lord went not in person among the wicked and the disobedient who had rejected the truth . . . but behold, from among the righteous He organized his forces . . . and commissioned them to go forth and carry the light of the gospel. . . .

". . . our Redeemer spent His time . . . in the world of spirits, instructing and preparing the faithful spirits . . . who had testified of Him in the flesh, that they might carry the message of redemption unto all the dead unto whom He could not go personally because of their rebellion and transgression. . . .

"I beheld that the faithful elders of this dispensation, when they depart from mortal life, continue their labors in the preaching of the gospel of repentance and redemption." [See D&C 138:29–30, 36–37, 57.]

Death, then, may be the opening of the door to opportunities, including that of teaching the gospel of Christ.[8]

In times of trial, we must trust in God.

Despite the fact that death opens new doors, we do not seek it. We are admonished to pray for those who are ill and use our priesthood power to heal them.

"And the elders of the church, two or more, shall be called, and shall pray for and lay their hands upon them in my name; and if they die they shall die unto me, and if they live they shall live unto me.

"Thou shalt live together in love, insomuch that thou shalt weep for the loss of them that die, and more especially for those that have not hope of a glorious resurrection.

"And it shall come to pass that those that die in me shall not taste of death, for it shall be sweet unto them;

"And they that die not in me, wo unto them, for their death is bitter.

"And again, it shall come to pass that he that hath faith in me to be healed, and is not appointed unto death, shall be healed." (D&C 42:44–48.)

We are assured by the Lord that the sick will be healed if the ordinance is performed, if there is sufficient faith, and if the ill one is "not appointed unto death." But there are three factors, all of which should be satisfied. Many do not comply with the ordinances, and great numbers are unwilling or incapable of exercising sufficient faith. But the other factor also looms important: If they are not appointed unto death.

Everyone must die. Death is an important part of life. Of course, we are never quite ready for the change. Not knowing

19

when it should come, we properly fight to retain our life. Yet we ought not be afraid of death. We pray for the sick, we administer to the afflicted, we implore the Lord to heal and reduce pain and save life and postpone death, and properly so, but not because eternity is so frightful. . . .

Just as Ecclesiastes (3:2) says, I am confident that there is a time to die, but I believe also that many people die before "their time" because they are careless, abuse their bodies, take unnecessary chances, or expose themselves to hazards, accidents, and sickness. . . .

God controls our lives, guides and blesses us, but gives us our agency. We may live our lives in accordance with his plan for us or we may foolishly shorten or terminate them.

I am positive in my mind that the Lord has planned our destiny. Sometime we'll understand fully, and when we see back from the vantage point of the future, we shall be satisfied with many of the happenings of this life that are so difficult for us to comprehend.

We sometimes think we would like to know what lies ahead, but sober thought brings us back to accepting life a day at a time and magnifying and glorifying that day. . . .

We knew before we were born that we were coming to the earth for bodies and experience and that we would have joys and sorrows, ease and pain, comforts and hardships, health and sickness, successes and disappointments, and we knew also that after a period of life we would die. We accepted all these eventualities with a glad heart, eager to accept both the favorable and unfavorable. We eagerly accepted the chance to come earthward even though it might be for only a day or a year. Perhaps we were not so much concerned whether we should die of disease, of accident, or of senility. We were willing to take life as it came and as we might organize and control it, and this without murmur, complaint, or unreasonable demands.

In the face of apparent tragedy we must put our trust in God, knowing that despite our limited view his purposes will not fail. With all its troubles life offers us the tremendous privilege to grow in knowledge and wisdom, faith and works, preparing to return and share God's glory.[9]

Suggestions for Study and Teaching

Consider these ideas as you study the chapter or as you prepare to teach. For additional help, see pages v–ix.

- Why doesn't the Lord protect us from all sorrow and suffering? (See pages 13–14.)

- Study pages 15–16, looking for what we would miss if the Lord did not permit us to experience trials. How should we respond to our trials and suffering? How has the Lord strengthened you in your trials?

- Read the paragraph that begins "There are people who . . ." on page 16. Why is it so difficult to see loved ones suffer? What can we do to avoid becoming bitter or discouraged at such times?

- Review pages 16–20, looking for teachings about priesthood blessings. When have you witnessed the healing or comforting power of the priesthood? In what ways can we respond when we learn that it is not the Lord's will for a loved one to be healed or for death to be postponed?

- How would you explain President Kimball's teachings about death to a child?

- President Kimball taught, "In the face of apparent tragedy we must put our trust in God" (page 20). When a person trusts in God, what might he or she do in a time of trial?

Related Scriptures: Psalm 116:15; 2 Nephi 2:11–16; 9:6; Alma 7:10–12; D&C 121:1–9; 122:1–9

Notes

1. In Edward L. Kimball and Andrew E. Kimball Jr., *Spencer W. Kimball* (1977), 43.
2. In *Spencer W. Kimball*, 46.
3. In *Spencer W. Kimball*, 46.
4. Joseph Robinson, in *Spencer W. Kimball*, 46.
5. *The Teachings of Spencer W. Kimball,* ed. Edward L. Kimball (1982), 40–41.
6. *Faith Precedes the Miracle* (1972), 95–96.
7. *Faith Precedes the Miracle*, 97–100.
8. *Faith Precedes the Miracle*, 100, 101, 102.
9. *Faith Precedes the Miracle*, 102–3, 105–6.

"I know that Jesus is the Christ, the Son of the living God."

⚬⚭ 🕯 ⚬⚭

Jesus Christ:
My Savior, My Lord

Jesus Christ is the Son of God and the Savior of mankind,
and we can receive all the blessings
He lived and died to give us.

From the Life of Spencer W. Kimball

Early in his service as an Apostle, Elder Spencer W. Kimball suffered three heart attacks within a period of about two weeks. After almost seven weeks of recovering at home, he "began looking for an escape from his monotonous house confinement." He arranged to recuperate among his beloved Navajo friends in the state of New Mexico.[1]

"One morning during this recuperative period, Elder Kimball's bed was discovered empty. Thinking that he had taken a morning stroll and would be back in time for breakfast, his attendants went about their duties. But when he hadn't returned by 10:00 A.M., they began to worry. A search began.

"He was finally discovered several miles away under a pine tree. His Bible lay next to him, opened to the last chapter of St. John. His eyes were closed, and when the search party came up to him he remained as still as when they first caught sight of him.

"Their frightened voices aroused him, however, and when he lifted his head they could see traces of tears on his cheeks. To their questions, he answered, '[Five] years ago today I was called to be an Apostle of the Lord Jesus Christ, and I just wanted to spend the day with Him whose witness I am.'"[2]

President Kimball bore witness of the Savior's divinity "again and again and again."[3] He declared: "No matter how much we say of him, it is still too little."[4] And the goodness of President Kimball's life matched the power of his testimony. Elder Neal A. Maxwell of

23

the Quorum of the Twelve Apostles observed: "President Kimball was the Lord's man and nobody else's. His deepest desires were to serve the Lord, and he refused to be compromised by other considerations."[5]

Teachings of Spencer W. Kimball

More than just a great teacher, Jesus Christ is the Son of the living God and the Savior of mankind.

In the magazine, *Time,* in a recent issue, a noted professor emeritus in one of our largest universities, was quoted at length on his rationalizing. To Jesus of Nazareth he gives human warmth; a great capacity for love; unusual understanding. He calls him a great humanist, a great teacher, a great dramatist. As a typical rationalization, he explains that Lazarus was not dead, but was merely ". . . brought 'back to health' by Jesus, the power of mind and learning, and by the 'therapy of his own abundant vitality!' "

I want to bear testimony today that Jesus is not only a great teacher, a great humanist, and a great dramatist, but is in very deed, the Son of the Living God, the Creator, the Redeemer of the world, the Savior of mankind.[6]

I know that Jesus is the Christ, the Son of the living God. I know that.[7]

The Christ declared himself to be the Lord God Almighty, Christ the Lord, the beginning and the end, the Redeemer of the world, Jesus the Christ, the mighty one of Israel, the Creator, the Son of the Living God, Jehovah.

The Father Elohim declares Jesus to be *Mine only Begotten Son, the word of my power.* And twice, at least, at the Jordan baptism and then on the Mount of Transfiguration, he declared:

"This is my beloved Son in whom I am well pleased" (see Mark 1:11; Luke 3:22) and stated that *"the worlds were made by him: Men were made by him: All things were made by him, and through him and of him."* [See D&C 93:10.][8]

We testify with John the Baptist, who, as he saw the Lord approaching to him, saith: ". . . Behold the Lamb of God, which taketh away the sin of the world." (John 1:29.) Not just a man of human warmth, but the Lamb of God.

We bear witness with Nathanael, an Israelite in whom was no guile: ". . . Rabbi, thou art the Son of God; thou art the King of Israel." (John 1:49.) Not merely a great teacher, but the very Son of God.

We testify again with John the Beloved, who seeing Jesus on the shore, said with conviction, "It is the Lord!" [See John 21:7.] Not only a great humanist, but the Lord God of heaven.

And with Simon Peter, who, when asked by the Lord, "But whom say ye that I am?" said, "Thou art the Christ, the Son of the living God," (Matt. 16:15, 16), and received this statement from the Savior: ". . . Blessed art thou, Simon Bar-jona: for flesh and blood hath not revealed it unto thee, but my Father which is in heaven." (Matt. 16:17.)

And finally, we bear witness with the Prophet Joseph Smith who was willing to give his life for his testimony.[9]

I know that Jesus Christ is the Son of the living God and that He was crucified for the sins of the world. He is my friend, my Savior, my Lord, and my God.[10]

The Savior's ministry extends through the eternities— past, present, and future.

I want to . . . testify that [Jesus Christ] not only lived in the meridian of time for approximately thirty-three years, but that he lived eternities before this, and will live eternities beyond it; and I bear testimony that he was not only the organizer of the kingdom of God upon the earth, but the Creator of this world, the Redeemer of mankind.[11]

Jesus Christ was the God of the Old Testament, and it was He who conversed with Abraham and Moses. It was He who inspired Isaiah and Jeremiah; it was He who foretold through those chosen men the happenings of the future, even to the latest day and hour.[12]

It was He, Jesus Christ, our Savior, who was introduced to surprised listeners at Jordan (see Matt. 3:13–17), at the holy Mount of Transfiguration (see Matt. 17:1–9), at the temple of the Nephites (see 3 Ne. 11–26), and in the grove at Palmyra, New York [see Joseph Smith—History 1:17–25]; and the introducing person was none other than his actual Father, the holy Elohim, in whose image he was and whose will he carried out.[13]

I know the Lord lives and I know that he's revealing his mind and will to us daily, so that we can be inspired as to the direction to go.[14]

He is the chief cornerstone. He is the head of the kingdom—these are his followers—this his Church—these his doctrines and ordinances—these his commandments.[15]

We look forward now to his second coming as he promised. This promise will be literally fulfilled as were his many other promises, and in the meantime, we praise his holy name and serve him, and bear testimony of the divinity of his mission, with the prophets through the generations! . . .

I know that Jesus, through eternities past and future, is the Creator, the Redeemer, the Savior, the Son of God.[16]

Through His Atonement, Jesus Christ saves all people from the effects of the Fall and saves the repentant from personal sins.

My beloved brothers and sisters, God lives, and I bear testimony of it. Jesus Christ lives, and he is the author of the true way of life and salvation.

This is the message of The Church of Jesus Christ of Latter-day Saints. It is the most important message in the world today. Jesus Christ is the son of God. He was chosen by the Father as the Savior of this world.[17]

When Adam intentionally and wisely partook of the forbidden fruit in the Garden of Eden, he brought upon all of us, his descendants, two deaths—the physical or "mortal death," and the spiritual death or the banishment from the presence of the Lord.[18]

In God's divine plan, provision was made for a redeemer to break the bonds of death and, through the resurrection, make possible the reunion of the spirits and bodies of all persons who had dwelt on earth.

Jesus of Nazareth was the one who, before the world was created, was chosen to come to earth to perform this service, to conquer mortal death. This voluntary action would atone for the fall of Adam and Eve and permit the spirit of man to recover his body, thereby reuniting body and spirit.[19]

This resurrection referred to is the work of Jesus Christ, the Savior, who, because he was both mortal (the son of Mary) and divine (the Son of God), was able to overcome the powers governing the flesh. He actually gave his life and literally took it up again as the "first fruits," to be followed by every soul that has ever lived [see 1 Corinthians 15:22–23]. Being a god, he gave his life. No one could take it from him. He had developed, through his perfection in overcoming all things, the power to take up his life again. Death was his last enemy, and he overcame even that and established the resurrection.[20]

It is because of Heavenly Father's gift of His Son that all men—past, present, and future—can return to live with Him who is the Father of our spirits. But to insure that that can happen, it was first necessary for Jesus to come to earth in the flesh to teach men by His example the correct way to live and then to willingly give up His life and, in some miraculous way, accept the burden for the sins of mankind.[21]

The purging out of sin would be impossible but for the total repentance of the individual and the kind mercy of the Lord Jesus Christ in his atoning sacrifice. Only by these means can man recover, be healed and washed and purged, and still be eligible for the glories of eternity. On the Savior's great role in this, Helaman reminded his sons of King Benjamin's comments:

". . . There is no other way nor means whereby man can be saved, only through the atoning blood of Jesus Christ, who shall come, yea, remember that he cometh to redeem the world." (Hel. 5:9.)

And, in recalling the words which Amulek spoke to Zeezrom, Helaman emphasized man's part in obtaining forgiveness—repenting from his sins:

"Death was his last enemy, and he overcame even that and established the resurrection."

". . . He said unto him that the Lord surely should come to redeem his people, but that he should not come to redeem them *in their sins,* but to redeem them *from their sins.*

"And he hath power given unto him from the Father to redeem them from their sins *because of repentance. . . ."* (Hel. 5:10–11. Italics added.)[22]

[The Savior] died a propitiation for our sins to open the way for our resurrection, to point the way to our perfection of life, to show the way to exaltation. He died purposefully, voluntarily. His birth was humble, his life was perfect, his example was compelling; his death opened doors, and man was offered every good gift and blessing.[23]

To receive all the blessings of the Savior's Atonement, we must join our efforts with His.

Every soul has his free agency. He can have all the blessings Christ lived and died to give him. But Christ's death and plan are all in vain and even worse than futile if we do not take advantage of them: "For behold, I, God, have suffered these things for all, that they might not suffer if they would repent" (D&C 19:16).

The Savior came "to bring to pass the immortality and eternal life of man" (Moses 1:39). His birth, death, and resurrection brought about the first. But we must join our efforts with his to bring about the second, to attain eternal life.[24]

When we think of the great sacrifice of our Lord Jesus Christ and the sufferings he endured for us, we would be ingrates if we did not appreciate it so far as our power made it possible. He suffered and died for us, yet if we do not repent, all his anguish and pain on our account are futile.[25]

His suffering before and on the cross and his great sacrifice can mean little or nothing to us unless we live his commandments. For he says:

". . . why call ye me, Lord, Lord, and do not the things which I say?" (Luke 6:46.)

"If ye love me, keep my commandments." (John 14:15.)[26]

Men who know God and love him and live his commandments and obey his true ordinances may yet in this life, or the life to come, see his face and know that he lives and will commune with them.[27]

We *believe,* and it is our testimony, and we proclaim it to the world "that there shall be no other name given nor any other way nor means whereby salvation can come unto the children of men, only in and through the name of Christ, the Lord Omnipotent" (Mosiah 3:17).

We *know,* and it is our testimony, and we also proclaim it to the world that to be saved men must "believe that salvation was, and is, and is to come, in and through the atoning blood of Christ, the Lord Omnipotent" (Mosiah 3:18).

Thus, with Nephi, "we labor diligently to write, to persuade our children, and also our brethren, to believe in Christ, and to be reconciled to God; for we know that it is by grace that we are saved, after all *we* can do. . . .

"And we talk of Christ, we rejoice in Christ, we preach of Christ, we prophesy of Christ, and we write according to our prophecies, that our children may know to what source they may look for a remission of their sins." (2 Ne. 25:23, 26; italics added.)[28]

We please the Lord when we live His gospel.

I can imagine the Lord Jesus Christ [during his mortal ministry,] smiling as he looked upon his people in their devotion. . . .

. . . I think the Lord Jesus Christ is smiling when he looks into the homes of this people and sees them on their knees in family prayer night and morning, the children participating also. I think he smiles when he sees young husbands and wives, and older ones, with deep affection for each other, who continue their courtship . . . , who continue to love each other with all their souls until the day they die and then accentuate it through eternity.

I think he is pleased with the families which sacrifice and share. . . . I think the Lord Jesus Christ is smiling when he looks down and sees [thousands] who were inactive a year ago, but today are happy in the kingdom, many of whom have been to the holy temple of God and had their endowments and their sealings, and who with tears of gratitude thank the Lord for his program.

I think I see tears of joy in his eyes and a smile on his lips as he sees the . . . new souls who have come unto him this year, who have professed his name, who have gone into the waters of baptism, and I think he loves those who helped to convert them also.

I see him smile as he sees his numerous people on their knees in repentance, changing their lives, making them brighter and cleaner, and more like their Heavenly Father and their Brother, Jesus Christ.

I think he is pleased and smiles as he sees youth as they organize their lives and protect and fortify themselves against the errors of the day. I think he is first grieved, and then perhaps pleased, when he sees, as he must have done a few days ago in my office, a young couple who had made serious error and were now on their knees together with their hands tightly clasped together. There must have been joy in his smile when he saw into their souls and saw that they were making the adjustment, as their tears bathed my hand which I had tenderly placed on theirs.

Oh, I love the Lord Jesus Christ. I hope that I can show to him and manifest my sincerity and devotion. I want to live close to him. I want to be like him, and I pray that the Lord will help all of us that we may so be as he said to his Nephite disciples, "Therefore, what manner of men ought ye to be?" and he answered his own question by saying, "Even as I am." (3 Nephi 27:27.)[29]

The Atonement gives us hope in this life and for the eternity that lies ahead.

We have a hope in Christ here and now. He died for our sins. Because of him and his gospel, our sins are washed away in the waters of baptism; sin and iniquity are burned out of our souls as though by fire; and we become clean, have clear consciences, and gain that peace which passeth understanding. (See Phil. 4:7.)

By living the laws of his gospel, we gain temporal prosperity and maintain health of body and strength of mind. The gospel blesses us today.

But today is just a grain of sand in the Sahara of eternity. We have also a hope in Christ for the eternity that lies ahead; otherwise, as Paul said, we would be "of all men most miserable" (1 Cor. 15:19).

How great would be our sorrow—and justly so—if there were no resurrection! How miserable we would be if there were no hope of life eternal! If our hope of salvation and eternal reward should fade away, we would certainly be more miserable than those who never had such an expectancy.

"But now is Christ risen from the dead, and become the first-fruits of them that slept" (1 Cor. 15:20).

Now the effects of his resurrection shall pass upon all men, "for as in Adam all die, even so in Christ shall all be made alive" (1 Cor. 15:22).

Now "as we have borne the image of the earthy, we shall also bear the image of the heavenly" (1 Cor. 15:49).

Now provision has been made whereby "this corruptible shall . . . put on incorruption, and this mortal shall . . . put on immortality, then shall be brought to pass the saying that is written, Death is swallowed up in victory" (1 Cor. 15:54). . . .

We have an eternal hope in Christ. We know this life is given us to prepare for eternity, "and that same sociality which exists among us here will exist among us there, only it will be coupled with eternal glory, which glory we do not now enjoy" (D&C 130:2).[30]

Suggestions for Study and Teaching

Consider these ideas as you study the chapter or as you prepare to teach. For additional help, see pages v–ix.

- Read the story on page 23. In what ways can we draw closer to the Lord and "spend the day" with Him, as President Kimball did?

- Review pages 24–25, looking for names and titles President Kimball used for Jesus Christ. What names and titles for Jesus Christ have special meaning for you and why? How would you respond to someone who claims that Jesus was just a great teacher?

- Ponder President Kimball's testimony of the Savior's premortal, mortal, and postmortal ministry (pages 25–26). Think about what you might do to deepen your testimony of the Savior's mission.

- Study pages 26–28, looking for reasons why we need a Savior. What difference has the Atonement of Jesus Christ made in your life?

- On pages 24–28, President Kimball testifies of the things the Savior has done for us. On pages 29–32, we learn of the things we must do to receive all the blessings of the Atonement. What are your feelings as you compare what the Savior has done for us with what He asks us to do?

- Review President Kimball's reflections about how we can please the Lord (pages 30–31). Think about how you feel when you know the Lord is pleased with you.

- President Kimball taught that we can have a hope in Christ both now and for the eternity that lies ahead (pages 31–32). How do people's lives change when they have a hope in Christ?

Related Scriptures: John 14:6, 21–23; 2 Nephi 9:5–13, 21–23; Moroni 7:41; 10:32–33; D&C 19:15–19

Notes

1. See Edward L. Kimball and Andrew E. Kimball Jr., *Spencer W. Kimball* (1977), 249–52.
2. In "The Gospel of Love: Stories about President Spencer W. Kimball," *Ensign,* Dec. 1985, 22–23.
3. In Conference Report, Apr. 1978, 9; or *Ensign,* May 1978, 7.
4. *The Teachings of Spencer W. Kimball,* ed. Edward L. Kimball (1982), 7.
5. "Spencer, the Beloved: Leader-Servant," *Ensign,* Dec. 1985, 15.
6. In Conference Report, Oct. 1946, 55–56.
7. In Conference Report, Oct. 1974, 163; or *Ensign,* Nov. 1974, 113.
8. In Conference Report, Apr. 1964, 94; or *Improvement Era,* June 1964, 496–97.
9. In Conference Report, Oct. 1946, 64.
10. In Conference Report, Oct. 1982, 6; or *Ensign,* Nov. 1982, 6.
11. *Faith Precedes the Miracle* (1972), 70.
12. In Conference Report, Apr. 1977, 113; or *Ensign,* May 1977, 76.
13. In Conference Report, Oct. 1977, 111; or *Ensign,* Nov. 1977, 73.
14. In Conference Report, Apr. 1977, 117; or *Ensign,* May 1977, 78.
15. *The Teachings of Spencer W. Kimball,* 6.
16. In Conference Report, Oct. 1946, 63, 64.
17. In Conference Report, Apr. 1978, 7; or *Ensign,* May 1978, 6.
18. *The Teachings of Spencer W. Kimball,* 68.
19. In Conference Report, Apr. 1978, 7; or *Ensign,* May 1978, 6.
20. "Absolute Truth," *Ensign,* Sept. 1978, 6.
21. "Christmas Message from the First Presidency to the Children of the World: Gifts That Endure," *Friend,* Dec. 1982, 3.
22. *The Miracle of Forgiveness* (1969), 339–40.
23. "Jesus of Nazareth," *Ensign,* Dec. 1980, 4.
24. *Ensign,* Dec. 1980, 4.
25. *The Miracle of Forgiveness,* 145.
26. In Conference Report, Apr. 1972, 26; or *Ensign,* July 1972, 37.
27. In Conference Report, Apr. 1964, 99; or *Improvement Era,* June 1964, 499.
28. In Conference Report, Oct. 1978, 109–10; or *Ensign,* Nov. 1978, 72.
29. In Conference Report, Apr. 1956, 120.
30. In Conference Report, Oct. 1978, 108–9; or *Ensign,* Nov. 1978, 72.

The Miracle of Forgiveness

Through sincere repentance and the Savior's redeeming power, we can experience the miracle of forgiveness.

From the Life of Spencer W. Kimball

President Spencer W. Kimball taught that "repentance is ever the key to a better, happier life. All of us need it."[1]

He also observed that "hope is . . . the great incentive to repentance, for without it no one would make the difficult, extended effort required." To illustrate this point, he told of an experience he had in helping a woman who came to him feeling despondent about the sin she had committed. She said: "I know what I have done. I have read the scriptures, and I know the consequences. I know that I am damned and can never be forgiven, and therefore why should I try now to repent?"

President Kimball responded: "My dear sister, you do not know the scriptures. You do not know the power of God nor his goodness. You *can* be forgiven for this heinous sin, but it will take much sincere repentance to accomplish it."

He then quoted to her several scriptures regarding the forgiveness that comes to those who sincerely repent and obey God's commandments. Continuing to instruct her, he saw hope awaken in her until finally she exclaimed: "Thank you, thank you! I believe you. I shall really repent and wash my filthy garments in the blood of the Lamb and obtain that forgiveness."

President Kimball recalled that the woman eventually returned to his office "a new person—bright of eye, light of step, full of hope as she declared to me that, since that memorable day when hope had seen a star and had clung to it, she had never reverted to [the sin] nor any approaches to it."[2]

Teachings of Spencer W. Kimball

The miracle of forgiveness brings peace and helps us grow closer to God.

There is a glorious miracle awaiting every soul who is prepared to change. Repentance and forgiveness make a brilliant day of the darkest night. When souls are reborn, when lives are changed—then comes the great miracle to beautify and warm and lift. When spiritual death has threatened and now instead there is resuscitation, when life pushes out death—when this happens it is the miracle of miracles. And such great miracles will never cease so long as there is one person who applies the redeeming power of the Savior and his own good works to bring about his rebirth. . . .

The essence of the miracle of forgiveness is that it brings peace to the previously anxious, restless, frustrated, perhaps tormented soul. In a world of turmoil and contention this is indeed a priceless gift.[3]

It is not easy to be at peace in today's troubled world. Necessarily peace is a personal acquisition. . . . It can be attained only through maintaining constantly a repentant attitude, seeking forgiveness of sins both large and small, and thus coming ever closer to God. For Church members this is the essence of their preparation, their readiness to meet the Savior when he comes. . . . Those who are ready will be at peace in their hearts. They will be partakers of the blessing the Savior promised to his apostles: "Peace I leave with you, my peace I give unto you: not as the world giveth, give I unto you. Let not your heart be troubled, neither let it be afraid." (John 14:27.)

[One of the purposes] of The Church of Jesus Christ of Latter-day Saints is to call people everywhere to repentance. Those who heed the call, whether members or nonmembers of the Church, can be partakers of the miracle of forgiveness. God will wipe away from their eyes the tears of anguish, and remorse, and consternation, and fear, and guilt. Dry eyes will replace the wet ones, and smiles of satisfaction will replace the worried, anxious look.

"Repentance and forgiveness make a brilliant day of the darkest night."

What relief! What comfort! What joy! Those laden with transgressions and sorrows and sin may be forgiven and cleansed and purified if they will return to their Lord, learn of him, and keep his commandments. And all of us needing to repent of day-to-day follies and weaknesses can likewise share in this miracle.[4]

We all need repentance.

". . . There cannot any unclean thing enter into the kingdom of God. . . ." (1 Ne. 15:34.) And again, ". . . no unclean thing can dwell with God. . . ." (1 Ne. 10:21.) To the prophets the term *unclean* in this context means what it means to God. To man the word may be relative in meaning—one minute speck of dirt does not make a white shirt or dress unclean, for example. But to God who is perfection, cleanliness means moral and personal cleanliness. Less

36

than that is, in one degree or another, uncleanliness and hence cannot dwell with God.

Were it not for the blessed gifts of repentance and forgiveness this would be a hopeless situation for man, since no one except the Master has ever lived sinless on the earth.[5]

There is never a day in any man's life when repentance is not essential to his well-being and eternal progress.

But when most of us think of repentance we tend to narrow our vision and view it as good only for our husbands, our wives, our parents, our children, our neighbors, our friends, the world—anyone and everyone except ourselves. Similarly there is a prevalent, perhaps subconscious, feeling that the Lord designed repentance only for those who commit murder or adultery or theft or other heinous crimes. This is of course not so. If we are humble and desirous of living the gospel we will come to think of repentance as applying to everything we do in life, whether it be spiritual or temporal in nature. Repentance is for every soul who has not yet reached perfection.[6]

Repentance is the key to forgiveness. It opens the door to happiness and peace and points the way to salvation in the kingdom of God. It unlocks the spirit of humility in the soul of man and makes him contrite of heart and submissive to the will of God.

"Sin is the transgression of the law" (1 John 3:4), and for such transgression a punishment is affixed under eternal law. Every normal individual is responsible for the sins he commits, and would be similarly liable to the punishment attached to those broken laws. However, Christ's death on the cross offers us exemption from the eternal punishment for most sins. He took upon himself the punishment for the sins of all the world, with the understanding that those who repent and come unto him will be forgiven of their sins and freed from the punishment.[7]

Recognition of sin and feeling godly sorrow are a part of true repentance.

Repentance is a kind and merciful law. It is far-reaching and all-inclusive. . . . It is composed of many elements, each one indispensable to complete repentance. . . .

There is *no royal road to repentance,* no privileged path to forgiveness. Every man must follow the same course whether he be rich or poor, educated or untrained, tall or short, prince or pauper, king or commoner. "For there is no respect of persons with God." (Rom. 2:11.) . . .

Before the many elements of repentance are set in motion there has to be a first step. That first step is the turning point at which the sinner consciously recognizes his sin. This is the awakening, the conviction of guilt. Without this there can be no true repentance because there is no acknowledgement of sin. . . .

When we have become aware of the gravity of our sin, we can condition our minds to follow such processes as will rid us of the effects of the sin. Alma tried to convey this to Corianton when he said: ". . . Let your sins trouble you, with that trouble which shall bring you down unto repentance. . . . Do not endeavor to excuse yourself in the least point. . . ." (Alma 42:29–30.)[8]

The Holy Ghost can play an important role in convincing the sinner of his error. He helps in making known "the truth of all things" (Moro. 10:5); in teaching all things and bringing all things to one's remembrance (John 14:26); and in reproving the world of sin (John 16:8).

Often people indicate that they have repented when all they have done is to express regret for a wrong act. But true repentance is marked by that godly sorrow that changes, transforms, and saves. To be sorry is not enough. . . . Paul put it this way to the Corinthian saints:

"Now I rejoice, not that ye were made sorry, but that ye sorrowed to repentance: for ye were made sorry after a godly manner, that ye might receive damage by us in nothing.

"For godly sorrow worketh repentance to salvation not to be repented of: but the sorrow of the world worketh death." (2 Cor. 7:9–10.)[9]

To every forgiveness there is a condition. The plaster must be as wide as the sore. The fasting, the prayers, the humility must be equal to or greater than the sin. There must be a broken heart and a contrite spirit. There must be "sackcloth and ashes." There must be tears and genuine change of heart.[10]

Abandonment of sin includes building a new life.

Of course, even the conviction of guilt is not enough. It could be devastating and destructive were it not accompanied by efforts to rid oneself of guilt. Accompanying the conviction, then, must be an earnest desire to clean up the guilt and compensate for the loss sustained through the error.[11]

There is one crucial test of repentance. This is abandonment of the sin. Providing that a person discontinues his sin with the right motives—because of a growing consciousness of the gravity of the sin and a willingness to comply with the laws of the Lord—he is genuinely repenting. This criterion has been set by the Lord: "By this ye may know if a man repenteth of his sins— behold, he will confess them and *forsake them*." (D&C 58:43. Italics added.)

In other words, it is not real repentance until one has abandoned the error of his way and started on a new path. . . . The saving power does not extend to him who merely *wants* to change his life. True repentance prods one to action.

One must not be surprised that effort is required, and not merely desire. After all, it is work which develops our moral as well as our physical muscles.[12]

In abandoning sin one cannot merely wish for better conditions. He must make them. He may need to come to hate the spotted garments and loathe the sin. He must be certain not only that he has abandoned the sin but that he has changed the situations surrounding the sin. He should avoid the places and conditions and circumstances where the sin occurred, for these could most readily breed it again. He must abandon the people with whom the sin was committed. He may not hate the persons involved but he must avoid them and everything associated with the sin. He must dispose of all letters, trinkets, and things which will remind him of the "old days" and the "old times." He must forget addresses, telephone numbers, people, places and situations from the sinful past, and build a new life. He must eliminate anything which would stir the old memories.[13]

"Confession brings peace."

In abandoning evil, transforming lives, changing personalities, molding characters or remolding them, we need the help of the Lord, and we may be assured of it if we do our part. The man who leans heavily upon his Lord becomes the master of self and can accomplish anything he sets out to do, whether it be to secure the brass plates, build a ship, overcome a habit, or conquer a deep-seated transgression.[14]

Confession lifts burdens.

The confession of sin is a necessary element in repentance and therefore in obtaining forgiveness. It is one of the tests of true repentance, for, "By this ye may know if a man repenteth of his sins—behold, *he will confess them* and forsake them." (D&C 58:43. Italics added.) . . .

Perhaps confession is one of the hardest of all the obstacles for the repenting sinner to negotiate. His shame often restrains him from making known his guilt and acknowledging his error. Sometimes his assumed lack of confidence in mortals to whom he should confess his sin justifies in his mind his keeping the secret locked in his own heart. . . .

Knowing the hearts of men, and their intents, and their abilities to repent and regenerate themselves, the Lord waits to forgive until the repentance has matured. The transgressor must have a "broken heart and a contrite spirit" and be willing to humble himself and do all that is required. The confession of his major sins to a proper Church authority is one of those requirements made by the Lord. These sins include adultery, fornication, other sexual transgressions, and other sins of comparable seriousness. This procedure of confession assures proper controls and protection for the Church and its people and sets the feet of the transgressor on the path of true repentance.

Many offenders in their shame and pride have satisfied their consciences, temporarily at least, with a few silent prayers to the Lord and rationalized that this was sufficient confession of their sins. "But I have confessed my sin to my Heavenly Father," they will insist, "and that is all that is necessary." This is not true where a major sin is involved. Then two sets of forgiveness are required to bring peace to the transgressor—one from the proper authorities of the Lord's Church, and one from the Lord himself. [See Mosiah 26:29.] . . .

. . . The ideal confession is voluntary, not forced. It is induced from within the offender's soul, not sparked by being found out in the sin. Such confession . . . is a sign of growing repentance. It indicates the sinner's conviction of sin and his desire to abandon the evil practices. The voluntary confession is infinitely more acceptable in the sight of the Lord than is forced admission, lacking humility, wrung from an individual by questioning when guilt is evident. Such forced admission is not evidence of the humble heart which calls forth the Lord's mercy: ". . . For I, the Lord, forgive sins, and am merciful unto those *who confess their sins* with humble hearts." (D&C 61:2. Italics added.)[15]

While the major sins such as those listed earlier . . . call for confession to the proper Church authorities, clearly such confession is neither necessary nor desirable for all sins. Those of lesser gravity but which have offended others—marital differences, minor fits of anger, disagreements and such—should instead be confessed to the person or persons hurt and the matter should be cleared

41

between the persons involved, normally without a reference to a Church authority.[16]

Confession brings peace. . . . Confession is not only the revealing of errors to proper authorities, but the sharing of burdens to lighten them. One lifts at least part of his burden and places it on other shoulders which are able and willing to help carry the load. Then there comes satisfaction in having taken another step in doing all that is possible to rid oneself of the burden of transgression.[17]

Restitution is a necessary part of repentance.

When a person has experienced the deep sorrow and humility induced by a conviction of sin; when he has cast off the sin and resolutely determined to abhor it henceforth; when he has humbly confessed his sin to God and to the proper persons on earth—when these things are done there remains the requirement of restitution. He must restore that which he damaged, stole, or wronged.[18]

The repentant sinner is required to make restitution insofar as it is possible. I say "insofar as it is possible" because there are some sins for which no adequate restitution can be made, and others for which only partial restitution is possible.

A thief or burglar may make partial restitution by returning that which was stolen. A liar may make the truth known and correct to some degree the damage done by the lie. A gossip who has slandered the character of another may make partial restitution through strenuous effort to restore the good name of the person he harmed. If by sin or carelessness the wrongdoer has destroyed property, he may restore or pay for it in full or in part.

If a man's actions have brought sorrow and disgrace to his wife and children, in his restitution he must make every effort to restore their confidence and love by an overabundance of . . . devotion and fidelity. This is true also of wives and mothers. Likewise if children have wronged their parents, a part of their . . . repentance must be to right those wrongs and to honor their parents.

As a rule there are many things which a repentant soul can do to make amends. "A broken heart and a contrite spirit" will usually find ways to restore to some extent. The true spirit of repentance demands that he who injures shall do everything in his power to right the wrong.[19]

In the process of repentance we must restore completely where possible, otherwise restore to the maximum degree attainable. And through it all we must remember that the pleading sinner, desiring to make restitution for his acts, must also forgive others of all offenses committed against him. The Lord will not forgive us unless our hearts are fully purged of all hate, bitterness and accusation against our fellowmen.[20]

True repentance includes a commitment to live the Lord's commandments.

In his preface to modern revelation, the Lord outlined what is one of the most difficult requirements in true repentance. For some it is the hardest part of repentance, because it puts one on guard for the remainder of his life. The Lord says:

". . . I the Lord cannot look upon sin with the least degree of allowance;

"Nevertheless, he that repents and *does the commandments of the Lord* shall be forgiven." (D&C 1:31–32. Italics added.)

This scripture is most precise. First, one repents. Having gained that ground he then must live the commandments of the Lord to retain his vantage point. This is necessary to secure complete forgiveness. . . .

Since all of us sin in greater or lesser degree, we are all in need of constant repentance, of continually raising our sights and our performance. One can hardly do the commandments of the Lord in a day, a week, a month or a year. This is an effort which must be extended through the remainder of one's years. . . .

. . . Repentance must involve an all-out, total surrender to the program of the Lord. That transgressor is not fully repentant who neglects his tithing, misses his meetings, breaks the Sabbath, fails in his family prayers, does not sustain the authorities of the

Church, breaks the Word of Wisdom, does not love the Lord nor his fellowmen. . . . God cannot forgive unless the transgressor shows a true repentance which spreads to all areas of his life. . . .

"Doing the commandments" includes the many activities required of the faithful. . . . General good works and devotion accompanied by constructive attitudes are what is needed. In addition, a sound way to neutralize the effects of sin in one's life is to bring the light of the gospel to others who do not now enjoy it. This can mean working with both inactive members of the Church and nonmembers—perhaps more usually the latter. Note how the Lord has related the forgiveness of sins to the bearing of testimony respecting the latter-day work:

"For I will forgive you of your sins with this commandment—that you remain steadfast in your minds in solemnity and the spirit of prayer, *in bearing testimony to all the world* of those things which are communicated unto you." (D&C 84:61. Italics added.)[21]

Can we not understand why the Lord has been pleading with man for these thousands of years to come unto him? Surely the Lord was speaking about forgiveness through repentance, and the relief that could come from the tenseness of guilt, when he followed his glorious prayer to his Father with this sublime entreaty and promise:

"Come unto me, all ye that labour and are heavy laden, and I will give you rest.

"Take my yoke upon you, and learn of me; for I am meek and lowly in heart: and ye shall find rest unto your souls.

"For my yoke is easy, and my burden is light." (Matt. 11:28–30.)

It is my hope and prayer that men and women everywhere will respond to this gentle invitation and thus let the Master work in their individual lives the great miracle of forgiveness.[22]

Suggestions for Study and Teaching

Consider these ideas as you study the chapter or as you prepare to teach. For additional help, see pages v–ix.

- President Kimball called forgiveness "the miracle of miracles" (page 35). In what ways is forgiveness a miracle? (For some examples, see pages 34–36.)

- As you read the section that begins on page 36, ponder what our condition would be without the Savior and His Atonement.

- Read the fifth, sixth, and seventh paragraphs on page 38. In what ways do you think "godly sorrow" is different from expressions of regret? What are some scriptural examples of godly sorrow that apply to us today?

- On pages 39–40 President Kimball gives examples of how to abandon sin and "build a new life." How might we apply this counsel to any sin we are trying to overcome—for example, pornography, profanity, or gambling?

- Review pages 40–42. Why do some consider confession so difficult? What blessings come from confession to the Lord? to the bishop or branch president? to others whom we have offended?

- Ponder the first paragraph on page 43. What does it mean to make restitution for sins? How can a repentant person best determine what to do to make restitution for his or her sins?

- How do President Kimball's teachings in this chapter differ from the false idea that repentance is the performance of a list of routine actions?

Related Scriptures: Isaiah 1:18; Mosiah 4:3; Alma 36:12–26; D&C 19:15–20; 64:8–9

Notes

1. *The Miracle of Forgiveness* (1969), 28.
2. See *The Miracle of Forgiveness,* 340–42.
3. *The Miracle of Forgiveness,* 362, 363.
4. *The Miracle of Forgiveness,* 366, 367–68.
5. *The Miracle of Forgiveness,* 19–20.
6. *The Miracle of Forgiveness,* 32–33.
7. *The Miracle of Forgiveness,* 133.
8. *The Miracle of Forgiveness,* 149, 150–51.
9. *The Miracle of Forgiveness,* 152–53.
10. *The Miracle of Forgiveness,* 353.
11. *The Miracle of Forgiveness,* 159.
12. *The Miracle of Forgiveness,* 163–64.
13. *The Miracle of Forgiveness,* 171–72.
14. *The Miracle of Forgiveness,* 176.
15. *The Miracle of Forgiveness,* 177, 178, 179, 181.
16. *The Miracle of Forgiveness,* 185.
17. *The Miracle of Forgiveness,* 187–88.
18. *The Miracle of Forgiveness,* 191.
19. *The Miracle of Forgiveness,* 194–95.
20. *The Miracle of Forgiveness,* 200.
21. *The Miracle of Forgiveness,* 201–2, 203, 204.
22. *The Miracle of Forgiveness,* 368.

"None of us should get so busy in our lives that we cannot contemplate with prayer."

CHAPTER 5

Prayer, the Passport to Spiritual Power

Through honest and heartfelt prayer, we receive love,
power, and strength from our Heavenly Father.

From the Life of Spencer W. Kimball

"I always have very tender feelings about prayers and the power and blessings of prayer," said President Spencer W. Kimball. "In my lifetime I have received more blessings than I can ever adequately give thanks for. The Lord has been so good to me. I have had so many experiences in sickness and in health that leave me with no shadow of doubt in my heart and mind that there is a God in heaven, that he is our Father, and that he hears and answers our prayers."[1]

One of these experiences came when President Kimball and his wife, Camilla, traveled to a conference in New Zealand. When they reached the city of Hamilton, they were so sick that President Kimball asked President N. Eldon Tanner, First Counselor in the First Presidency, to represent him at a cultural event planned for that evening. Some hours later, President Kimball "awakened with a start and asked Dr. Russell Nelson, who sat watching over him, 'Brother Nelson, what time was that program to begin this evening?'

"'At seven o'clock, President Kimball.'

"'What time is it now?'

"'It is almost seven.'

"Spencer was soaked with perspiration. His fever had broken. . . . He said, 'Tell Sister Kimball we're going.'

"Camilla got out of bed, and they both hurriedly dressed and then drove the short distance to the stadium where the program had just convened. President Tanner had explained at the beginning of the meeting that they were too sick to attend. In the opening prayer a young New Zealander petitioned fervently, 'We three thousand New Zealand youth have gathered here prepared to sing and to dance for thy prophet. Wilt thou heal him and deliver him here.' As the prayer ended, the car carrying Spencer and Camilla entered and the stadium erupted in a spontaneous, deafening shout at the answer to their prayer."[2]

Teachings of Spencer W. Kimball

We are required to pray, just as we are required to keep any other commandment.

Prayer is not an optional activity; it is basic to our religion.[3]

Why should we pray? Because we are the sons and daughters of our Heavenly Father, on whom we depend for everything we enjoy—our food and clothing, our health, our life itself, our sight and hearing, our voices, our locomotion, even our brains.

. . . Do you give to yourself your breath, your life, your being? Can you lengthen your days by a single hour? Are you so strong without the gifts of heaven? Are your brains made by self, and did you fashion them? Can you give life or give it prolongation? Do you have power to do without your Lord? Yet I find that many fail to pray. . . .

You who pray sometimes, why not pray more regularly, more often, more devoutly? Is time so precious, life so short, or faith so scant? . . .

We all are under heavy obligation to our Lord. None of us has reached perfection. None of us is free from error. To pray is required of all men like chastity is required, and Sabbath observance, and tithing, and living the Word of Wisdom, attending meetings, and entering into celestial marriage. As truly as any other, this is a commandment of the Lord.[4]

When I used to travel throughout the stakes and missions of the Church in earlier years, I often met people who were in trouble or who had great need. My first question to them was, "What about your prayers? How often? How deeply involved are you when you pray?" I have observed that sin generally comes when communication lines are down. For this reason the Lord said to the Prophet Joseph Smith, "What I say unto one I say unto all; pray always lest that wicked one have power in you." (D&C 93:49.)[5]

There is a great need in the world today for prayer which can keep us in touch with God and keep open the channels of communication. None of us should get so busy in our lives that we cannot contemplate with prayer. Prayer is the passport to spiritual power.[6]

Our prayers should include expressions of gratitude and humble pleading for Heavenly Father to bless us and those around us.

About what shall we pray in our prayers? We should express joyful and sincere gratitude for past blessings. The Lord has said, "And ye must give thanks unto God in the Spirit for whatsoever blessing ye are blessed with." (D&C 46:32.) A wonderful and assuring spirit comes over us as we express sincere gratitude to Heavenly Father for our blessings—for the gospel and the knowledge of it that we have been blessed to receive, for the efforts and labors of parents and others in our behalf, for our families and friends, for opportunities, for mind and body and life, for experiences good and helpful throughout our lives, for all of our Father's helps and kindnesses and answered prayers.

We can pray for our leaders. Paul wrote:

"I exhort therefore, that, first of all, supplications, prayers, intercessions, and giving of thanks, be made for all men;

"For kings, and for all that are in authority." (1 Tim. 2:1–2.)

We will develop loyalty to country and to the laws that govern us if we so pray. And we will develop love and faith in our Church leadership, and our children will come to respect them. For one can hardly be critical of Church officers if honest prayers are offered for them. It is a joy to me that all my life I have sustained my leaders, prayed for their welfare. And in recent years, I have felt a great power coming to me because of similar prayers of the Saints, raised to heaven in my behalf.

The all-encompassing missionary work should be the constant object of our prayers. We pray that the doors of nations will be opened to receive the gospel. We pray for opportunity and guidance to share the glorious gospel news with others. When each child prays all his life for the missionary cause, he will be a good missionary.

. . . We pray for that person we felt was an enemy, for we remember the beautiful and powerful counsel of our Lord: "But I say unto you which hear, Love your enemies, do good to them which hate you, Bless them that curse you, and pray for them which despitefully use you." (Luke 6:27–28.) Can anyone long have an enemy when he prays for persons around him about whom he may have hard feelings?

We pray for wisdom, for judgment, for understanding. We pray for protection in dangerous places, for strength in moments of temptation. We remember loved ones and friends. We utter momentary prayers in word or thought, aloud or in deepest silence. We always have a prayer in our hearts that we may do well in the activities of our day. Can one do evil when honest prayers are in his heart and on his lips?

We pray over our marriages, our children, our neighbors, our jobs, our decisions, our church assignments, our testimonies, our feelings, our goals. Indeed, we take Amulek's great counsel and we pray for mercy, we pray over our means of livelihood, over our households and against the power of our enemies; we pray "against the devil, who is an enemy to all righteousness," and over the crops of our fields. And when we do not cry unto the Lord, we "let [our] hearts be full, drawn out in prayer unto him continually for [our] welfare, and also for the welfare of those who are around [us]." (See Alma 34:18–27.)[7]

We pray for forgiveness. I have interviewed numerous prospective missionaries. Too often I find them not praying, even though they have unforgiven follies. "Why don't you pray," I have asked, "when you have such a great obligation to repay? Do you think you can merely write it off and shrug your shoulders and rationalize that it is just a common practice? Are you ashamed to kneel, ashamed of Christ? Is there some disbelief in

"We pray over our marriages, our children, our neighbors, our jobs, our decisions, our church assignments, our testimonies, our feelings, our goals."

God? Do you not know he lives and loves, forgives when repentance is forthcoming? Do you know that sins cannot be erased, transgressions cannot be forgiven through evasion and mere forgetfulness?" . . .

We pray for everything that is needed and dignified and proper. I heard a boy about fourteen years of age in family prayer imploring the Lord to protect the family sheep upon the hill. It was snowing and bitterly cold. I heard a family pray for rain when a severe drought was on and conditions were desperate. I heard a young girl praying for help in her examinations that were coming up that day.

Our petitions are also for the sick and afflicted. The Lord will hear our sincere prayers. He may not always heal them, but he may give them peace or courage or strength to bear up. We do not forget in our prayers the folks who need blessings almost more than the physically imperfect—the frustrated and confused people, the tempted, the sinful, the disturbed.

Our prayers are for our children's welfare. Sometimes as children grow up, there comes into their lives a rebellious attitude in spite of all that we can say and do. Alma found his admonitions futile with his [son] and he prayed for [him], and his prayers were mighty ones. Sometimes that is about all there is left for parents to do. The prayer of a righteous man availeth much, says the scripture, and so it did in this case [see James 5:16; Mosiah 27:14].[8]

It is such a privilege and joy to pray to our Father in Heaven, such a blessing for us. But our experience is not finished after our prayer is completed. Amulek correctly taught: "And now behold, my beloved brethren, . . . after ye have [prayed], if ye turn away the needy, and the naked, and visit not the sick and afflicted, and impart of your substance, if ye have, to those who stand in need—I say unto you, if ye do not any of these things, behold, your prayer is vain, and availeth you nothing, and ye are as hypocrites who do deny the faith." (Alma 34:28.) We must never forget that we are to live the gospel as honestly and earnestly as we pray.[9]

In our private, personal prayers, we can commune with God and learn His will.

Some things are best prayed about in private, where time and confidentiality are not considerations. Prayer in solitude is rich and profitable. Praying alone helps us to shed shame or pretense, any lingering deceit; it helps us open our hearts and be totally honest and honorable in expressing all of our hopes and attitudes.

I have long been impressed about the need for privacy in our personal prayers. The Savior at times found it necessary to slip away into the mountains or desert to pray. Similarly, the Apostle Paul turned to the desert and solitude after his great call. Enos found himself in solitary places to commune with God. Joseph Smith found his privacy in the grove with only birds and trees and God to listen to his prayer. Observe some keys in his story: "So, in accordance with this, my determination to ask of God, I *retired* to the woods to make the attempt. . . . It was the first time

It has sorrowed me that some of us have not learned the meaning of that calm, spiritual warmth, for it is a witness to us that our prayers have been heard. And since our Father in Heaven loves us with more love than we have even for ourselves, it means that we can trust in his goodness, we can trust in him; it means that if we continue praying and living as we should, our Father's hand will guide and bless us.

And so in our prayers we say, "Thy will be done"—and mean it. We would not ask a leader for advice, then disregard it. We must not ask the Lord for blessings and then ignore the answer. Thus, we pray, "Thy will be done, O Lord. Thou knowest best, kind Father. I will accept and follow thy direction gracefully."[25]

We should pray in faith, but with awareness that when the Lord answers it may not be with the answer we expect or desire. Our faith must be that God's choice for us is right.[26]

After a lifetime of prayers, I know of the love and power and strength that comes from honest and heartfelt prayer. I know of the readiness of our Father to assist us in our mortal experience, to teach us, to lead us, to guide us. Thus, with great love, our Savior has said, "What I say unto one I say unto all; pray always." (D&C 93:49.)

If we will do so, we shall gain for ourselves personal knowledge that our Father in Heaven truly hears and answers prayers. This knowledge he wants each of us to have. Seek it, my beloved brothers and sisters! Seek it![27]

Suggestions for Study and Teaching

Consider these ideas as you study the chapter or as you prepare to teach. For additional help, see pages v–ix.

- How might your life be different if you did not pray? Ponder the reasons why the Lord commands us to pray (pages 48–49).

- Review pages 49–52. In what ways are we influenced when we express gratitude in prayer? when we pray for others?

- Review the second paragraph on page 52. Why are our prayers incomplete if we do not "live the gospel as honestly and earnestly as we pray"?

- President Kimball said, "Prayer in solitude is rich and profitable" (page 52). What can we do to make time for meaningful personal prayers? Why do you think it is helpful at times to pray aloud in our personal prayers? Why is listening an important part of prayer?

- On pages 54–55 President Kimball tells of blessings that come as a result of family prayers. What experiences have you had with these blessings? What can families do to make time for family prayer every morning and every night?

- President Kimball taught that prayers in group settings should be appropriate for the occasion (page 56). When we are asked to offer such prayers, what is our responsibility? What can we learn from the example of the young New Zealander in the story on pages 47–48?

- Read the paragraph that begins at the bottom of page 56. How has prayer influenced your relationship with Heavenly Father?

Related Scriptures: Psalm 55:17; Matthew 6:5–15; James 1:5–6; 2 Nephi 32:8–9; 3 Nephi 18:18–21

Notes

1. In Conference Report, Oct. 1979, 5; or *Ensign*, Nov. 1979, 5.
2. Caroline Eyring Miner and Edward L. Kimball, *Camilla: A Biography of Camilla Eyring Kimball* (1980), 182–84.
3. *Faith Precedes the Miracle* (1972), 200.
4. "Prayer," *New Era*, Mar. 1978, 15, 17, 18.
5. "Pray Always," *Ensign*, Oct. 1981, 3.
6. In Conference Report, Apr. 1979, 7; or *Ensign*, May 1979, 6–7.
7. *Ensign*, Oct. 1981, 4–5.
8. *Faith Precedes the Miracle*, 205, 206.
9. *Ensign*, Oct. 1981, 6.
10. *Ensign*, Oct. 1981, 4.
11. In Conference Report, Oct. 1979, 5; or *Ensign*, Nov. 1979, 4.
12. *Faith Precedes the Miracle*, 207.
13. *Ensign*, Oct. 1981, 5.
14. *Faith Precedes the Miracle*, 200–201.
15. "Therefore I Was Taught," *Ensign*, Jan. 1982, 4.
16. *Faith Precedes the Miracle*, 201.
17. *The Miracle of Forgiveness* (1969), 253.
18. *Faith Precedes the Miracle*, 207.
19. Quoted by James E. Faust, in Conference Report, Oct. 1990, 41; or *Ensign*, Nov. 1990, 33.
20. *Ensign*, Oct. 1981, 4.
21. "Family Prayer," *Children's Friend*, Jan. 1946, 30.
22. *Ensign*, Oct. 1981, 4.
23. *Faith Precedes the Miracle*, 201.
24. *The Teachings of Spencer W. Kimball*, ed. Edward L. Kimball (1982), 119–20.
25. *Ensign*, Oct. 1981, 5.
26. *Faith Precedes the Miracle*, 207.
27. *Ensign*, Oct. 1981, 6.

Discovering the Scriptures
for Ourselves

*Each of us can come to enjoy the blessings of immersing
ourselves in the scriptures.*

From the Life of Spencer W. Kimball

When Spencer W. Kimball was 14 years old, he heard Brigham
Young's daughter Susa Young Gates speak at a stake conference
on the subject of reading the scriptures. He recalled: "She gave
a rousing talk on the reading of the scriptures and making them
our own; then she stopped her dissertation to ask this mixed
congregation, about a thousand of us, 'How many of you have
read the Bible through?'

". . . An accusing guilt complex spread over me. I had read
many books by that time, the funny papers, and light books, but
my accusing heart said to me, 'You, Spencer Kimball, you have
never read that holy book. Why?' I looked around me at the people in front and on both sides of the hall to see if I was alone in
my failure to read the sacred book. Of the thousand people,
there were perhaps a half dozen who proudly raised their hands.
I slumped down in my seat. I had no thought for the others who
had also failed, but only a deep accusing thought for myself. I
don't know what other people were doing and thinking, but I
heard no more of the sermon. It had accomplished its work.
When the meeting closed, I sought the large double exit door
and rushed to my home a block east of the chapel; and I was grit-
ting my teeth and saying to myself, 'I will. I will. I will.'

"Entering the back door of our family home, I went to the
kitchen shelf where we kept the coal oil lamps, selected one that
was full of oil and had a newly trimmed wick, and climbed the
stairs to my attic room. There I opened my Bible and began on

As a young man, Spencer W. Kimball determined to read the entire Bible.

Genesis, first chapter and first verse, and I read well into the night with Adam and Eve and Cain and Abel, and Enoch and Noah and through the flood even to Abraham."[1]

Approximately one year later, Spencer finished reading the Bible: "What a satisfaction it was to me to realize I had read the Bible through from beginning to end! And what exultation of spirit! And what joy in the over-all picture I had received of its contents!"[2] The experience made a lasting impression, and later in life he referred to it often in general and area conferences.

President Kimball continued to enjoy the blessings of scripture study throughout his days and encouraged others to do likewise. Elder Richard G. Scott, later a member of the Quorum of the Twelve Apostles, recalled: "Elder Spencer W. Kimball supervised our area when I was mission president. I observed how well he understood and used the Book of Mormon in his inspiring messages to members and missionaries alike. . . . At a missionary zone meeting on one occasion, he said, 'Richard, you used a scripture from the Book of Mormon today that I had never thought of using in that way.' That was the careful preparation for a very significant lesson he wanted me to learn. He then added, 'And to think that I have read that book more than seventy-six times.' He didn't have to point out specifically that I knew very little about the scriptures, and that I needed to spend a lifetime in pondering and applying them. That single comment has motivated me to a lifelong goal of increased understanding of the sacred word of God."[3]

Teachings of Spencer W. Kimball

The scriptures are a rare possession that we must each discover for ourselves.

Sometimes it seems we take the scriptures too much for granted because we do not fully appreciate how rare a thing it is to possess them, and how blessed we are because we do have them. We seem to have settled so comfortably into our experiences in this world and become so accustomed to hearing the gospel taught among us that it is hard for us to imagine it could ever have been otherwise.

But we need to understand that it has [not] been [many] years since the world emerged from the long night of spiritual darkness that we call the Great Apostasy. We need to sense something of the depth of the spiritual darkness that prevailed before that day in the spring of 1820 when the Father and the Son appeared to Joseph Smith—a darkness which was foreseen by the prophet Nephi and described as "that awful state of blindness" in which the gospel was withheld from man. (See 1 Ne. 13:32.) . . .

. . . The fact that I was not born in the times of spiritual darkness in which the heavens were silent and the Spirit withdrawn fills my soul with gratitude. Truly, to be without the word of the Lord to direct us is to be as wanderers in a vast desert who can find no familiar landmarks, or in the dense darkness of a cavern with no light to show us the way to escape. . . .

. . . Isaiah made direct reference to the end of darkness and the coming forth of the Book of Mormon [see Isaiah 29:11–12]. . . .

And thus began the marvelous work, "even a marvellous work and a wonder" which the Lord promised he would proceed to do. (See Isa. 29:14.)

Since the beginning of the restoration of the gospel through the prophet Joseph Smith, [millions of] copies of the Book of Mormon have been printed and distributed. . . . An untold number of Bibles have been printed, far outstripping all other published works in quantity. We also have the Doctrine and Covenants and the Pearl of Great Price. In addition to our access to these precious works of scripture, we have, to an extent unknown at any other time in the history of the world, the education and the ability to use them, if we will.

The ancient prophets knew that after the darkness there would come light. We live in that light—but do we fully comprehend it? With the doctrines of salvation easily within our grasp, I fear that some are still overcome with the "spirit of slumber, eyes that they should not see, and ears that they should not hear." (Rom. 11:8.)

. . . I ask us all to honestly evaluate our performance in scripture study. It is a common thing to have a few passages of scripture at our disposal, floating in our minds, as it were, and thus to have the illusion that we know a great deal about the gospel. In this sense, having a little knowledge can be a problem indeed. I am convinced that each of us, at some time in our lives, must discover the scriptures for ourselves—and not just discover them once, but rediscover them again and again.[4]

Our commitment to serve the Lord deepens when we turn to the scriptures.

The story of King Josiah in the Old Testament is a most profitable one to "liken . . . unto [our]selves." (1 Ne. 19:24.) To me, it is one of the finest stories in all of the scriptures.

Josiah was only eight years old when he began to reign in Judah, and although his immediate progenitors were extremely wicked, the scriptures tell us that "he did that which was right in the sight of the Lord, and walked in all the way of David his father, and turned not aside to the right hand or to the left." (2 Kings 22:2.) This is all the more surprising when we learn that by that time (just two generations before the destruction of Jerusalem in 587 B.C.) the written law of Moses had been lost and was virtually unknown, even among the priests of the temple!

But in the eighteenth year of his reign, Josiah directed that the temple be repaired. At that time Hilkiah, the high priest, found the book of the law, which Moses had placed in the ark of the covenant, and delivered it to King Josiah.

When the book of the law was read to Josiah, he "rent his clothes" and wept before the Lord.

"Great is the wrath of the Lord that is kindled against us," he said, "because our fathers have not hearkened unto the words of this book, to do according unto all that which is written concerning us." (2 Kings 22:13.)

The king then read the book before all the people, and at that time they all made a covenant to obey all the Lord's commandments "with all their heart and all their soul." (2 Kings 23:3.) Then Josiah proceeded to clean up the kingdom of Judah, removing all the idols, the groves, the high places, and all the abominations that had accumulated during the reign of his fathers, defiling the land and its people. . . .

"And like unto him was there no king before him, that turned to the Lord with all his heart, and with all his soul, and with all his might, according to all the law of Moses; neither after him arose there any like him." [2 Kings 23:25.]

I feel strongly that we must all of us return to the scriptures just as King Josiah did and let them work mightily within us, impelling us to an unwavering determination to serve the Lord.

Josiah had the law of Moses only. In our scriptures we have the gospel of Jesus Christ in its fulness; and if a taste is sweet, in fulness there is joy.

The Lord is not trifling with us when he gives us these things, for "unto whomsoever much is given, of him shall be much required." (Luke 12:48.) Access to these things means responsibility for them. We must study the scriptures according to the Lord's commandment (see 3 Ne. 23:1–5); and we must let them govern our lives and the lives of our children.[5]

We learn lessons of life through scripture study.

Every lesson in ethical standards and in proper spiritual living is found in the standard works. Here will be found the rewards of righteousness and the penalties of sin.[6]

We learn the lessons of life more readily and surely if we see the results of wickedness and righteousness in the lives of others. . . . To come to know Job well and intimately is to learn to keep faith through the greatest of adversities. To know well the strength of Joseph in the luxury of ancient Egypt when he was tempted by a voluptuous woman, and to see this clean young man resist all the powers of darkness embodied in this one seductive person, certainly should fortify the intimate reader against such sin. To see the forbearance and fortitude of Paul when he was giving his life to his ministry is to give courage to those who feel they have been injured and tried. He was beaten many times, imprisoned frequently for the cause, stoned near to death, shipwrecked three times, robbed, nearly drowned, the victim of false and disloyal brethren. While starving, choking, freezing, poorly clothed, Paul was yet consistent in his service. He never wavered once after the testimony came to him following his supernatural experience. To see the growth of Peter with the gospel as the catalyst moving him from a lowly fisherman— uncultured, unlearned, and ignorant, as they rated him—blossoming out into a great organizer, prophet, leader, theologian, teacher. . . .

Our children may learn the lessons of life through the perseverance and personal strength of Nephi; the godliness of the three Nephites; the faith of Abraham; the power of Moses; the deception and perfidy of Ananias; the courage even to death of the unresisting Ammonites; the unassailable faith of the

"I am convinced that each of us, at some time in our lives, must discover the scriptures for ourselves—and not just discover them once, but rediscover them again and again."

Lamanite mothers transmitted down through their sons, so powerful that it saved Helaman's striplings. Not a single one came to his death in that war.

All through the scriptures every weakness and strength of man has been portrayed, and rewards and punishments have been recorded. One would surely be blind who could not learn to live life properly by such reading. The Lord said, "Search the scriptures; for in them ye think ye have eternal life: and they are they which testify of me." (John 5:39.) And it was this same Lord and master in whose life we find every quality of goodness: godliness, strength, controls, perfection. And how can students study this great story without capturing some of it in their lives?[7]

65

Here [in the standard works] are the biographies of the prophets and of leaders and of the Lord himself, giving example and direction so that men can, by following those examples, be perfected, happy, full of joy, and with eternity their goal and expectation.[8]

Spiritual knowledge is available to all who study and search the scriptures.

There are still many of the Saints who are not reading and pondering the scriptures regularly, and who have little knowledge of the Lord's instructions to the children of men. Many have been baptized and received a testimony, and have "gotten into this straight and narrow path," yet have failed to take the further required step—to "press forward, *feasting upon the word of Christ,* and endure to the end." (2 Ne. 31:19, 20; italics added.)

Only the faithful will receive the promised reward, which is eternal life. For one cannot receive eternal life without becoming a "doer of the word" (see James 1:22) and being valiant in obedience to the Lord's commandments. And one cannot become a "doer of the word" without first becoming a "hearer." And to become a "hearer" is not simply to stand idly by and wait for chance bits of information; it is to seek out and study and pray and comprehend. Therefore the Lord said, "Whoso receiveth not my voice is not acquainted with my voice, and is not of me." (D&C 84:52.)[9]

The years have taught me that if we will energetically pursue this worthy personal goal [to study the scriptures] in a determined and conscientious manner, we shall indeed find answers to our problems and peace in our hearts. We shall experience the Holy Ghost broadening our understanding, find new insights, witness an unfolding pattern of all scripture; and the doctrines of the Lord shall come to have more meaning to us than we ever thought possible. As a consequence, we shall have greater wisdom with which to guide ourselves and our families.[10]

I ask all to begin now to study the scriptures in earnest, if you have not already done so.[11]

As we immerse ourselves in the scriptures, we come to know and love Heavenly Father and Jesus Christ.

I find that when I get casual in my relationships with divinity and when it seems that no divine ear is listening and no divine voice is speaking, that I am far, far away. If I immerse myself in the scriptures the distance narrows and the spirituality returns. I find myself loving more intensely those whom I must love with all my heart and mind and strength, and loving them more, I find it easier to abide their counsel.[12]

I find that all I need to do to increase my love for my Maker and the gospel and the Church and my brethren is to read the scriptures. I have spent many hours in the scriptures. . . . I cannot see how anyone can read the scriptures and not develop a testimony of their divinity and of the divinity of the work of the Lord, who is the spokesman in the scriptures.[13]

Few of the billions [on] earth can walk with God as did Adam and Abraham and Moses, yet, in the world in which we live, the scriptures are available to nearly every soul, and, through them, men can become intimately acquainted with their Heavenly Father, his Son Jesus Christ, and with conditions and opportunities and expectations of life eternal.[14]

No amount of human study can find out God, but he has revealed himself to his servants the prophets, and they have taught us of his nature. We can each have a confirmation of the truth through our own fasting and prayer. The theological storms around us find us calm in the center of tempest with a simple, sure knowledge of the Father and the Son derived from the ancient and modern scriptures and affirmed by the Spirit. In this knowledge we have hope of eternal life.[15]

Suggestions for Study and Teaching

Consider these ideas as you study the chapter or as you prepare to teach. For additional help, see pages v–ix.

- Ponder the stories on pages 59–61. How do these stories influence you? Ask yourself how you are doing in reading, understanding, and applying the scriptures. Consider your personal goals for scripture study.

- As you review the section beginning on page 61, imagine your life without the scriptures. How would your life be different? What are some consequences of taking the scriptures "too much for granted"?

- Why is it insufficient merely to have a few favorite scripture passages "floating in our minds"? (page 62). What do you think it means to discover the scriptures for yourself and to "rediscover them again and again"?

- President Kimball encouraged us to liken the story of King Josiah to ourselves (pages 62–64; see also 2 Kings 22–23). What similarities and differences do you see between your life and the lives of King Josiah and his people?

- Think of some "lessons of life" you have learned through scripture study. (For some examples, see pages 64–66.)

- Review the fourth paragraph on page 66. What are some scripture passages that have helped you find answers to your problems and peace in your heart?

- Read the first and second paragraphs on page 67. How has scripture study affected your relationship with God? your relationships with family members? your service in Church callings?

Related Scriptures: Amos 8:11–12; 1 Nephi 19:23; Alma 37:8; D&C 1:37; 18:33–36

Notes

1. "Read the Scriptures," *Friend,* Dec. 1985, inside front cover; see also "What I Read as a Boy," *Children's Friend,* Nov. 1943, 508.

2. *Children's Friend,* Nov. 1943, 508.

3. "The Power of the Book of Mormon in My Life," *Ensign,* Oct. 1984, 9.

4. "How Rare a Possession—the Scriptures!" *Ensign,* Sept. 1976, 2, 4.

5. *Ensign,* Sept. 1976, 4–5.

6. "The Power of Books" (written with Camilla E. Kimball), *Relief Society Magazine,* Oct. 1963, 729.

7. *The Teachings of Spencer W. Kimball,* ed. Edward L. Kimball (1982), 131, 132–33.

8. *Relief Society Magazine,* Oct. 1963, 729.

9. *Ensign,* Sept. 1976, 2.

10. "Always a Convert Church: Some Lessons to Learn and Apply This Year," *Ensign,* Sept. 1975, 3.

11. *Ensign,* Sept. 1976, 5.

12. *The Teachings of Spencer W. Kimball,* 135.

13. *The Teachings of Spencer W. Kimball,* 135.

14. *Relief Society Magazine,* Oct. 1963, 730.

15. *Faith Precedes the Miracle* (1972), 67.

Personal Testimony

A sure knowledge of the truthfulness of the gospel is an
open door to great rewards and joys unspeakable.

From the Life of Spencer W. Kimball

In 1947 Elder Spencer W. Kimball received a letter from his son Andrew, who was serving a full-time mission. Andrew wrote: "I told one fellow . . . that I knew of the truthfulness of what I told him, and said that the Holy Ghost had borne witness of it to me. . . . When I thought about it later I was a little concerned that I should do such a thing." Because of his concern he said, "I've carefully avoided bearing my testimony to anyone beyond the point of saying 'I feel, I believe, etc.'"

Elder Kimball wrote back to his son. "I think I know exactly how you felt," he said, "for I went through the same experience in my mission. I wanted to be very honest with myself and with the program and with the Lord. For a time I couched my words carefully to try to build up others without actually committing myself to a positive, unequivocal statement that I *knew*. I felt a little hesitant about it, too, for when I was in tune and doing my duty I felt the Spirit. I *really* wanted to say that which I really felt, that I knew, but I was reticent. When I approached a positive declaration, it frightened me and yet when I was wholly in tune and spiritually inspired, I wanted to testify. I thought I was being honest, very honest, but then I decided that I was fooling myself. . . .

"Undoubtedly, the day you testified to your investigator that you KNEW it was true, the Lord was trying so hard to reveal this truth to you through the power of the Holy Ghost. While you were in the Spirit and in tune and defending the holy program, you felt it deeply, but after you were 'out of the Spirit' and began to reason with yourself and check yourself and question your-self, you wanted to back out. . . .

"I have no question in my mind of your testimony. I am sure that you (like I did) have countless golden threads of testimony all through your being only waiting for the hand of the Master Weaver to assemble and weave them into a tapestry of exquisite and perfect design. Now my son, take my advice and QUENCH NOT THE SPIRIT, but whenever the Spirit whispers, follow its holy promptings. Keep in tune spiritually and listen for the promptings and when you are impressed speak out boldly your impressions. The Lord will magnify your testimony and touch hearts. I hope that you will know that there is no criticism herein, but only attempted helpfulness. . . .

"I cannot close my epistle to you without bearing you my tes-timony. I know that it is true—that Jesus is the Creator and Redeemer; that the Gospel taught by us and our 3,000 mission-aries is restored and revealed through the real Prophet, Joseph Smith, and is of God, and I have consecrated the balance of my life to 'preaching the kingdom.' I [have borne] my testimony boldly . . . and I reaffirm it again and again. I am sure your testi-mony is the same except perhaps your golden threads need only to be woven into a complete tapestry which will quickly be accomplished in your missionary work as you turn your heart loose and let it rule your mind.

"May God help you to weave into a beautiful pattern the golden threads of your experience and inspiration and may you with always increasing power continue . . . to live and teach the everlasting truth."[1]

Teachings of Spencer W. Kimball

Each of us can receive a testimony—a revelation from Heavenly Father through the Holy Ghost.

Peter was asked by the Savior, "But whom say ye that I am?" And Peter, speaking for his brethren, the other Apostles, said, "Thou art the Christ, the Son of the living God." The Savior's next remark is a most significant one. He said, "Blessed art thou,

In response to Peter's testimony, the Savior said, "Blessed art thou,
Simon Bar-jona: for flesh and blood hath not revealed it unto thee,
but my Father which is in heaven" (Matthew 16:17).

Simon Bar-jona: for flesh and blood hath not revealed it unto
thee, but my Father which is in heaven" (Matt. 16:13–17).

Who revealed this startling truth to him? Our Father in
Heaven. How did he do it? By revelation. This basic knowledge
that Jesus was the Christ, the Redeemer, the Savior, came not
from any man or from any book or from any college. Peter
received it directly from our Heavenly Father through the ministrations of the Holy Ghost. . . .

. . . Every soul in this world may have a revelation, the same
one that Peter had. That revelation will be a testimony, a knowledge that Christ lives, that Jesus Christ is the Redeemer of this
world. Every soul may have this assurance, and when he gets this
testimony, it will have come from God and not from study alone.
Study is an important element, of course, but there must be

associated with study much prayer and reaching, and then this revelation comes.

When you individually know that Jesus was not only a great philosopher but that he was verily the Son of God, that he came into the world in the way that we claim he did, and that he went out of the world for the purpose that we claim he did—when you know that positively, and know that Joseph Smith was a prophet of God and that this is the divine Church established by Jesus Christ, then you have had a revelation.[2]

There are people who pride themselves on their keen minds, who think they can delve into mysteries, but they can never define or explain or understand the spiritual things through their logic or through their mental processes. The spiritual things can be understood only through the Spirit. It must come through the heart and that is where the testimony is lodged.[3]

A sure knowledge of the spiritual is an open door to great rewards and joys unspeakable. To ignore the testimony is to grope in caves of impenetrable darkness, to creep along in fog over hazardous highways. That person is to be pitied who may still be walking in darkness at noonday, who is tripping over obstacles that can be removed, and who dwells in the dim flickering candlelight of insecurity and skepticism when he need not. The spiritual knowledge of truth is the electric light illuminating the cavern; the wind and sun dissipating the fog; the power equipment removing boulders from the road.[4]

A testimony is obtained and maintained by intense strivings.

A testimony is a personal revelation—one of the important gifts—and may be enjoyed by every soul who will pay the price.[5]

It is a good question which has been asked by millions since Joseph Smith phrased it: How am I to know which of all, if any, of the organizations is authentic, divine, and recognized by the Lord?

He has given the key. You may *know.* You need not be in doubt. . . . The necessary procedure is: study, think, pray, and do.

Revelation is the key. God will make it known to you once you have capitulated and have become humble and receptive. Having dropped all pride of your mental stature, having acknowledged before God your confusion, having subjected your egotism, and having surrendered yourself to the teaching of the Holy Spirit, you are ready to begin to learn.[6]

We can have positive certainty of the reality of a personal God; the continued active life of the Christ, separate from but like his Father; the divinity of the restoration through Joseph Smith and other prophets of the organization and doctrines of God's church on earth; and the power of the divine, authoritative priesthood given to men through revelations from God. These can be known by every responsible person as surely as the knowledge that the sun shines. To fail to attain this knowledge is to admit that one has not paid the price. Like academic degrees, it is obtained by intense strivings. That soul who is clean through repentance and the ordinances receives it if he desires and reaches for it, investigates conscientiously, studies, and prays faithfully.[7]

The Redeemer declared:

"My doctrine is not mine, but his that sent me.

"If any man will do his will, he shall know of the doctrine, whether it be of God, or whether I speak of myself." (John 7:16–17.)

What is it to *know* of the doctrine? It is an unwavering assurance. The Lord has offered a rich reward but has provided that it can be had only by meeting certain requirements. In this case the blessing promised is a *knowledge of the divinity of the doctrine.* And in this case the law or requirement is that one must "do his will." . . .

. . . Mere passive acceptance of the doctrines will not give the testimony; no casual half-compliance with the program will bring that assurance, but an all-out effort to live his commandments.

We often see this in the lives of members of the Church. One said to me in a stake I visited, "I assiduously avoid all testimony meetings. I can't take the sentimental and emotional statements

73

For those seeking a testimony,
"the necessary procedure is: study, think, pray, and do."

that some of the people make. I can't accept these doctrines unless I can in an intellectual and rational way prove every step." I knew this type of man as I have met others like him. In no case had they gone all-out to live the commandments: little or no tithing, only occasional attendance at meetings, considerable criticism of the doctrines, the organizations, and the leaders, and we know well why they could have no testimony. Remember that the Lord said:

"I, the Lord, am bound when ye do what I say; but when ye do not what I say, ye have no promise" (D&C 82:10).

Such people have failed to "do what he says," so of course, they have no promise. . . .

. . . It is not blind loyalty but faithful observance and turning of keys which open the storehouse of spiritual knowledge. The Lord will not discriminate between his children but delights to own and bless us all, if we will let him.[8]

What are you going to do with your testimony? Are you going to keep it sharpened like the knife with which our mothers cut the meat? Are you going to let it get dull and rusty? . . . It is a little like a rose. Just keep the rain off it; just keep the irrigation water off it for a little while and what happens to your rose? It dies. Your testimony dies. Your love dies. Everything has to be fed. You feed your body three times a day. The Lord says to keep your testimony, to keep your spirit alive, you have to feed it every day. . . . That is why he says pray every night and morning. That is why he says pray continually so that you keep that line open.[9]

We need to participate in testimony meetings.

Testimony meetings are some of the best meetings in the [Church] in the whole month, if you have the spirit. If you are bored at a testimony meeting, there is something the matter with *you,* and not the other people. You can get up and bear your testimony and you think it is the best meeting in the month; but if you sit there and count the grammatical errors and laugh at the man who can't speak very well, you'll be bored. . . . Don't forget it! You have to *fight* for a testimony. You have to *keep* fighting!

The Lord says in the 60th section of the Doctrine and Covenants, "With some I am not well pleased for they will not open their mouths" (D&C 60:2). What does he mean? He says that if they do not use it, they will lose what he has given them. They lose their spirit. They lose their testimony. And this priceless thing that you have can slip right out of your life.

Every month the First Presidency and the Twelve meet with all the General Authorities in the temple. They bear testimony and they tell each other how they love one another just like all of you. Why do the General Authorities need a testimony meeting? The same reason that you need a testimony meeting. Do you think that you can go three, and six, and nine, and twelve months without bearing your testimony and still keep its full value? . . .

You know this testimony is a tremendous thing, a most important thing. Any minister or priest can quote scripture and present dialogues. But not every priest or minister can bear his testimony. Don't you sit there in your fast meeting and cheat yourself and say, "I guess I won't bear my testimony today. I guess that wouldn't be fair to these other members because I have had so many opportunities." You bear your testimony. And one minute is long enough to bear it.

You have a testimony! It needs building and lifting and enlarging, of course; and that is what you are doing. Every time you bear your testimony it becomes strengthened.[10]

Testimonies are expressed in words that are simple but powerful.

"I know it is true." Because those few words have been said a billion times by millions of people does not make it trite. It will never be worn out. I feel sorry for people who try to couch it in other words, because there are no words like "I know." There are no words which express the deep feelings which can come from the human heart like "I know."[11]

Some of our good people get so terrified at triteness that they try to steer around and away from their testimonies by getting out on the fringes. Don't you ever worry about triteness in testimony. When the President of the Church bears his testimony, he says, "I know that Joseph Smith was called of God, a divine representative. I know that Jesus is the Christ, the Son of the living God." You see, the same thing every one of you says. That is a testimony. It never gets old, never gets old! Tell the Lord frequently how much you love him.

A testimony is not an exhortation; a testimony is not a sermon (none of you are there to exhort the rest); it is not a travelogue. You are there to bear your own witness. It is amazing what you can say in 60 seconds by way of testimony, or 120, or 240, or whatever time you are given, if you confine yourselves to testimony. We'd like to know how you feel. Do you love the work, really? Are you happy in your work? Do you love the Lord? Are you glad that you are a member of the Church?[12]

Just tell how you feel inside. That is the testimony. The moment you begin preaching to others, your testimony ended. Just tell us how you feel, what your mind and heart and every fiber of your body tells you.[13]

Knowing full well that before long, in the natural course of events, I must stand before the Lord and give an accounting of my words, I now add my personal and solemn testimony that God, the Eternal Father, and the risen Lord, Jesus Christ, appeared to the boy Joseph Smith. I testify that the Book of Mormon is a translation of an ancient record of nations who once lived in [the] western hemisphere, where they prospered and became mighty when they kept the commandments of God, but who were largely destroyed through terrible civil wars when they forgot God. This book bears testimony of the living reality of the Lord Jesus Christ as the Savior and Redeemer of mankind.

I testify that the holy priesthood, both Aaronic and Melchizedek, with authority to act in the name of God, was restored to the earth by John the Baptist, and Peter, James, and John; that other keys and authority were subsequently restored; and that the power and authority of those various divine bestowals are among us today. Of these things I bear solemn witness to all within the sound of my voice. I promise in the name of the Lord that all who give heed to our message, and accept and live the gospel, will grow in faith and understanding. They will have an added measure of peace in their lives and in their homes and by the power of the Holy Ghost will speak similar words of testimony and truth.[14]

Suggestions for Study and Teaching

Consider these ideas as you study the chapter or as you prepare to teach. For additional help, see pages v–ix.

- Review the letter Elder Spencer W. Kimball wrote to his son Andrew (pages 69–70), noting the comparison of a testimony to a tapestry. What experiences and feelings make up your personal "golden threads of testimony"? Consider what the Lord has done to help you weave your threads of testimony into a tapestry.

- How do you think it helped Andrew Kimball to receive the letter from his father? What opportunities do parents have to share their testimonies with their children? How can we help young people receive and recognize the spiritual promptings that lead to a testimony?

- Briefly review pages 71–76, looking for words and phrases President Kimball used to describe our efforts to obtain and strengthen our testimonies. If a person feels that his or her testimony is wavering, what can that person do?

- Study President Kimball's counsel about fast and testimony meetings (pages 75–76). Why do you think we have these meetings? Why do our testimonies grow stronger when we share them? What can we do to ensure that testimony meeting will be one of the best meetings of the month for us?

- Review President Kimball's counsel on how we should bear our testimonies (pages 76–77). Why do the words "I know" contain so much power?

Related Scriptures: 1 Corinthians 12:3; 1 Peter 3:15; Alma 5:45–46; Moroni 10:4–7; D&C 42:61; 62:3

Notes

1. Letter from Spencer W. Kimball to Andrew E. Kimball, 1947; from the personal collection of Andrew E. Kimball.
2. "President Kimball Speaks Out on Testimony," *New Era,* Aug. 1981, 4.
3. In H. Stephen Stoker and Joseph C. Muren, comps., *Testimony* (1980), 167–68.
4. *Faith Precedes the Miracle* (1972), 14.
5. "The Significance of Miracles in the Church Today," *Instructor,* Dec. 1959, 396.
6. "Absolute Truth," *Ensign,* Sept. 1978, 7–8.
7. *Faith Precedes the Miracle,* 13–14.
8. *New Era,* Aug. 1981, 4, 6, 7.
9. *The Teachings of Spencer W. Kimball,* ed. Edward L. Kimball (1982), 141–42.
10. *New Era,* Aug. 1981, 6–7.
11. *The Teachings of Spencer W. Kimball,* 141.
12. *New Era,* Aug. 1981, 6.
13. In Stoker and Muren, *Testimony,* 139.
14. In Conference Report, Apr. 1980, 78; or *Ensign,* May 1980, 54.

Selfless Service

As we lose ourselves in service to others,
we find greater spirituality and happiness.

From the Life of Spencer W. Kimball

President Spencer W. Kimball urged Latter-day Saints to engage in "simple acts of service" that would bless others' lives as well as their own.[1] He often found opportunities to offer such service himself, as the following account shows:

"A young mother on an overnight flight with a two-year-old daughter was stranded by bad weather in Chicago airport without food or clean clothing for the child and without money. She was . . . pregnant and threatened with miscarriage, so she was under doctor's instructions not to carry the child unless it was essential. Hour after hour she stood in one line after another, trying to get a flight to Michigan. The terminal was noisy, full of tired, frustrated, grumpy passengers, and she heard critical references to her crying child and to her sliding her child along the floor with her foot as the line moved forward. No one offered to help with the soaked, hungry, exhausted child.

"Then, the woman later reported, 'someone came towards us and with a kindly smile said, "Is there something I could do to help you?" With a grateful sigh I accepted his offer. He lifted my sobbing little daughter from the cold floor and lovingly held her to him while he patted her gently on the back. He asked if she could chew a piece of gum. When she was settled down, he carried her with him and said something kindly to the others in the line ahead of me, about how I needed their help. They seemed to agree and then he went up to the ticket counter [at the front of the line] and made arrangements with the clerk for me to be put on a flight leaving shortly. He walked with us to a bench, where we chatted a moment, until he was assured that I would

*President Kimball's simple act of kindness in a Chicago airport
had far-reaching effects.*

be fine. He went on his way. About a week later I saw a picture of
Apostle Spencer W. Kimball and recognized him as the stranger in
the airport.' "[2]

Several years later, President Kimball received a letter that
read, in part:

"Dear President Kimball:

"I am a student at Brigham Young University. I have just
returned from my mission in Munich, West Germany. I had a
lovely mission and learned much. . . .

"I was sitting in priesthood meeting last week, when a story
was told of a loving service which you performed some twenty-
one years ago in the Chicago airport. The story told of how you

met a young pregnant mother with a . . . screaming child, in . . . distress, waiting in a long line for her tickets. She was threatening miscarriage and therefore couldn't lift her child to comfort her. She had experienced four previous miscarriages, which gave added reason for the doctor's orders not to bend or lift.

"You comforted the crying child and explained the dilemma to the other passengers in line. This act of love took the strain and tension off my mother. I was born a few months later in Flint, Michigan.

"I just want to *thank you* for your love. *Thank you* for your example!"[3]

Teachings of Spencer W. Kimball

We should follow the Savior's example of selfless service.

[The Savior] gave himself for his followers. . . . He was ever conscious of doing what was right and of meeting the real and true needs of those he served.[4]

He put himself and his own needs second and ministered to others beyond the call of duty, tirelessly, lovingly, effectively. So many of the problems in the world today spring from selfishness and self-centeredness in which too many make harsh demands of life and others in order to meet their demands.[5]

The more we understand what really happened in the life of Jesus of Nazareth in Gethsemane and on Calvary, the better able we will be to understand the importance of sacrifice and self-lessness in our lives.[6]

If we follow in [the Savior's] footsteps, we can live by faith rather than by fear. If we can share his perspective about people, we can love them, serve them, and reach out to them—rather than feeling anxious and threatened by others.[7]

God often meets others' needs through our small acts of service.

We need to help those we seek to serve to know for themselves that God not only loves them, but he is ever mindful of them and of their needs. . . .

God does notice us, and he watches over us. But it is usually through another person that he meets our needs. Therefore, it is vital that we serve each other in the kingdom. The people of the Church need each other's strength, support, and leadership in a community of believers as an enclave of disciples. In the Doctrine and Covenants we read about how important it is to ". . . succor the weak, lift up the hands which hang down, and strengthen the feeble knees." (D&C 81:5.) So often, our acts of service consist of simple encouragement or of giving mundane help with mundane tasks, but what glorious consequences can flow from mundane acts and from small but deliberate deeds! . . .

If we focus on simple principles and simple acts of service, we will see that organizational lines soon lose some of their significance. Too often in the past, organizational lines in the Church have become walls that have kept us from reaching out to individuals as completely as we should. We will also find as we become less concerned with getting organizational or individual credit that we will become more concerned with serving the one whom we are charged to reach. We will also find ourselves becoming less concerned with our organizational identity and more concerned with our true and ultimate identity as a son or daughter of our Father in heaven and helping others to achieve the same sense of belonging.[8]

We should use our talents and abilities to serve others.

None of us should become so busy in our formal Church assignments that there is no room left for quiet Christian service to our neighbors.[9]

It is easy for us to fit into the old established programs, to do the things that we are required to do, to put in a certain number of hours, to sing so many times and pray so many times, but you remember the Lord said it is a slothful servant that waits to be commanded in all things [see D&C 58:26].[10]

"Verily I say, men should be anxiously engaged in a good cause, and do many things of their own free will, and bring to pass much righteousness." (D&C 58:27.)

All men have been given special powers and within certain limitations should develop those powers, give vent to their own imaginations, and not become rubber stamps. They should develop their own talents and abilities and capacities to their limit and use them to build up the kingdom.[11]

The Church member who has the attitude of leaving it to others will have much to answer for. There are many who say: "My wife does the Church work!" Others say: "I'm just not the religious kind," as though it does not take effort for most people to serve and do their duty. But God has endowed us with talents and time, with latent abilities and with opportunities to use and develop them in his service. He therefore expects much of us, his privileged children.[12]

In the account of the barren fig tree (see Matt. 21:19) the unproductive tree was cursed for its barrenness. What a loss to the individual and to humanity if the vine does not grow, the tree does not bear fruit, the soul does not expand through service! One must live, not only exist; he must do, not merely be; he must grow, not just vegetate. We must use our talents in behalf of our fellowmen, rather than burying them in the tomb of a self-centered life.[13]

Some observers might wonder why we concern ourselves with such simple things as service to others in a world surrounded by such dramatic problems. Yet, one of the advantages of the gospel of Jesus Christ is that it gives us perspective about the people on this planet, including ourselves, so that we can see the things that truly matter and avoid getting caught up in the multiplicity of lesser causes that vie for the attention of mankind. . . .

May I counsel you that when you select causes for which you give your time and talents and treasure in service to others, be careful to select good causes. There are so many of these causes to which you can give yourself fully and freely and which will produce much joy and happiness for you and for those you serve. There are other causes, from time to time, which may seem more fashionable and which may produce the applause of the world, but these are usually more selfish in nature. These latter causes tend to arise out of what the scriptures call "the commandments of men" [Matthew 15:9] rather than the commandments of God. Such causes have some virtues and some usefulness, but they are not as important as those causes which grow out of keeping the commandments of God.[14]

Youth will thrive on opportunities to give meaningful service.

We should not be afraid to ask our youth to render service to their fellowmen or to sacrifice for the kingdom. Our youth have a sense of intrinsic idealism, and we need have no fear in appealing to that idealism when we call them to serve.[15]

As we read of delinquency and crime, . . . and as we note many are committed by girls and boys, we ask ourselves what is the cause and what are the cures? In an adequate survey it was learned that a majority of youth wish responsibility and will thrive on it.

"What can we do?" [the youth] ask. . . .

Do the shopping, work in the hospital, help the neighbors . . . , wash dishes, vacuum the floors, make the beds, get the meals, learn to sew.

Read good books, repair the furniture, make something needed in the home, clean the house, press your clothes, rake the leaves, shovel the snow.[16]

We are concerned . . . with our need to provide continually significant opportunities for our young men to stretch their souls in service. Young men do not usually become inactive in the Church because they are given too many significant things to do. No young man who has really witnessed for himself that the gospel works in the lives of the people will walk away from his duties in the kingdom and leave them undone.[17]

I hope our young women of the Church will establish early in their lives a habit of Christian service. When we help other people with their problems, it puts ours in fresh perspective. We encourage the sisters of the Church—young and older—to be "anxiously engaged" [D&C 58:27] in quiet acts of service for friends and neighbors. Every principle of the gospel carries within itself its own witness that it is true. So it is that acts of

"We should not be afraid to ask our youth to render service to their fellowmen or to sacrifice for the kingdom."

service help not only the beneficiaries of the service, but they enlarge the giver.[18]

Giving selfless service leads us to the abundant life.

Service to others deepens and sweetens this life while we are preparing to live in a better world. It is by serving that we learn how to serve. When we are engaged in the service of our fellowmen, not only do our deeds assist them, but we put our own problems in a fresher perspective. When we concern ourselves more with others, there is less time to be concerned with ourselves! In the midst of the miracle of serving, there is the promise of Jesus that by losing ourselves, we find ourselves! [See Matthew 10:39.]

Not only do we "find" ourselves in terms of acknowledging divine guidance in our lives, but the more we serve our fellowmen in appropriate ways, the more substance there is to our souls. We become more significant individuals as we serve others. We become more substantive as we serve others—indeed, it is easier to "find" ourselves because there is so much more of us to find! . . .

. . . The abundant life noted in the scriptures [see John 10:10] is the spiritual sum that is arrived at by the multiplying of our service to others and by investing our talents in service to God and to man. Jesus said, you will recall, that on the first two commandments hang all the law and the prophets, and those two commandments involve developing our love of God, of self, of our neighbors, and of all men [see Matthew 22:36–40]. There can be no real abundance in life that is not connected with the keeping and the carrying out of those two great commandments.

Unless the way we live draws us closer to our Heavenly Father and to our fellowmen, there will be an enormous emptiness in our lives. It is frightening for me to see, for instance, how the life-style of so many today causes them to disengage from their families and their friends and their peers toward a heedless pursuit of pleasure or materialism. So often loyalty to family, to community, and to country is pushed aside in favor of other pursuits which are wrongly thought to be productive of happiness when, in fact, selfishness is so often the pursuit of questionable pleasure which passes so quickly. One of the differences between true joy and mere pleasure is that certain pleasures are realized only at the cost of someone else's pain. Joy, on the other hand, springs out of selflessness and service, and it benefits rather than hurts others.[19]

I know a man whose every thought through three quarters of a century had been for and of himself. . . . He had sought to keep his life for himself, and to gather all the good things of life for his own development and enjoyment. Strangely enough, trying to keep his life for himself, . . . he has shrunk, has lost his friends, and his own people shun him as a bore.

And now, as life is ebbing out gradually, he finds himself standing alone, forsaken, bitter, unloved, and unsung; and with self-pity, he can still think of only one person, himself. He has sought to save for himself his time, talents, and his means. He has lost the abundant life.

On the other hand, I know another man who has never given thought to himself. His every desire was for the protection and pleasure of those about him. No task was too great, no sacrifice too much for him to make for his fellowmen. His means brought relief from physical suffering; his kind work and thoughtfulness brought comfort and cheer and courage. Wherever people were in distress, he was on hand, cheering the discouraged, burying the dead, comforting the bereaved, and proving himself a friend in need. His time, his means, and his energies were lavished upon those needing assistance. Having given himself freely, by that same act he has added to his mental, physical, and moral stature until today he stands in his declining years a power for good, an example and an inspiration to many. He has developed and grown until he is everywhere acclaimed, loved, and appreciated. He has given life and in a real way has truly found the abundant life.[20]

As the contrasts between the ways of the world and the ways of God become sharpened by circumstance, the faith of the members of the Church will be tried even more severely. One of the most vital things we can do is to express our testimonies through service, which will, in turn, produce spiritual growth, greater commitment, and a greater capacity to keep the commandments. . . .

There is great security in spirituality, and we cannot have spirituality without service![21]

If we seek true happiness, we must expend our energies for purposes larger than our own self-interests. Let us ponder prayerfully how we may effectively and lovingly give service to our families, neighbors, and fellow Saints.[22]

Suggestions for Study and Teaching

Consider these ideas as you study the chapter or as you prepare to teach. For additional help, see pages v–ix.

- Review the story on pages 79–81. Consider the effects of President Kimball's simple act of kindness. What can we learn from the manner in which he provided the service?

- How would you describe the way in which the Savior served others? (For some examples, see page 81.) What can we do to follow His example?

- Read the first paragraph on page 82. When has God met your needs through other people? What can we do to be ready to meet the needs of others?

- Briefly review pages 82–84, looking for obstacles that can hinder us from giving selfless service. How can we overcome these obstacles?

- President Kimball taught that youth need opportunities to serve (pages 84–85). Why is this so? What can parents and Church leaders do to provide youth with significant opportunities to serve?

- What do you think it means to have "the abundant life"? (For some examples, see pages 85–87.) Why does selfless service lead to the abundant life?

Related Scriptures: Matthew 25:40; James 1:27; Mosiah 2:17; 4:14–16; D&C 88:123

Notes

1. See "Small Acts of Service," *Ensign,* Dec. 1974, 7.
2. Edward L. Kimball and Andrew E. Kimball Jr., *Spencer W. Kimball* (1977), 334.
3. In Gordon B. Hinckley, "Do Ye Even So to Them," *Ensign,* Dec. 1991, 5.
4. Regional representatives' seminar, Mar. 30, 1979, Archives of The Church of Jesus Christ of Latter-day Saints, 3.
5. "Jesus: The Perfect Leader," *Ensign,* Aug. 1979, 6.
6. "The Abundant Life," *Ensign,* July 1978, 7.
7. *Ensign,* July 1978, 5–6.
8. *Ensign,* Dec. 1974, 4, 5, 7.
9. In Conference Report, Apr. 1976, 71; or *Ensign,* May 1976, 47.
10. *The Teachings of Spencer W. Kimball,* ed. Edward L. Kimball (1982), 257.
11. "How to Evaluate Your Performance," *Improvement Era,* Oct. 1969, 16.
12. *The Miracle of Forgiveness* (1969), 100.
13. "President Kimball Speaks Out on Service to Others," *New Era,* Mar. 1981, 49.
14. *Ensign,* July 1978, 4, 5.
15. "President Kimball Speaks Out on Being a Missionary," *New Era,* May 1981, 48.
16. In Conference Report, Oct. 1963, 38–39; or *Improvement Era,* Dec. 1963, 1073.
17. In Conference Report, Apr. 1976, 68–69; or *Ensign,* May 1976, 45.
18. "Privileges and Responsibilities of Sisters," *Ensign,* Nov. 1978, 104.
19. *Ensign,* July 1978, 3, 4.
20. *The Teachings of Spencer W. Kimball,* 250–51.
21. *Ensign,* Dec. 1974, 5.
22. "Seek Learning, Even by Study and Also by Faith," *Ensign,* Sept. 1983, 6.

Forgiving Others with All Our Hearts

The Lord commands us to forgive others so that
we may be forgiven of our own sins and be blessed
with peace and joy.

From the Life of Spencer W. Kimball

When President Spencer W. Kimball taught about seeking forgiveness, he also emphasized the vital principle of forgiving others. In imploring all people to strive to develop the spirit of forgiveness, he related the following experience:

"I was struggling with a community problem in a small ward . . . where two prominent men, leaders of the people, were deadlocked in a long and unrelenting feud. Some misunderstanding between them had driven them far apart with enmity. As the days, weeks, and months passed, the breach became wider. The families of each conflicting party began to take up the issue and finally nearly all the people of the ward were involved. Rumors spread and differences were aired and gossip became tongues of fire until the little community was divided by a deep gulf. I was sent to clear up the matter. . . . I arrived at the frustrated community about 6 p.m., Sunday night, and immediately went into session with the principal combatants.

"How we struggled! How I pleaded and warned and begged and urged! Nothing seemed to be moving them. Each antagonist was so sure that he was right and justified that it was impossible to budge him.

"The hours were passing—it was now long after midnight, and despair seemed to enshroud the place; the atmosphere was still one of ill temper and ugliness. Stubborn resistance would

President Kimball counseled Church members: "Forgive and forget, don't let old grievances change your souls and affect them, and destroy your love and lives."

not give way. Then it happened. I aimlessly opened my Doctrine and Covenants again and there before me it was. I had read it many times in past years and it had had no special meaning then. But tonight it was the very answer. It was an appeal and an imploring and a threat and seemed to be coming direct from the Lord. I read [section 64] from the seventh verse on, but the quarreling participants yielded not an inch until I came to the ninth verse. Then I saw them flinch, startled, wondering. Could that be right? The Lord was saying to us—to all of us—'Wherefore, I say unto you, that ye ought to forgive one another.'

"This was an obligation. They had heard it before. They had said it in repeating the Lord's Prayer. But now: '. . . for he that forgiveth not his brother his trespasses standeth condemned before the Lord . . .'

"In their hearts, they may have been saying: 'Well, I might forgive if he repents and asks forgiveness, but he must make the first move.' Then the full impact of the last line seemed to strike them: 'For there remaineth in him the greater sin.'

"What? Does that mean I must forgive even if my antagonist remains cold and indifferent and mean? There is no mistaking it.

"A common error is the idea that the offender must apologize and humble himself to the dust before forgiveness is required. Certainly, the one who does the injury should totally make his adjustment, but as for the offended one, he must forgive the offender regardless of the attitude of the other. Sometimes men get satisfactions from seeing the other party on his knees and grovelling in the dust, but that is not the gospel way.

"Shocked, the two men sat up, listened, pondered a minute, then began to yield. This scripture added to all the others read brought them to their knees. Two a.m. and two bitter adversaries were shaking hands, smiling and forgiving and asking forgiveness. Two men were in a meaningful embrace. This hour was holy. Old grievances were forgiven and forgotten, and enemies became friends again. No reference was ever made again to the differences. The skeletons were buried, the closet of dry bones was locked and the key was thrown away, and peace was restored."[1]

Throughout his ministry, President Kimball exhorted Church members to be forgiving: "If there be misunderstandings, clear them up, forgive and forget, don't let old grievances change your souls and affect them, and destroy your love and lives. Put your houses in order. Love one another and love your neighbors, your friends, the people who live near you, as the Lord gives this power to you."[2]

Teachings of Spencer W. Kimball

We must forgive to be forgiven.

Since forgiveness is an absolute requirement in attaining eternal life, man naturally ponders: How can I best secure that forgiveness? One of many basic factors stands out as indispensable immediately: One must forgive to be forgiven.[3]

"For if ye forgive men their trespasses, your heavenly Father will also forgive you:

"But if ye forgive not men their trespasses, neither will your Father forgive your trespasses." (Matt. 6:14–15.)

Hard to do? Of course. The Lord never promised an easy road, nor a simple gospel, nor low standards, nor a low norm. The price is high, but the goods attained are worth all they cost. The Lord himself turned the other cheek; he suffered himself to be buffeted and beaten without remonstrance; he suffered every indignity and yet spoke no word of condemnation. And his question to all of us is: "Therefore, what manner of men ought ye to be?" And his answer to us is: "Even as I am." (3 Ne. 27:27.)[4]

Our forgiveness of others must be heartfelt and complete.

The command to forgive and the condemnation which follows failure to do so could not be stated more plainly than in this modern revelation to the Prophet Joseph Smith:

"My disciples, in days of old, sought occasion against one another and forgave not one another in their hearts; and for this evil they were afflicted and sorely chastened.

"Wherefore, I say unto you, that ye ought to forgive one another; for he that forgiveth not his brother his trespasses standeth condemned before the Lord; for there remaineth in him the greater sin.

"I, the Lord, will forgive whom I will forgive, but of you it is required to forgive all men." (D&C 64:8–10.) . . .

The lesson stands for us today. Many people, when brought to a reconciliation with others, say that they forgive, but they continue to hold malice, continue to suspect the other party, con-

*Jesus Christ taught, "If ye forgive men their trespasses,
your heavenly Father will also forgive you" (Matthew 6:14).*

tinue to disbelieve the other's sincerity. This is sin, for when a
reconciliation has been effected and when repentance is
claimed, each should forgive and forget, build immediately the
fences which have been breached, and restore the former com-
patibility.

The early disciples evidently expressed words of forgiveness,
and on the surface made the required adjustment, but "forgave
not one another in their hearts." This was not a forgiveness, but
savored of hypocrisy and deceit and subterfuge. As implied in
Christ's model prayer, it must be a heart action and a purging of
one's mind [see Matthew 6:12; see also verses 14–15]. Forgiveness
means forgetfulness. One woman had "gone through" a reconciliation in a branch and had made the physical motions and verbal
statements indicating it, and expressed the mouthy words [of] forgiving. Then with flashing eyes, she remarked, "I will forgive her,
but I have a memory like an elephant. I'll never forget." Her

pretended adjustment was valueless and void. She still harbored the bitterness. Her words of friendship were like a spider's web, her rebuilt fences were as straw, and she herself continued to suffer without peace of mind. Worse still, she stood "condemned before the Lord," and there remained in her an even greater sin than in the one who, she claimed, had injured her.

Little did this antagonistic woman realize that she had not forgiven at all. She had only made motions. She was spinning her wheels and getting nowhere. In the scripture quoted above, the phrase *in their hearts* has deep meaning. It must be a purging of feelings and thoughts and bitternesses. Mere words avail nothing.

"For behold, if a man being evil giveth a gift, he doeth it grudgingly; wherefore it is counted unto him the same as if he had retained the gift; wherefore he is counted evil before God." (Moro. 7:8.)

Henry Ward Beecher expressed the thought this way: "I can forgive but I cannot forget is another way of saying I cannot forgive."

I may add that unless a person forgives his brother his trespasses *with all his heart* he is unfit to partake of the sacrament.[5]

We should leave judgment to the Lord.

To be in the right we must forgive, and we must do so *without regard to whether or not our antagonist repents,* or how sincere is his transformation, or whether or not he asks our forgiveness. We must follow the example and the teaching of the Master, who said: ". . . Ye ought to say in your hearts—let God judge between me and thee, and reward thee according to thy deeds." (D&C 64:11.) But men often are unwilling to leave it to the Lord, fearing perhaps that the Lord might be too merciful, less severe than is proper in the case.[6]

Some people not only cannot or will not forgive and forget the transgressions of others, but go to the other extreme of hounding the alleged transgressor. Many letters and calls have come to me from individuals who are determined to take the sword of justice in their own hands and presume to see that a transgressor is punished. "That man should be excommunicated," a woman declared, "and I'm never going to rest till he has been properly dealt with." Another said, "I can never rest, so long as that person is a member of the Church." Still another said: "I will never enter the chapel so long as that person is permitted to enter. I want him tried for his membership." One man even made many trips to Salt Lake City and wrote several long letters to protest against the bishop and the stake president who did not take summary disciplinary action against a person who, he claimed, was breaking the laws of the Church.

To such who would take the law into their own hands, we read again the positive declaration of the Lord: ". . . there remaineth in him the greater sin." (D&C 64:9.) The revelation continues: "And ye ought to say in your hearts—let God judge between me and thee, and reward thee according to thy deeds." (D&C 64:11.) When known transgressions have been duly reported to the proper ecclesiastical officers of the Church, the individual may rest the case and leave the responsibility with the Church officers. If those officers tolerate sin in the ranks, it is an awesome responsibility for them and they will be held accountable.[7]

The Lord will judge with the same measurements meted out by us. If we are harsh, we should not expect other than harshness. If we are merciful with those who injure us, he will be merciful with us in our errors. If we are unforgiving, he will leave us weltering in our own sins.

While the scriptures are plain in their declaration that man shall have meted out to him the same measure that he gives his fellowmen, the meting out even of warranted judgment is not for the layman, but for proper authorities in Church and state. The Lord will do the judging in the final analysis. . . .

The Lord can judge men by their thoughts as well as by what they say and do, for he knows even the intents of their hearts; but this is not true of humans. We hear what people say, we see what they do, but being unable to discern what they think or intend, we often judge wrongfully if we try to fathom the meaning and motives behind their actions and place on them our own interpretation.[8]

Though it may seem difficult, we can forgive.

In the context of the spirit of forgiveness, one good brother asked me, "Yes, that is what ought to be done, but how do you do it? Doesn't that take a superman?"

"Yes," I said, "but we are commanded to be supermen. Said the Lord, 'Be ye therefore perfect, even as your Father which is in heaven is perfect.' (Matt. 5:48.) We are gods in embryo, and the Lord demands perfection of us."

"Yes, the Christ forgave those who injured him, but he was more than human," he rejoined.

And my answer was: "But there are many humans who have found it possible to do this divine thing."

Apparently there are many who, like this good brother, hold the comfortable theory that the forgiving spirit . . . is more or less the monopoly of scriptural or fictional characters and can hardly be expected of practical people in today's world. This is not the case.[9]

I knew a young mother who lost her husband by death. The family had been in poor circumstances and the insurance policy was only $2,000, but it was like a gift from heaven. The company promptly delivered the check for that amount as soon as proof of death was furnished. The young widow concluded she should save this for emergencies, and accordingly deposited it in the bank. Others knew of her savings, and one kinsman convinced her that she should lend the $2,000 to him at a high rate of interest.

Years passed, and she had received neither principal nor interest. She noticed that the borrower avoided her and made evasive promises when she asked him about the money. Now she needed the money and it could not be had.

"How I hate him!" she told me, and her voice breathed venom and bitterness and her dark eyes flashed. To think that an able-bodied man would defraud a young widow with a family to support! "How I loathe him!" she repeated over and over. Then I told her [a] story, where a man forgave the murderer of his father. She listened intently. I saw she was impressed. At the conclusion there were tears in her eyes, and she whispered: "Thank you. Thank you sincerely. Surely I, too, must forgive my enemy. I will now cleanse my heart of its bitterness. I do not expect ever to receive the money, but I leave my offender in the hands of the Lord."

Weeks later, she saw me again and confessed that those intervening weeks had been the happiest of her life. A new peace had overshadowed her and she was able to pray for the offender and forgive him, even though she never received back a single dollar.[10]

When we forgive others, we free ourselves from hatred and bitterness.

Why does the Lord ask you to love your enemies and to return good for evil? That you might have the benefit of it. It does not injure the one you hate so much when you hate a person, especially if he is far removed and does not come in contact with you, but the hate and the bitterness canker your unforgiving heart. . . .

Perhaps Peter had met people who continued to trespass against him, and he asked:

"Lord, how oft shall my brother sin against me, and I forgive him? . . ."

And the Lord said:

"I say not unto thee, Until seven times: but, Until seventy times seven." (Matthew 18:21–22.) . . .

. . . When they have repented and come on their knees to ask forgiveness, most of us can forgive, but the Lord has required that we shall forgive even if they do not repent nor ask forgiveness of us. . . .

It must be very clear to us, then, that we must still forgive without retaliation or vengeance, for the Lord will do for us such as is necessary. . . . Bitterness injures the one who carries it; it hardens and shrivels and cankers.[11]

It frequently happens that offenses are committed when the offender is not aware of it. Something he has said or done is misconstrued or misunderstood. The offended one treasures in his heart the offense, adding to it such other things as might give fuel to the fire and justify his conclusions. Perhaps this is one of

*"Forgiveness is the miraculous ingredient that assures harmony
and love in the home or the ward."*

the reasons why the Lord requires that the offended one should make the overtures toward peace.

"And if thy brother or sister offend thee, thou shalt take him or her between him or her and thee alone; and if he or she confess thou shalt be reconciled." (D&C 42:88.) . . .

Do we follow that command or do we sulk in our bitterness, waiting for our offender to learn of it and to kneel to us in remorse?[12]

We may get angry with our parents, or a teacher, or the bishop, and dwarf ourselves into nameless anonymity as we shrivel and shrink under the venom and poison of bitterness and hatred. While the hated one goes on about his business, little realizing the suffering of the hater, the latter cheats himself. . . .

. . . To terminate activity in the Church just to spite leaders or to give vent to wounded feelings is to cheat ourselves.[13]

In the midst of discordant sounds of hate, bitterness and revenge expressed so often today, the soft note of forgiveness comes as a healing balm. Not least is its effect on the forgiver.[14]

As we forgive others, we are blessed with joy and peace.

Inspired by the Lord Jesus Christ, Paul has given to us the solution to the problems of life which require understanding and forgiveness. "And be ye kind one to another, tender-hearted, forgiving one another, even as God for Christ's sake hath forgiven you." (Eph. 4:32.) If this spirit of kindly, tender-hearted forgiveness of one another could be carried into every home, selfishness, distrust and bitterness which break so many homes and families would disappear and men would live in peace.[15]

Forgiveness is the miraculous ingredient that assures harmony and love in the home or the ward. Without it there is contention. Without understanding and forgiveness there is dissension, followed by lack of harmony, and this breeds disloyalty in homes, in branches and in wards. On the other hand, forgiveness is harmonious with the spirit of the gospel, with the Spirit of Christ. This is the spirit we must all possess if we would receive forgiveness of our own sins and be blameless before God.[16]

Frequently, pride gets in our way and becomes our stumbling block. But each of us needs to ask himself the question: "Is your pride more important than your peace?"

All too frequently, one who has done many splendid things in life and made an excellent contribution will let pride cause him to lose the rich reward to which he would be entitled otherwise. We should always wear the sackcloth and ashes of a forgiving heart and a contrite spirit, being willing always to exercise genuine humility, as did the publican [see Luke 18:9–14], and ask the Lord to help us to forgive.[17]

So long as mortality exists we live and work with imperfect people; and there will be misunderstandings, offenses, and injuries to sensitive feelings. The best of motives are often misunderstood. It is gratifying to find many who, in their bigness of soul have straightened out their thinking, swallowed their pride, forgiven what they had felt were personal slights. Numerous others who have walked critical, lonely, thorny paths in abject misery, have finally accepted correction, acknowledged errors, cleansed their hearts of bitterness, and have come again to peace, that coveted peace which is so conspicuous in its absence. And the frustrations of criticism, bitterness, and the resultant estrangements have given place to warmth and light and peace.[18]

It can be done. Man can conquer self. Man can overcome. Man can forgive all who have trespassed against him and go on to receive *peace* in this life and eternal life in the world to come.[19]

If we would sue for peace, taking the initiative in settling differences—if we would forgive and forget with all our hearts—if we would cleanse our own souls of sin, bitterness, and guilt before we cast a stone or accusation at others—if we would forgive all real or fancied offenses before we asked forgiveness for our own sins—if we would pay our own debts, large or small, before we pressed our debtors—if we would manage to clear our own eyes of the blinding beams before we magnified the motes in the eyes of others—what a glorious world this would be! Divorce would be reduced to a minimum; courts would be freed from disgusting routines; family life would be heavenly; the building of the kingdom would go forward at an accelerated pace; and that peace which passeth understanding [see Philippians 4:7] would bring to us all a joy and happiness that has hardly "entered into the heart of man." [See 1 Corinthians 2:9.][20]

May the Lord bless us all that we may continually carry in our hearts the true spirit of repentance and forgiveness until we shall have perfected ourselves, looking toward the glories of exaltation awaiting the most faithful.[21]

Suggestions for Study and Teaching

Consider these ideas as you study the chapter or as you prepare to teach. For additional help, see pages v–ix.

- Review the story on pages 89–91. Why is it sometimes so difficult for people to forgive one another? What do the words "For there remaineth in him the greater sin" (D&C 64:9) mean to you?

- Review Matthew 6:14–15, quoted by President Kimball on page 92. Why do you think we must forgive others in order to receive the Lord's forgiveness?

- What are some attitudes and actions that indicate our forgiveness of another is heartfelt and complete? (See pages 92–94.) Why must forgiveness be "a heart action"?

- Review the section that begins on page 94. What gospel teachings can help us be willing to leave judgment to the Lord?

- As you read the story about the young mother on pages 96–97, look for what prevented her, at first, from forgiving and what enabled her to finally forgive. How can we overcome the obstacles that interfere with our desires and efforts to forgive others?

- What are some consequences of refusing to forgive? (See pages 97–98.) What blessings have you experienced as you have forgiven another? Consider how you might apply the spirit of forgiveness in your relationships.

Related Scriptures: Matthew 5:43–48; Luke 6:36–38; Colossians 3:12–15; D&C 82:23

Notes

1. *The Miracle of Forgiveness* (1969), 281–82.
2. *The Teachings of Spencer W. Kimball*, ed. Edward L. Kimball (1982), 243.
3. *The Miracle of Forgiveness*, 261.
4. In Conference Report, Oct. 1977, 71; or *Ensign*, Nov. 1977, 48.
5. *The Miracle of Forgiveness*, 262–64.
6. *The Miracle of Forgiveness*, 283.
7. *The Miracle of Forgiveness*, 264.
8. *The Miracle of Forgiveness*, 267, 268.
9. *The Miracle of Forgiveness*, 286–87.
10. In Conference Report, Oct. 1977, 68–69; or *Ensign*, Nov. 1977, 46. See also *The Miracle of Forgiveness*, 293–94.
11. *Faith Precedes the Miracle* (1972), 191, 192.
12. *Faith Precedes the Miracle*, 194, 195.
13. "On Cheating Yourself," *New Era*, Apr. 1972, 33, 34.
14. *The Miracle of Forgiveness*, 266.
15. *The Miracle of Forgiveness*, 298.
16. *The Miracle of Forgiveness*, 275.
17. *The Miracle of Forgiveness*, 297.
18. In Conference Report, Apr. 1955, 98.
19. *The Miracle of Forgiveness*, 300.
20. *Faith Precedes the Miracle*, 195–96.
21. In Conference Report, Oct. 1949, 134.

President Kimball taught that if we will yield "to the sweet influence and pleadings of the Spirit," we will be blessed with "protection, power, freedom and joy."

Fortifying Ourselves against Evil Influences

The gospel of Jesus Christ offers us power and protection against the evils of our day.

From the Life of Spencer W. Kimball

President Spencer W. Kimball taught that the fight against Satan and his forces "is not a little skirmish with a half-willed antagonist, but a battle royal with an enemy so powerful, entrenched, and organized that we are likely to be vanquished if we are not strong, well-trained, and watchful."[1]

As a young missionary serving in the Central States Mission, he recorded in his diary an experience illustrating his resolve to withstand temptation. He was traveling on a train to Chicago, Illinois, when a man approached him. "[He] tried to get me to read a vulgar book with obscene pictures. I told him it didn't appeal to me. He began tempting me then to go with him in Chicago and I knew he'd lead me down to hell. I shut him up but after he was gone I could feel myself blush for an hour. I thought—'Oh! how hard Satan, through his imps, tries to lead young people astray.' I thanked the Lord that I had power to overcome it."[2]

Teachings of Spencer W. Kimball

Satan is real and will use any means to try to destroy us.

In these days of sophistication and error men depersonalize not only God but the devil. Under this concept Satan is a myth, useful for keeping people straight in less enlightened days but outmoded in our educated age. Nothing is further from reality. Satan is very much a personal, individual spirit being, but without a mortal body. His desires to seal each of us his are no less ardent in wickedness than our Father's are in righteousness to attract us to his own eternal kingdom.[3]

To know where the danger is and to be able to recognize it in all of its manifestations provides protection. The evil one is alert. He is always ready to deceive and claim as his victims every unwary one, every careless one, every rebellious one.[4]

Regardless of who is getting the adversary's special attention at any given time, he seeks to make all people "miserable like unto himself" (2 Ne. 2:27). Indeed, he seeks "the misery of all mankind" (2 Ne. 2:18). He is undeviating in his purposes and is clever and relentless in his pursuit of them.[5]

Peter cautioned us: "Be sober, be vigilant; because your adversary the devil, as a roaring lion, walketh about, seeking whom he may devour" (1 Pet. 5:8).

And the Savior said that the very elect would be deceived by Lucifer if it were possible [see Joseph Smith—Matthew 1:22]. [Lucifer] will use his logic to confuse and his rationalizations to destroy. He will shade meanings, open doors an inch at a time, and lead from purest white through all the shades of gray to the darkest black.[6]

The arch deceiver has studied every way possible to achieve his ends, using every tool, every device possible. He takes over, distorts, and changes and camouflages everything created for the good of man, . . . so he may take over their minds and pervert their bodies and claim them his.

He never sleeps—he is diligent and persevering. He analyzes carefully his problem and then moves forward diligently, methodically to reach that objective. He uses all five senses and man's natural hunger and thirst to lead him away. He anticipates resistance and fortifies himself against it. He uses time and space and leisure. He is constant and persuasive and skillful. He uses such useful things as radio, television, the printed page, the airplane, and the car to distort and damage. He uses the gregariousness of man, his loneliness, his every need to lead him astray. He does his work at the most propitious time in the most impressive places with the most influential people. He overlooks nothing that will deceive and distort and prostitute. He uses money, power, force. He entices man and attacks at his weakest spot. He takes the good and creates ugliness. . . . He uses every teaching art to subvert man.[7]

The adversary is subtle. He is cunning. He knows that he cannot induce good men and women to do major evils immediately, so he moves slyly, whispering half-truths until he has his intended captives following him.[8]

With the Lord's help, we can withstand evil influences.

If we would escape [the] deadly thrusts of the evil one and keep our homes and families free and solidly fortified against all destructive influences so rampant about us, we must have the help of . . . the Creator himself. There is only one sure way and that is through the gospel of the Lord Jesus Christ and being obedient to its profound and inspired teachings.[9]

In the life of everyone there comes the conflict between good and evil, between Satan and the Lord. Every person who has reached or passed the age of accountability of eight years, and who with a totally repentant heart is baptized properly, positively will receive the Holy Ghost. If heeded, this member of the Godhead will guide, inspire, and warn, and will neutralize the promptings of the evil one.[10]

He who has greater strength than Lucifer, he who is our fortress and our strength, can sustain us in times of great temptation. While the Lord will never forcibly take anyone out of sin or out of the arms of the tempters, he exerts his Spirit to induce the sinner to do it with divine assistance. And the man who yields to the sweet influence and pleadings of the Spirit and does all in his power to stay in a repentant attitude is guaranteed protection, power, freedom and joy.[11]

Satan . . . contended for the subservience of Moses. . . .

"Moses, son of man, worship me," the devil tempted, with promise of worlds and luxuries and power. . . .

. . . The prophet demanded: "Get thee hence, Satan. . . ." (Moses 1:16.) The liar, the tempter, the devil unwilling to give up this possible victim, now in rage and fury "cried with a loud voice, and rent upon the earth, and commanded, saying: I am the Only Begotten, worship me." (Moses 1:19.)

Moses recognized the deception and saw the power of darkness and the "bitterness of hell." Here was a force not easily reckoned with nor evicted. Terrified, he called upon God, then commanded with new power:

"I will not cease to call upon God . . . for his glory has been upon me, wherefore I can judge between him and thee. . . . In the name of the Only Begotten, depart hence, Satan." (Moses 1:18, 21.)

Not even Lucifer, . . . the arch-enemy of mankind, can withstand the power of the priesthood of God. Trembling, quaking, cursing, weeping, wailing, gnashing his teeth, he departed from the victorious Moses.[12]

We must be prepared to make a bold stand before Satan . . . and against principalities and powers and the rulers of darkness. We need the whole armor of God that we may withstand. [See Ephesians 6:12–13.][13]

"Put on the whole armour of God," as Paul admonished [Ephesians 6:11]. With this divine influence and protection, we may be able to discern the adversary's deceptions in whatever appealing words and rationalizations and we may be "able to withstand the evil day, and having done all, to stand." [See Ephesians 6:13.][14]

We must not yield to even the smallest temptations.

Serious sin enters into our lives as we yield first to little temptations. Seldom does one enter into deeper transgression without first yielding to lesser ones, which open the door to the greater. Giving an example of one type of sin, someone said, "An honest man doesn't suddenly become dishonest any more than a clean field suddenly becomes weedy."

It is extremely difficult, if not impossible, for the devil to enter a door that is closed. He seems to have no keys for locked doors. But if a door is slightly ajar, he gets his toe in, and soon this is followed by his foot, then by his leg and his body and his head, and finally he is in all the way.

This situation is reminiscent of the fable of the camel and his owner who were traveling across the desert sand dunes when a wind storm came up. The traveler quickly set up his tent and moved in, closing the flaps to protect himself from the cutting, grinding sands of the raging storm. The camel was of course left outside, and as the violent wind hurled the sand against his body and into his eyes and nostrils he found it unbearable and finally begged for entrance into the tent.

"There is room only for myself," said the traveler.

"But may I just get my nose in so I can breathe air not filled with sand?" asked the camel.

"Well, perhaps you could do that," replied the traveler, and he opened the flap ever so little and the long nose of the camel entered. How comfortable the camel was now! But soon the camel became weary of the smarting sand on his eyes and ears . . . :

"The wind-driven sand is like a rasp on my head. Could I put just my head in?"

Again, the traveler rationalized that to acquiesce would do him no damage, for the camel's head could occupy the space at the top of the tent which he himself was not using. So the camel put his head inside and the beast was satisfied again—but for a short while only.

"Just the front quarters," he begged, and again the traveler relented and soon the camel's front shoulders and legs were in the tent. Finally, by the same processes of pleading and of yielding, the camel's torso, his hind quarters and all were in the tent. But now it was too crowded for the two, and the camel kicked the traveler out into the wind and storm.

Like the camel, Lucifer readily becomes the master when one succumbs to his initial blandishments. Soon then the conscience is stilled completely, the evil power has full sway, and the door to salvation is closed until a thorough repentance opens it again.

The importance of not accommodating temptation in the least degree is underlined by the Savior's example. Did not he recognize the danger when he was on the mountain with his fallen brother, Lucifer, being sorely tempted by that master tempter? He could have opened the door and flirted with danger by saying, "All right, Satan, I'll listen to your proposition. I need not succumb, I need not yield, I need not accept—but I'll listen."

Christ did not so rationalize. He positively and promptly closed the discussion, and commanded: "Get thee hence, Satan," meaning, likely, "Get out of my sight—get out of my presence— I will not listen—I will have nothing to do with you." Then, we read, "the devil leaveth him." [Matthew 4:10–11.]

This is our proper pattern, if we would prevent sin rather than be faced with the much more difficult task of curing it. As I study the story of the Redeemer and his temptations, I am certain he spent his energies fortifying himself against temptation rather than battling with it to conquer it.[15]

Right decisions now can help us withstand temptations later.

One of the basic tasks for each individual is the making of decisions. A dozen times a day we come to a fork in the road and must decide which way we will go. Some alternatives are long and hard, but they take us in the right direction toward our ultimate goal; others are short, wide, and pleasant, but they go off in the wrong direction. It is important to get our ultimate objectives clearly in mind so that we do not become distracted at each fork in the road by the irrelevant questions: Which is the easier or more pleasant way? or, Which way are others going?

Right decisions are easiest to make when we make them well in advance, having ultimate objectives in mind; this saves a lot of anguish at the fork, when we're tired and sorely tempted.

When I was young, I made up my mind unalterably that I would never taste tea, coffee, tobacco, or liquor. I found that this rigid determination saved me many times throughout my varied experiences. There were many occasions when I could have sipped or touched or sampled, but the unalterable determination firmly established gave me good reason and good strength to resist.

. . . The time to decide that we will settle for nothing less than an opportunity to live eternally with our Father is now, so that every choice we make will be affected by our determination to let nothing interfere with attaining that ultimate goal.[16]

Develop discipline of self so that, more and more, you do not have to decide and redecide what you will do when you are confronted with the same temptation time and time again. You only need to decide some things *once!*

How great a blessing it is to be free of agonizing over and over again regarding a temptation. To do such is time-consuming and very risky.[17]

We can push some things away from us once and have done with them! We can make a single decision about certain things that we will incorporate in our lives and then make them ours—without having to brood and redecide a hundred times what it is we will do and what we will not do.

Indecision and discouragement are climates in which the Adversary lives to function, for he can inflict so many casualties among mankind in those settings. . . . If you have not done so yet, decide to decide![18]

How wonderful it would be if we could just get every Latter-day Saint boy and girl to make up his mind or her mind during childhood to say, "I will never yield to Satan or to anybody who would want me to destroy myself."[19]

The time to quit evil ways is before they start. The secret of the good life is in protection and prevention. Those who yield to evil are usually those who have placed themselves in a vulnerable position.[20]

We resist the adversary as we acknowledge our weaknesses and strive to overcome them.

Having been reared on the farm, I know that when the pigs got out, I looked first for the holes through which they had previously escaped. When the cow was out of the field looking for greener pastures elsewhere, I knew where to look first for the place of her escape. It was most likely to be the place where she had jumped the fence before, or where the fence had been broken. Likewise the devil knows where to tempt, where to put in his telling blows. He finds the vulnerable spot. Where one was weak before, he will be most easily tempted again.[21]

It seems that evil is always about us. . . . Accordingly, we must be alert constantly. We catalogue our weaknesses and move in against them to overcome them.[22]

Most of us have vulnerable spots through which disaster can overtake us unless we are properly safeguarded and immunized. . . .

History provides many . . . examples of strength and pride, both individual and national, which succumbed to attack on the vulnerable spot. While these spots were often, on the surface at least, physical, Lucifer and his followers know the habits, weaknesses, and vulnerable spots of everyone and take advantage of them to lead us to spiritual destruction. With one person it may be thirst for liquor; another may have an insatiable hunger; another has permitted his sex urges to dominate; another loves money, and the luxuries and comforts it can buy; another craves power; and so on.[23]

Let him who has evil tendencies be honest and acknowledge his weakness. I tell you the Lord places no sin in our lives. He has made no man wicked. . . . Sin was permitted in the world, and Satan permitted to tempt us, but we have our free agency. We may sin or live righteously, but we cannot escape responsibility. To blame our sin upon the Lord, saying it is inherent and cannot be controlled, is cheap and cowardly. To blame our sins upon our parents and our upbringing is the way of the escapist. One's parents may have failed; our own backgrounds may have been frustrating, but as sons and daughters of a living God we have within ourselves the power to rise above our circumstances, to change our lives.[24]

We plead with our people everywhere, "Submit yourselves therefore to God. Resist the devil, and he will flee from you." (James 4:7.) . . .

There may be some who have a general feeling of uneasiness because of world conditions and lengthening shadows of evil,

President Kimball said that in order for us to guard against the adversary, we need to "hold fast to the iron rod."

but the Lord said, ". . . if ye are prepared ye shall not fear" (D&C 38:30), and again, "Peace I leave with you. . . . Let not your heart be troubled, neither let it be afraid." (John 14:27.)[25]

As Latter-day Saints we must ever be vigilant. The way for each person and each family to guard against the slings and arrows of the Adversary and to prepare for the great day of the Lord is to hold fast to the iron rod, to exercise greater faith, to repent of our sins and shortcomings, and to be anxiously engaged in the work of His kingdom on earth, which is The Church of Jesus Christ of Latter-day Saints. Herein lies the only true happiness for all our Father's children.[26]

Suggestions for Study and Teaching

Consider these ideas as you study the chapter or as you prepare to teach. For additional help, see pages v–ix.

• Which teachings of President Kimball about Satan and his methods do you find helpful and why? (See pages 103–5.)

• Review the section beginning on page 105. In what ways can the Lord help us withstand evil? (For an example, see the story on page 103.) When have you received this kind of help?

• Read the fable on page 107. Why do you think the traveler allowed the camel into his tent? Consider how the Savior resisted temptation (see pages 107–8). What are some ways parents can help their children recognize and resist even the smallest temptations?

• Review the second full paragraph on page 108. Compare the process of preventing sin with the process of curing it.

• President Kimball said, "Right decisions are easiest to make when we make them well in advance" (page 108). How might our lives be affected by early decisions to keep such commandments as the Word of Wisdom? (For an example, see page 108.) What are some decisions related to gospel living that you have unalterably made?

• Consider President Kimball's observations about his pigs and his cow (pages 109–10). What do we gain by acknowledging our weaknesses and accepting responsibility for them?

Related Scriptures: 1 Corinthians 10:13; 1 Nephi 15:23–25; Helaman 5:12; Ether 12:27; D&C 10:5

Notes

1. In Conference Report, Brisbane Australia Area Conference 1976, 19.
2. In "The Mission Experience of Spencer W. Kimball," *Brigham Young University Studies,* fall 1985, 126.
3. *The Miracle of Forgiveness* (1969), 21.
4. *The Miracle of Forgiveness,* 213.
5. "The Role of Righteous Women," *Ensign,* Nov. 1979, 104.
6. "President Kimball Speaks Out on Morality," *Ensign,* Nov. 1980, 94.
7. "How to Evaluate Your Performance," *Improvement Era,* Oct. 1969, 12.
8. "The Gospel of Repentance," *Ensign,* Oct. 1982, 2.
9. In Conference Report, Apr. 1979, 5; or *Ensign,* May 1979, 6.
10. *The Miracle of Forgiveness,* 14–15.
11. *The Miracle of Forgiveness,* 176.

12. *Faith Precedes the Miracle* (1972), 87, 88.

13. "The Blessings and Responsibilities of Womanhood," *Ensign,* Mar. 1976, 71.

14. *Faith Precedes the Miracle,* 219.

15. *The Miracle of Forgiveness,* 215–17.

16. "Decisions: Why It's Important to Make Some Now," *New Era,* Apr. 1971, 3.

17. "President Kimball Speaks Out on Planning Your Life," *New Era,* Sept. 1981, 50.

18. In Conference Report, Apr. 1976, 70; or *Ensign,* May 1976, 46.

19. In Conference Report, Manila Philippines Area Conference 1975, 5.

20. *The Miracle of Forgiveness,* 15.

21. *The Miracle of Forgiveness,* 171.

22. *The Miracle of Forgiveness,* 209–10.

23. *The Miracle of Forgiveness,* 218–19.

24. *An Apostle Speaks to Youth—Be Ye Clean: Steps to Repentance and Forgiveness* (pamphlet, 1970), 13.

25. In Conference Report, Apr. 1974, 6; or *Ensign,* May 1974, 6.

26. In Conference Report, Oct. 1982, 4; or *Ensign,* Nov. 1982, 5.

"Let us practice the principles of personal and family preparedness in our daily lives."

114

Provident Living: Applying Principles of Self-Reliance and Preparedness

Wise and provident living is a lifestyle that builds character and increases our temporal, social, emotional, and spiritual well-being.

From the Life of Spencer W. Kimball

As a young couple, Spencer W. Kimball and his wife, Camilla, "knew they weren't rich. But they had work and ability. They knew how to manage their own money, living within their income, saving for the future."[1]

The Kimballs lived through times of widespread economic difficulties—World War I (1914–18), the Great Depression (1929–39), and World War II (1939–45). Having experienced these challenges, President Kimball concluded, "What I have seen with my own eyes makes me afraid not to do what I can to protect against the calamities."[2]

Among the things he saw were the struggles of others: "All my life from childhood I have heard the Brethren saying, 'get out of debt and stay out of debt.' I was employed for some years in the banks and I saw the terrible situation that many people were in because they had ignored that important counsel."

In addition to his bank work, Spencer kept the account books for some of the local stores. "One of the shocking things of my life was to find on the books the accounts of many of the people in the community that I knew. I knew them. I knew approximately what their income was, and then I saw them wear it away. In other words, I saw they were buying their clothes, their shoes, everything they had 'on time.'

"And I found that it was my duty to make the bills at the end of the month for them. And many of them couldn't pay at the end of the month. They couldn't pay even the installments that were arranged for them. And having been reared in a home that took care of its funds, I couldn't understand it. I could understand how a person could buy a home on time or perhaps could even buy an automobile on time. But I never could quite understand how anybody would wear clothes they didn't own. Or eat food that they had to buy 'on time.' "[3]

In his teachings President Kimball addressed not only financial issues but also other matters related to provident living, such as personal responsibility, work, and home food production and storage. He said: "Let us practice the principles of personal and family preparedness in our daily lives. 'If ye are prepared ye shall not fear' (D&C 38:30)."[4]

Teachings of Spencer W. Kimball

We are responsible for our own social, emotional, spiritual, physical, and economic well-being.

The Church and its members are commanded by the Lord to be self-reliant and independent. (See D&C 78:13–14.)

The responsibility for each person's social, emotional, spiritual, physical, or economic well-being rests first upon himself, second upon his family, and third upon the Church if he is a faithful member thereof.

No true Latter-day Saint, while physically or emotionally able, will voluntarily shift the burden of his own or his family's well-being to someone else. So long as he can, under the inspiration of the Lord and with his own labors, he will supply himself and his family with the spiritual and temporal necessities of life. (See 1 Timothy 5:8.)[5]

As we travel and visit the people throughout the world, we recognize the great temporal needs of our people. And as we long to help them, we realize the vital importance of their learning this great lesson: that the highest achievement of spirituality comes as we conquer the flesh. We build character as we encourage people to care for their own needs.[6]

No amount of philosophizing, excuses, or rationalizing will ever change the fundamental need for self-reliance. This is so because:

"All truth is independent in that sphere in which God has placed it, . . . as all intelligence also; otherwise there is no existence." (D&C 93:30.) The Lord declares that herein lies "the agency of man" (see D&C 93:31), and with this agency comes the responsibility for self. With this agency we can rise to glory or fall to condemnation. May we individually and collectively be ever self-reliant. This is our heritage and our obligation.[7]

We have placed considerable emphasis on personal and family preparedness. I hope that each member of the Church is responding appropriately to this direction. I also hope that we are understanding and accentuating the positive and not the negative. I like the way the Relief Society teaches personal and family preparedness as "provident living." This implies the husbanding [prudent managing] of our resources, the wise planning of financial matters, full provision for personal health, and adequate preparation for education and career development, giving appropriate attention to home [food] production and storage as well as the development of emotional resiliency.[8]

We have been counseled to participate in home food production and storage.

The Lord has urged that his people save for the rainy days, prepare for the difficult times, and put away for emergencies, a year's supply or more of bare necessities so that when comes the flood, the earthquake, the famine, the hurricane, the storms of life, our families can be sustained through the dark days.[9]

We encourage you to grow all the food that you feasibly can on your own property. Berry bushes, grapevines, fruit trees— plant them if your climate is right for their growth. Grow vegetables and eat them from your own yard. Even those residing in apartments or condominiums can generally grow a little food in

117

pots and planters. Study the best methods of providing your own foods. Make your garden as neat and attractive as well as productive. If there are children in your home, involve them in the process with assigned responsibilities.[10]

I hope that we understand that, while having a garden . . . is often useful in reducing food costs and making available delicious fresh fruits and vegetables, it does much more than this. Who can gauge the value of that special chat between daughter and Dad as they weed or water the garden? How do we evaluate the good that comes from the obvious lessons of planting, cultivating, and the eternal law of the harvest? And how do we measure the family togetherness and cooperating that must accompany successful canning? Yes, we are laying up resources in store, but perhaps the greater good is contained in the lessons of life we learn as we *live providently*.[11]

We encourage families to have on hand this year's supply; and we say it over and over and over and repeat over and over the scripture of the Lord where He says, "Why call ye me, Lord, Lord, and do not the things which I say?" [Luke 6:46.] How empty it is as they put their spirituality, so-called, into action and call him by his important names, but fail to do the things which he says.[12]

As we become more affluent and our bank accounts enlarge, there comes a feeling of security, and we feel sometimes that we do not need the supply that has been suggested by the Brethren. . . . We must remember that conditions could change and a year's supply of basic commodities could be very much appreciated by us or others. So we would do well to listen to what we have been told and to follow it explicitly.[13]

We should work for what we receive.

With regard to all phases of our lives, I believe that men should help themselves. They should plow and plant and cultivate and harvest and not expect their faith to bring them bread.[14]

Work is a spiritual necessity as well as an economic necessity.[15]

Work brings happiness, self-esteem, and prosperity. It is the means of all accomplishment; it is the opposite of idleness. We

*"Work brings happiness, self-esteem, and prosperity.
It is the means of all accomplishment; it is the opposite of idleness."*

are commanded to work. (See Gen. 3:19.) Attempts to obtain our temporal, social, emotional, or spiritual well-being by means of a dole violate the divine mandate that we should work for what we receive.[16]

We cannot be too often reminded that Church welfare assistance is spiritual at heart and that these spiritual roots would wither if we ever permitted anything like the philosophy of the dole to enter into our Welfare Services ministrations. Everyone assisted can do something. Let us follow the order of the Church in this regard and insure that all who receive give of themselves in return. May we be on guard against accepting worldly substitutes for the plan to care for his poor in this, the Lord's own way.[17]

The Lord's way builds individual self-esteem and develops and heals the dignity of the individual, whereas the world's way depresses the individual's view of himself and causes deep resentment.

The Lord's way causes the individual to hasten his efforts to become economically independent again, even though he may have temporary need, because of special conditions, for help and assistance. The world's way deepens the individual's dependency on welfare programs and tends to make him demand more rather than encouraging him to return to economic independence.

The Lord's way helps our members get a testimony for themselves about the gospel of work. For work is important to human happiness as well as productivity. The world's way, however, places greater and greater emphasis on leisure and upon the avoidance of work.[18]

It is right to work. Every man and woman and child should work. Even little children should learn how to share, to help do the housework and the yardwork, to plant gardens, to plant trees, to pick fruit, and to do everything that needs to be done, because that makes strong characters out of them and builds their faith and character.

We want you parents to create work for your children. Insist on them learning their lessons in school. Do not let them play all the time. There is a time for play, there is a time to work, and there is a time to study. Be sure your children grow up like you know they ought to grow.[19]

Work should be the ruling principle in the lives of our Church membership. (See D&C 42:42; 75:29; 68:30–32; 56:17.)[20]

We can become economically self-reliant by saving, avoiding debt, and living within our means.

Are you prepared for and protected against death, illness, a long-continuing, crippling illness of the breadwinner? How long can you go if the income stops? What are your reserves? How long could you make your many payments on home, car, implements, appliances? . . .

The first reaction is: We just cannot do it. We can hardly get by using every cent of income monthly. . . . If you can hardly get by when you are earning increasingly, well employed, well, productive, young, then how can you meet emergencies with employment curtailed, illness and other unlooked-for problems arising?[21]

You must not spend all you make. Money must be put aside for missions and for schooling for your children. They can assume responsibilities and take little jobs whereby they can also help to raise these funds and instead of spending those little accumulations, they will save them for these great purposes. It may mean that the parents of today will go without many things that they would like, but tomorrow will come the harvest.[22]

Avoid debt. . . . Today everything is seemingly geared toward debt. "Get your cards, and buy everything on time": you're encouraged to do it. But the truth is that we *don't* need to do it to live.[23]

We wonder what our people will do who have been spending their all and more. If employment and income should reduce, what then? Are you living beyond your means? Do you owe what you cannot pay if times became perilous? Are your shock absorbers in condition to take a shock?[24]

Plan and work in a way that will permit you to be happy even as you do without certain things that in times of affluence may have been available to you. Live within your means and not beyond them. . . . Purchase your essentials wisely and carefully. Strive to save a portion of that which you earn. Do not mistake many wants for basic needs.[25]

Let us as individuals, as families, and as wards and stakes learn to live within our means. There is strength and salvation in this principle. Someone has said that we are rich in proportion to that with which we can do without. As families and as a Church, we can and should provide that which is *truly essential* for our people, but we must be careful not to extend beyond that which is essential or for purposes which are not directly related to our families' welfare and the basic mission of the Church.[26]

Preparedness is a way of life that brings its own rewards.

Preparedness, when properly pursued, is a way of life, not a sudden, spectacular program.[27]

121

We could refer to all the components of personal and family preparedness, not in relation to holocaust or disaster, but in cultivating a life-style that is on a day-to-day basis its own reward.

Let's do these things because they are right, because they are satisfying, and because we are obedient to the counsels of the Lord. In this spirit we will be prepared for most eventualities, and the Lord will prosper and comfort us. It is true that difficult times will come—for the Lord has foretold them—and, yes, stakes of Zion are "for a defense, and for a refuge from the storm." (D&C 115:6.) But if we live wisely and providently, we will be as safe as in the palm of His hand.[28]

Suggestions for Study and Teaching

Consider these ideas as you study the chapter or as you prepare to teach. For additional help, see pages v–ix.

- Given that our lives are connected with family, friends, the Church, and the community, what do you think it means to be self-reliant and independent? (See pages 116–17.)

- President Kimball taught that "social, emotional, spiritual, physical, [and] economic well-being" are elements of provident living (page 116). In what ways does spiritual well-being relate to the other elements?

- As you study the section that begins on page 117, think about how well prepared you are for "the storms of life." How can we become better prepared?

- What benefits can a garden bring to a family beyond providing food? (See page 118.)

- President Kimball said that "work is a spiritual necessity" (page 118). What spiritual benefits have you experienced through work? In what ways can we help our children learn the importance of work?

- What do you think the difference is between a want and a need? What attitudes can help us manage our wants? (For some examples, see pages 120–21 and the stories on pages 115–16.) What benefits are there in having a budget? What help is available to guide us in budgeting our resources?

- Read the section that begins on page 121. In what ways does preparedness bring day-to-day rewards?

Related Scriptures: Genesis 41:14–57; 2 Nephi 5:17; D&C 29:8–11

Notes

1. Edward L. Kimball and Andrew E. Kimball Jr., *Spencer W. Kimball* (1977), 99.

2. *The Teachings of Spencer W. Kimball,* ed. Edward L. Kimball (1982), 372.

3. In Conference Report, Apr. 1975, 166–67.

4. In Conference Report, Oct. 1978, 114; or *Ensign,* Nov. 1978, 75.

5. In Conference Report, Oct. 1977, 124; or *Ensign,* Nov. 1977, 77–78.

6. In Conference Report, Oct. 1977, 123; or *Ensign,* Nov. 1977, 77.

7. In Conference Report, Apr. 1978, 120; or *Ensign,* May 1978, 79.

8. In Conference Report, Oct. 1977, 125; or *Ensign,* Nov. 1977, 78.

9. *The Teachings of Spencer W. Kimball,* 374.

10. In Conference Report, Apr. 1976, 170–71; or *Ensign,* May 1976, 124.

11. In Conference Report, Oct. 1977, 125; or *Ensign,* Nov. 1977, 78.

12. In Conference Report, Apr. 1976, 171; or *Ensign,* May 1976, 125.

13. In Conference Report, Apr. 1976, 170; or *Ensign,* May 1976, 124.

14. *The Teachings of Spencer W. Kimball,* 370.

15. In Conference Report, Apr. 1981, 107; or *Ensign,* May 1981, 80.

16. In Conference Report, Oct. 1977, 124; or *Ensign,* Nov. 1977, 77.

17. In Conference Report, Apr. 1978, 119–20; or *Ensign,* May 1978, 79.

18. In Conference Report, Apr. 1976, 172; or *Ensign,* May 1976, 125.

19. *The Teachings of Spencer W. Kimball,* 360–61.

20. In Conference Report, Oct. 1977, 124; or *Ensign,* Nov. 1977, 77.

21. *The Teachings of Spencer W. Kimball,* 372.

22. *The Teachings of Spencer W. Kimball,* 371–72.

23. In Conference Report, Apr. 1976, 171; or *Ensign,* May 1976, 125.

24. In Conference Report, Oct. 1974, 7; or *Ensign,* Nov. 1974, 7.

25. In Conference Report, Apr. 1981, 107, 108; or *Ensign,* May 1981, 80.

26. In Conference Report, Apr. 1981, 63; or *Ensign,* May 1981, 46.

27. Regional representatives' seminar, Sept. 30, 1976, Archives of The Church of Jesus Christ of Latter-day Saints, 8.

28. In Conference Report, Oct. 1977, 125–26; or *Ensign,* Nov. 1977, 78.

Daniel was "a captive and slave but also a prophet of God who was willing to die for his convictions. Was integrity ever placed on a higher plane?"

Integrity

*Let us develop in ourselves integrity—that quality of soul
we prize so highly in others.*

From the Life of Spencer W. Kimball

Before his call as an Apostle, Spencer W. Kimball was active in business and community life in Arizona. He was co-owner of an insurance and real estate business and participated in local and statewide service organizations. In these matters, he was known for his honesty and integrity. It has been written of him: "Personal rectitude lay at the heart of the perceptions others had of Spencer W. Kimball. . . . He was always a straight arrow, delivering what he promised and negotiating with candor and without devious motives."[1]

Integrity was part of his character from the days of his youth, as the following account demonstrates: "Spencer and some of the boys borrowed a horse and an old buggy to use when their science class at school went on a field trip. On the rough road a buggy spring broke. The next day Spencer explained to his friends, 'We ought to all pitch in some money to pay for the broken spring,' but no one offered to help. He persuaded them, saying, 'That spring's going to be paid for, if I have to do it myself.' "[2]

Speaking at a general priesthood meeting in October 1974, President Marion G. Romney, Second Counselor in the First Presidency, pointed to President Kimball's example: "Throughout the years he has been a pattern of integrity. No one doubts that he would discharge the sacred trust the Lord has placed upon him at the peril of his life. . . . How glorious, men of the priesthood, it would be if all of us possessed the integrity of a President Kimball."[3]

Teachings of Spencer W. Kimball

Integrity is fundamental to good character.

Integrity (the willingness and ability to live by our beliefs and commitments) is one of the foundation stones of good character, and without good character one cannot hope to enjoy the presence of God here or in the eternities.[4]

Integrity is a state or quality of being complete, undivided, or unbroken. It is wholeness and unimpaired. It is purity and moral soundness. It is unadulterated genuineness and deep sincerity. It is courage, a human virtue of incalculable value. It is honesty, uprightness, and righteousness. Take these away and there is left but an empty shell. . . .

Integrity in individuals and corporate bodies is not to ask, "What will others think of me, and my practices?" but, "What do I think of myself if I do this or fail to do that?" Is it proper? Is it right? Would the Master approve? . . .

Integrity in man should bring inner peace, sureness of purpose, and security in action. Lack of it brings the reverse: disunity, fear, sorrow, unsureness.[5]

It would be well if all of us would take frequent inventory to see if hidden away under the rugs and in the corners of our lives there might be some vestige of hypocrisy and ugliness or error. Or could there be hidden under the blankets of personal excuse and rationalization some small eccentricities and dishonesties? Are there any cobwebs in ceilings and corners which we think will not be noticed? Are we trying to cover up the small pettinesses and the small gratifications we secretly allow ourselves— rationalizing the while that they are insignificant and inconsequential? Are there areas in our thoughts and actions and attitudes which we would like to hide from those we respect most?[6]

We show integrity by keeping our covenants with honor.

When we make a covenant or agreement with God, we must keep it at whatever cost. Let us not be like the student who agrees to live by certain standards of conduct and who then breaks his oath and tries to see how long he can get away with his deceit. Let us not be like the missionary who agrees to serve the Lord for two years, then wastes his time with laziness and rationalization. Let us not be like the Church member who partakes of the sacrament in the morning, then defiles the Sabbath that afternoon.[7]

By taking our covenants lightly, we will wound our own eternal selves. . . . Self-justification is easy and rationalization seductive, but the Lord explains in modern revelation that "when we undertake to cover our sins, or to gratify our pride, [or] our vain ambition . . . the heavens withdraw themselves; the Spirit of the Lord is grieved; and . . . [man] is left unto himself, to kick against the pricks" (D&C 121:37–38).

Of course, we can choose; the free agency is ours, but we cannot escape the consequences of our choices. And if there is a chink in our integrity, that is where the devil concentrates his attack.[8]

The covenants we make with God involve promises to *do*, not merely to refrain from doing, to work righteousness as well as to avoid evil. The children of Israel made such covenants through Moses, saying, "All that the Lord hath spoken *we will do*" (Exodus 19:8, italics added), though hardly was Moses' back turned until they had broken their promise through wrongdoing. In the baptismal waters we give a similar undertaking and we repledge it in the ordinance of the sacrament. Not to honor these pledges, to refuse to serve or to accept responsibility and do less than one's best at it, is a sin of omission. . . .

Melchizedek Priesthood holders and those who have received their temple endowments have made further and specific pledges to *do*, to work righteousness. The Lord has expressed the mutual pledges between our Heavenly Father and the priesthood holders as an "oath and covenant." [D&C 84:39.] . . . One breaks the priesthood covenant by transgressing commandments—but also by leaving undone his duties. Accordingly, *to break this covenant one needs only to do nothing.*[9]

"The covenants we make with God involve promises to do, not merely to refrain from doing, to work righteousness as well as to avoid evil."

Keep your promises. Maintain your integrity. Abide by your covenants. Give the Lord this year and every year your high fidelity and fullest expression of faith. Do it "on your honor" and you will be blessed now and forever.[10]

If we are dishonest, we cheat ourselves.

Almost all dishonesty owes its existence and growth to that inward distortion we call self-justification. It is the first, and worst, and most insidious form of cheating: We are cheating ourselves.[11]

Self-justification is the enemy of repentance. God's Spirit continues with the honest in heart to strengthen, to help, and to save, but invariably the Spirit of God ceases to strive with the man who excuses himself in his wrong doing.[12]

Our Creator said in the carved message on Sinai, "Thou shalt not steal." [Exodus 20:15.] Again it was reiterated in the basis of the Restoration, "Thou shalt not steal." (D&C 59:6.)

In public office and private lives, the word of the Lord thunders: "Thou shalt not steal; . . . nor do anything like unto it." (D&C 59:6.)

We find ourselves rationalizing in all forms of dishonesty, including shoplifting, which is a mean, low act indulged in by millions who claim to be honorable, decent people.

Dishonesty comes in many other forms: . . . in playing upon private love and emotions for filthy lucre; in robbing money tills or stealing commodities of employers; in falsifying accounts; . . . in taking unreal exemptions; in taking out government or private loans without intent to repay; in declaring unjust, improper bankruptcies to avoid repayment of loans; in robbing on the street or in the home money and other precious possessions; in stealing *time,* giving less than a full day of honest labor for a full day's compensation; in riding public transportation without paying the fare; and all forms of dishonesty in all places and in all conditions. . . .

"Everybody's doing it" is often given as an excuse. No society can be healthy without honesty, trust, and self-restraint.[13]

He is dishonest who buys more than he can reasonably expect to pay for. This is defrauding. He has little honor who fails to pay his honest debts. It would seem to me that every luxury one enjoys at the expense of a creditor is not wholly honest. . . . It is not always dishonorable to be in debt, but certainly it is to ignore debts.[14]

The theft of pennies or dollars or commodities may impoverish little the one from whom the goods are taken, but it is a shrivelling, dwarfing process to the one who steals.[15]

Our standard of integrity influences our families and others.

A parent who understates the age of the child to avoid adult prices in shows and planes and trains and buses is forcefully teaching the child to be dishonest. He will not forget these lessons. Some parents permit the child to break the law as to firecrackers, the use of guns, fishing and hunting without license. The children are permitted to drive without a license or to falsify their ages. Those who take little things without accounting for

129

them, such as fruit from the neighbor's yard, a pen from a desk, a package of gum from the help-yourself shelf, all are being taught silently that little thefts and dishonesties are not so bad.[16]

Parents who "cover up" for their children, excuse them and pay for their misappropriations, miss an important opportunity to teach a lesson and thereby do untold damage to their offspring. If the child is required to return the coin or the pencil or the fruit with an appropriate apology, it is likely that his tendencies to steal will be curbed. But if he is lionized and made a little hero, if his misappropriation is made a joke, he is likely to continue in ever-increasing thefts.[17]

Parents can develop respect for others' property and rights in their growing children by example and precept. Parents who require their youngsters to apologize and make good and return—perhaps even double or triple—that which they have taken, broken, or destroyed—those children will be honorable citizens and will bring honor and glory to their parents. Those parents who themselves respect law and order and observe all the rules can, by that pattern and by their expression of approval or disapproval, discipline and protect their children against disorder and rebellion.[18]

We urge you to teach your children honor and integrity and honesty. Is it possible that some of our children do not know how sinful it is to steal? It is unbelievable—the extent of vandalism, thievery, robbery, stealing. Protect your family against it by proper teaching.[19]

Let us be sure that we inject into our home evenings a lesson on honesty and integrity.[20]

We may be bucking a strong tide, but we must teach our children that sin is sin. Children are permitted to get by with inaccuracies in sports and cheating in games. This cheating goes on into college and into the professions and into businesses. In addition to its being wrong, very wrong, it undermines the very fabric of their culture and their characters.[21]

On the train from New York to Baltimore we sat in the dining car opposite a businessman and commented, "It seldom rains like this in Salt Lake City."

The conversation soon led naturally into the golden question: "How much do you know about the Church?"

"I know little about the Church," he said, "but I know one of its people." He was developing subdivisions in New York. "There is a sub-contractor working for me," he continued. "He is so honest and full of integrity that I never [require] him to bid on a job. He is the soul of honor. If the Mormon people are like this man, I'd like to know about a church that produces such honorable men." We left him literature and sent the missionaries to teach him.[22]

The scriptures provide examples of great courage and integrity.

How one's admiration soars for Peter . . . as he is seen standing at full height and with boldness and strength before those magistrates and rulers who could imprison him, flog him, and perhaps even take his life. We seem to hear those fearless words as he faced his foes and said: "We ought to obey God rather than men." (Acts 5:29.)

Peter looked into the eyes of the crowd and bore his testimony to them of the God they had crucified [see Acts 3:13–15]. . . .

Of those who heard this testimony and charge, 5,000 men saw this courage superior and integrity supreme! And 5,000 men believed.

Turn back to Daniel, a captive and slave but also a prophet of God who was willing to die for his convictions. Was integrity ever placed on a higher plane? The gospel was Daniel's life. . . . In the king's court, he could be little criticized, but even for a ruler he would not drink the king's wine nor gorge himself with meat and rich foods. His moderation and his purity of faith brought him health and wisdom and knowledge and skill and understanding, and his faith linked him closely to his Father in heaven, and revelations came to him as often as required. His revealing of the dreams of the king and the interpretations thereof brought him honor and acclaim and gifts and high position such as many men would sell their souls to get. But when the choice was put to him of ceasing to pray or of being cast into a den of lions, he prayed openly and submitted to the punishment. [See Daniel 1–2, 6.]

We remind ourselves of the integrity of the three Hebrews, Shadrach, Meshach, and Abednego, who like Daniel defied men and rulers, to be true to themselves and to keep faith with their faith. They were required by decree of the emperor to kneel down and worship a monumental image of gold that the king had set up. In addition to losing caste, losing position, and angering the king, they faced the fiery furnace rather than deny their God.

. . . When the prearranged sounds of the cornet, flute, harp, and other instruments reverberated through the area and the masses of men and women everywhere filled their homes and

Shadrach, Meshach, and Abednego "faced the fiery furnace rather than deny their God." The Lord delivered them from the fire.

the streets with kneeling worshipers of the huge golden image, three men refused to insult their true God. They prayed to God, and when confronted by the raging and furious emperor king, they courageously answered in the face of what could be certain death:

"If it be so, our God whom we serve is able to deliver us from the burning fiery furnace, and he will deliver us out of thine hand, O king.

"But if not, be it known unto thee, O king, that we will not serve thy gods, nor worship the golden image which thou hast set up." (Daniel 3:17–18.)

Integrity! The promises of eternal life from God supersede all promises of men to greatness, comfort, immunities. These men of courage and integrity were saying, "We do not have to live, but we must be true to ourselves and God.". . .

No virtues in the perfection we strive for are more important than integrity and honesty. Let us then be complete, unbroken, pure, and sincere, to develop in ourselves that quality of soul we prize so highly in others.[23]

Suggestions for Study and Teaching

Consider these ideas as you study the chapter or as you prepare to teach. For additional help, see pages v–ix.

- Review the second paragraph on page 125. What qualities of character did young Spencer's reaction reveal? What similar experiences might we have today?

- Study the first four paragraphs on page 126, looking for words President Kimball used to define integrity. When have you seen that integrity brings "inner peace, sureness of purpose, and security in action"? When have you seen that lack of integrity brings "disunity, fear, sorrow, unsureness"?

- What are some attitudes about covenants that hinder a person from having integrity? (For some examples, see pages 126–27.) How can we overcome these attitudes? Ponder the integrity with which you keep your covenants.

- In what ways are we "cheating ourselves" if we are dishonest? (For some examples, see pages 128–29.)

- Review President Kimball's examples of dishonesty and honesty in parents (pages 129–30). Consider what you are doing to teach children integrity.

- Read the story that begins with the last paragraph on page 130. How has your life been influenced by the integrity of others?

- Study the fifth paragraph on page 126. Consider taking an inventory of your life, as President Kimball counseled. Ask yourself the questions he asked.

Related Scriptures: Job 27:5–6; Proverbs 20:7; Alma 53:20–21; D&C 97:8; 136:20, 25–26

Notes

1. Francis M. Gibbons, *Spencer W. Kimball: Resolute Disciple, Prophet of God* (1995), 106.
2. Edward L. Kimball and Andrew E. Kimball Jr., *The Story of Spencer W. Kimball: A Short Man, a Long Stride* (1985), 23.
3. In Conference Report, Oct. 1974, 103, 106; or *Ensign,* Nov. 1974, 73, 75.
4. "Give the Lord Your Loyalty," *Ensign,* Mar. 1980, 2.
5. *The Teachings of Spencer W. Kimball,* ed. Edward L. Kimball (1982), 192.
6. In Conference Report, Mexico City Mexico Area Conference 1972, 32.
7. "The Example of Abraham," *Ensign,* June 1975, 6.
8. *Ensign,* Mar. 1980, 2.
9. *The Miracle of Forgiveness* (1969), 94–95, 96.
10. "On My Honor," *Ensign,* Apr. 1979, 5.
11. *Ensign,* Apr. 1979, 5.
12. *Faith Precedes the Miracle* (1972), 234.
13. "A Report and a Challenge," *Ensign,* Nov. 1976, 6.
14. *The Teachings of Spencer W. Kimball,* 196.
15. *The Teachings of Spencer W. Kimball,* 198.
16. *The Teachings of Spencer W. Kimball,* 343.
17. *The Miracle of Forgiveness,* 50.
18. "Train Up a Child," *Ensign,* Apr. 1978, 4.
19. In Conference Report, Oct. 1974, 5; or *Ensign,* Nov. 1974, 5.
20. In Conference Report, Temple View New Zealand Area Conference 1976, 29.
21. "What I Hope You Will Teach My Grandchildren," address to seminary and institute personnel, Brigham Young University, July 11, 1966, Archives of The Church of Jesus Christ of Latter-day Saints, 2.
22. *Faith Precedes the Miracle,* 240–41.
23. *Faith Precedes the Miracle,* 244–46, 248.

Obedience Born of Faith in God

Faith in the Lord can help us live the commandments with a willing heart and receive countless blessings.

From the Life of Spencer W. Kimball

In March 1972, when Spencer W. Kimball was Acting President of the Quorum of the Twelve Apostles, he was experiencing serious heart problems. At the time, one of his doctors was Russell M. Nelson, who would later become a member of the Quorum of the Twelve. Elder Nelson recounted:

"When President Kimball's heart was failing and he sensed that death was nigh, he obtained a conference with his file leaders in the Church, the First Presidency. To provide medical information as requested, he invited his devoted cardiologist, Dr. Ernest L. Wilkinson, and me.

"President Kimball breathlessly began, 'I am a dying man. I can feel my life slipping. At the present rate of deterioration I believe that I can live only about two more months. Now I would like my doctor to present his views.'

"Dr. Wilkinson then reaffirmed President Kimball's feelings, concluding that recovery would be unlikely and death would ensue in the not-too-distant future.

"Then President Kimball called on me as a cardiac surgeon and asked, 'What can surgery offer?'

"I indicated that an operation, if it were to be done, would consist of two components. First, an aortic valve replacement would be required. Second, an important coronary artery with a blockage should be treated with a bypass graft.

*Abraham showed "exceeding faith" when he responded
to the "test [that] was applied to him."*

"President Harold B. Lee of the First Presidency then asked the crucial question, 'What would be the risks with such a procedure?'

"'I don't know,' I replied. 'In a man aged seventy-seven, the risk of either of these operations is significant. But to do both on one whose heart is failing would entail risk so high that the operation cannot be recommended. . . .'

"As a weary President Kimball responded, 'I am an old man and ready to die,' President Lee interrupted. He rose to his feet, pounded his fist to the desk, and said, with his prophetic power, 'Spencer, you have been called! You are not to die! You are to do everything you need to do to care for yourself and continue to live.'

"President Kimball replied, 'Then I will have the operation.'

"He underwent that complex operation not because it was deemed to be reasonably safe in the opinion of his medical advisers, but because he was obedient to the counsel of the Lord, expressed through the leaders of the Church—regardless of personal risk.

"The outcome is well known. He was blessed to survive the operation which reversed the tide of his deterioration."[1]

Through his example and his counsel to the Saints, President Kimball taught that we are blessed as we show our faith in God by being obedient to His will.

Teachings of Spencer W. Kimball

True faith motivates us to do the will of God.

The exercising of faith is a willingness to accept without total regular proof and to move forward and perform works. "Faith without works is dead" [James 2:26] and a dead faith will not lead one to move forward to adjust a life or to serve valiantly. A real faith pushes one forward to constructive and beneficial acts as though he knew in absoluteness.[2]

One may enjoy the benefits of the miracles in the physical world without a complete knowledge of the underlying principles

President Kimball compared faith to tuning a radio.

involved. He may turn darkness into light by pushing a button and read in the darkest night. He need not be able to develop the electricity, nor to have the knowledge to wire the home. But he must have the faith sufficient to secure lamps and faith to turn the switch. He then may receive the light. . . . He may turn a dial and enjoy sweet music from afar without being able to fashion a radio or understand fully its workings, but the blessing will never be his unless he connects his set with the power, and turns the dial correctly. In like manner, one may receive spiritual blessings and manifestations, by establishing contact turning the dial. Faith manifested by prayer and works is that key.[3]

We pray for enlightenment, then go to with all our might and our books and our thoughts and righteousness to get the inspiration. We ask for judgment, then use all our powers to act wisely and develop wisdom. We pray for success in our work and then study hard and strive with all our might to help answer our prayers. When we pray for health we must live the laws of health and do all in our power to keep our bodies well and vigorous. We pray for protection and then take reasonable precaution to avoid danger. There must be works with faith.[4]

There must be a faith in God that will cause men to cleanse their lives; to forget themselves in the service of their fellow men and to overcome all weaknesses of the flesh; a faith that will bring about a repentance which is total, continuing and which will bring them to baptism, the priesthood, and temple ordinances.[5]

Herein lies the genius of the gospel of Jesus Christ, perceived by only the spiritual eye. Under the gospel's beneficent laws, everyone—rich or poor, learned or unlearned—is encouraged first to perceive with the eye of faith and then, through effort, to express that faith in a higher, nobler life.[6]

Obedience based on faith is not blind obedience.

We render intelligent, constructive obedience when we voluntarily, humbly, and happily obey the commands of our Lord.[7]

To obey! To hearken! What a difficult requirement! Often we hear: "Nobody can tell me what clothes to wear, what I shall eat or drink. No one can outline my Sabbaths, appropriate my earnings, nor in any way limit my personal freedoms! I do as I please! I give no *blind obedience!*"

Blind obedience! How little they understand! . . .

When men obey commands of a creator, it is not blind obedience. How different is the cowering of a subject to his totalitarian monarch and the dignified, willing obedience one gives to his God. The dictator is ambitious, selfish, and has ulterior motives. God's every command is righteous, every directive purposeful, and all for the good of the governed. The first may be blind obedience, but the latter is certainly faith obedience. . . .

Is it blind obedience when one regards the sign "High Voltage—Keep Away" or is it the obedience of faith in the judgment of experts who know the hazard?

Is it blind obedience when the air traveler fastens his seat belt as that sign flashes or is it confidence in the experience and wisdom of those who know more of hazards and dangers?

Is it blind obedience when the little child gleefully jumps from the table into the strong arms of its smiling father, or is this implicit trust in a loving parent who feels sure of his catch and who loves the child better than life itself? . . .

139

Is it then blind obedience when we, with our limited vision, elementary knowledge, selfish desires, ulterior motives, and carnal urges, accept and follow the guidance and obey the commands of our loving Father who . . . created a world for us, loves us, and has planned a constructive program for us, wholly without ulterior motive, whose greatest joy and glory is to "bring to pass the immortality and eternal life" of all his children? [See Moses 1:39.][8]

It is not blind obedience, even without total understanding, to follow a Father who has proved himself.[9]

The scriptures provide examples of obedience born of faith.

Our righteous and wise parents, Adam and Eve, were exemplary in the matter of obedience born of childlike faith:

". . . And Adam was obedient unto the commandments of the Lord.

"And after many days an angel of the Lord appeared unto Adam, saying: Why dost thou offer sacrifices unto the Lord? And Adam said unto him: I know not, save the Lord commanded me.

"And then the angel spake, saying: This thing is a similitude of the sacrifice of the Only Begotten of the Father, which is full of grace and truth." (Moses 5:5–7.)

Blind obedience? Assuredly not. They had known Jehovah, heard his voice, walked with him in the Garden of Eden, and knew of his goodness, justice, and understanding. And so for "many days" they killed the blemishless lambs and offered them without knowing why, but in total confidence that there was righteous purpose in the law and that the reason would unfold later after compliance.[10]

Paul speaking to the Hebrews said:

"By faith Noah, being warned of God of things not seen as yet, moved with fear, prepared an ark to the saving of his house." (Heb. 11:7.)

As yet there was no evidence of rain and flood. His people mocked and called him a fool. His preaching fell on deaf ears.

His warnings were considered irrational. There was no precedent; never had it been known that a deluge could cover the earth. How foolish to build an ark on dry ground with the sun shining and life moving forward as usual! But time ran out. The ark was finished. The floods came. The disobedient and rebellious were drowned. The miracle of the ark followed the faith manifested in its building.

Paul said again:

"Through faith also Sara herself received strength to conceive seed, and was delivered of a child when she was past age, because she judged him faithful who had promised." (Heb. 11:11.) . . .

So absurd it was to be told that children could be born of centenarians that even Sarah doubted at first. But the faith of a noble pair prevailed, and the miracle son was born to father multitudes of nations.

Exceeding faith was shown by Abraham when the superhuman test was applied to him. His young "child of promise," destined to be the father of empires, must now be offered upon the sacrificial altar. It was God's command, but it seemed so contradictory! How could his son, Isaac, be the father of an uncountable posterity if in his youth his mortal life was to be terminated? Why should he, Abraham, be called upon to do this revolting deed? It was irreconcilable, impossible! And yet he believed God. His undaunted faith carried him with breaking heart toward the land of Moriah with this young son. . . .

"He staggered not at the promise of God through unbelief; but was strong in faith, giving glory to God;

"And being fully persuaded that, what he had promised, he was able also to perform." (Rom. 4:20–21.)

Father Abraham and Mother Sarah knew—knew the promise would be fulfilled. *How*—they did not know and did not demand to know. Isaac positively would live to be the father of a numerous posterity. They knew he would, even though he might need to die. They knew he could still be raised from the dead to fulfil the promise, and faith here preceded the miracle.[11]

Remember that Abraham, Moses, Elijah, and others could not see clearly the end from the beginning. They . . . walked by faith and without sight. Remember again that no gates were open; Laban was not drunk; and no earthly hope was justified at the moment Nephi exercised his faith and set out finally to get the plates. No asbestos clothes or other ordinary protective devices were in the fiery furnace to protect the three Hebrews from death; there were no leather nor metal muzzles for the mouths of the lions when Daniel was locked in the den. . . .

. . . Remember there were no towns and cities, no farms and gardens, no homes and storehouses, no blossoming desert in Utah when the persecuted pioneers crossed the plains. And remember that there were no heavenly beings in Palmyra, on the Susquehanna or on Cumorah when the soul-hungry Joseph slipped quietly into the Grove, knelt in prayer on the river bank, and climbed the slopes of the sacred hill.[12]

Faith precedes the miracle.

In faith we plant the seed, and soon we see the miracle of the blossoming. Men have often misunderstood and have reversed the process. They would have the harvest before the planting, the reward before the service, the miracle before the faith. . . . Many of us would have the vigor without the observance of the health laws, prosperity through the opened windows of heaven without the payment of our tithes. We would have the close communion with our Father without fasting and praying; we would have rain in due season and peace in the land without observing the Sabbath and keeping the other commandments of the Lord. We would pluck the rose before planting the roots; we would harvest the grain before its planting and cultivating.

If we could only realize as Moroni writes:

"For if there be no faith among the children of men, God can do no miracle among them. . . .

"And neither at any time hath any wrought miracles until after their faith; wherefore they first believed in the Son of God." (Ether 12:12, 18.)[13]

If we can walk now by faith, if we can believe in the rich promises of God, if we can obey and patiently wait, the Lord will fulfil all his rich promises to us:

". . . Eye hath not seen, nor ear heard, neither have entered into the heart of man, the things which God hath prepared for them that love him." (1 Cor. 2:9.)[14]

It takes a great faith to pay tithes when funds are scarce and demands are great. It takes faith to fast and have family prayers and to observe the Word of Wisdom. It takes faith to do home teaching, [member] missionary work, and other service, when sacrifice is required. It takes faith to fill full-time missions. But know this—that all these are of the planting, while faithful, devout families, spiritual security, peace, and eternal life are the harvest. . . .

. . . Just as undaunted faith has stopped the mouths of lions, made ineffective fiery flames, opened dry corridors through rivers and seas, protected against deluge and drouth, and brought heavenly manifestations at the instance of prophets, so in each of our lives faith can heal the sick, bring comfort to those who mourn, strengthen resolve against temptation, relieve from the bondage of harmful habits, lend the strength to repent and change our lives, and lead to a sure knowledge of the divinity of Jesus Christ. Indomitable faith can help us live the commandments with a willing heart and thereby bring blessings unnumbered, with peace, perfection, and exaltation in the kingdom of God.[15]

Suggestions for Study and Teaching

Consider these ideas as you study the chapter or as you prepare to teach. For additional help, see pages v–ix.

- Look at the title of this chapter. Why is obedience an act of faith?

- Read about the decision President Kimball had to make in March 1972 (pages 135, 137). What gospel principles do you think apply when we are faced with difficult decisions?

- As you read President Kimball's comparison between "blind obedience" and "faith obedience," what differences do you see? (See pages 139–40.) What do we know about Heavenly Father that can help us obey Him "voluntarily, humbly, and happily"? What might you say to a person who claims that Church members blindly follow their leaders?

- Review the scripture stories on pages 140–42. What are some things the people in these stories have in common? What do you have in common with them? What can you learn from them?

- When have you seen that faith precedes the miracle? (For some examples, see pages 142–43.) How can we teach our families that faith precedes the miracle?

Related Scriptures: Joshua 22:5; James 2:14–26; Ether 12:4–21; Moroni 7:33; D&C 130:20–21

Notes

1. "Spencer W. Kimball: Man of Faith," *Ensign*, Dec. 1985, 40.
2. "The Fourth Article of Faith," *Instructor,* Apr. 1955, 109.
3. *The Teachings of Spencer W. Kimball*, ed. Edward L. Kimball (1982), 62.
4. *The Teachings of Spencer W. Kimball*, 122.
5. "Beloved Youth, Study and Learn," in *Life's Directions* (1962), 188–89.
6. In Conference Report, London England Area Conference 1976, 36.
7. In Conference Report, Oct. 1954, 55.
8. In Conference Report, Oct. 1954, 51, 52, 53.
9. *The Teachings of Spencer W. Kimball*, 59.
10. In Conference Report, Oct. 1954, 54.
11. In Conference Report, Oct. 1952, 48, 49.
12. In Conference Report, Oct. 1952, 51.
13. In Conference Report, Oct. 1952, 47.
14. In Conference Report, Apr. 1952, 22.
15. *Faith Precedes the Miracle* (1972), 11, 12.

"Thou Shalt Have No Other Gods before Me"

We must put the Lord and His cause first and refrain from worshiping false gods.

From the Life of Spencer W. Kimball

President Spencer W. Kimball exhorted Latter-day Saints to put the Lord first in their lives and not set their hearts on the things of the world. He taught that putting such things as material possessions, business, recreation, and prestige ahead of the Lord is to worship false gods. He emphasized that false gods or idols include "everything which entices a person away from duty, loyalty, and love for and service to God."[1]

Wholehearted commitment to the Lord was at the foundation of President Kimball's life and the lives of his parents. In the late 1890s, when Spencer was a small boy, his father, Andrew, received a call to be stake president in southeastern Arizona. Leaving the relative comforts of Salt Lake City to live in a desert frontier would not be easy for the Kimball family, but for Andrew Kimball "there was but one answer and that was to go."[2]

Several years later, Spencer W. Kimball showed similar devotion to the Lord when he was called to be second counselor in a stake presidency. He and his wife, Camilla, "had talked of his going back to college to become an accountant or teacher," but accepting the Church position meant setting such plans aside.[3]

When President Kimball was ordained an Apostle, President Heber J. Grant's counsel to him reinforced this principle of putting the Lord and His kingdom first: "Set your heart upon the service of the Lord thy God. From this very moment resolve to make this cause and this labor first and foremost in all your thoughts."[4]

Teachings of Spencer W. Kimball

When we place our hearts and trust in anything above the Lord, we are worshiping our own false gods.

As I study ancient scripture, I am more and more convinced that there is significance in the fact that the commandment "Thou shalt have no other gods before me" is the first of the Ten Commandments.

Few men have ever knowingly and deliberately chosen to reject God and his blessings. Rather, we learn from the scriptures that because the exercise of faith has always appeared to be more difficult than relying on things more immediately at hand, carnal man has tended to transfer his trust in God to material things. Therefore, in all ages when men have fallen under the power of Satan and lost the faith, they have put in its place a hope in the "arm of flesh" and in "gods of silver, and gold, of brass, iron, wood, and stone, which see not, nor hear, nor know" (Dan. 5:23)—that is, in idols. This I find to be a dominant theme in the Old Testament. Whatever thing a man sets his heart and his trust in most is his god; and if his god doesn't also happen to be the true and living God of Israel, that man is laboring in idolatry.

It is my firm belief that when we read these scriptures and try to "liken them unto [our]selves," as Nephi suggested (1 Ne. 19:24), we will see many parallels between the ancient worship of graven images and behavioral patterns in our very own experience.[5]

Idolatry is among the most serious of sins. . . .

Modern idols or false gods can take such forms as clothes, homes, businesses, machines, automobiles, pleasure boats, and numerous other material deflectors from the path to godhood. . . .

Intangible things make just as ready gods. Degrees and letters and titles can become idols. . . .

Many people build and furnish a home and buy the automobile first—and then find they "cannot afford" to pay tithing. Whom do they worship? Certainly not the Lord of heaven and earth. . . .

"Gods of power, wealth, and influence . . . are quite as real as the golden calves of the children of Israel in the wilderness."

Many worship the hunt, the fishing trip, the vacation, the weekend picnics and outings. Others have as their idols the games of sport, baseball, football, the bullfight, or golf. . . .

Still another image men worship is that of power and prestige. . . . These gods of power, wealth, and influence are most demanding and are quite as real as the golden calves of the children of Israel in the wilderness.[6]

Becoming attached to worldly things can make us vulnerable to Satan's influence.

In spite of our delight in defining ourselves as modern, and our tendency to think we possess a sophistication that no people in the past ever had—in spite of these things, we are, on the whole, an idolatrous people—a condition most repugnant to the Lord.[7]

I am reminded of an article I read some years ago about a group of men who had gone to the jungles to capture monkeys. They tried a number of different things to catch the monkeys, including nets. But finding that the nets could injure such small creatures, they finally came upon an ingenious solution. They built a large number of small boxes, and in the top of each they bored a hole just large enough for a monkey to get his hand into. They then set these boxes out under the trees and in each one they put a nut that the monkeys were particularly fond of.

When the men left, the monkeys began to come down from the trees and examine the boxes. Finding that there were nuts to be had, they reached into the boxes to get them. But when a monkey would try to withdraw his hand with the nut, he could not get his hand out of the box because his little fist, with the nut inside, was now too large.

At about this time, the men would come out of the under-brush and converge on the monkeys. And here is the curious thing: When the monkeys saw the men coming, they would shriek and scramble about with the thought of escaping; but as easy as it would have been, they would not let go of the nut so that they could withdraw their hands from the boxes and thus escape. The men captured them easily.

And so it often seems to be with people, having such a firm grasp on things of the world—that which is telestial—that no amount of urging and no degree of emergency can persuade them to let go in favor of that which is celestial. Satan gets them in his grip easily. If we insist on spending all our time and resources building up for ourselves a worldly kingdom, that is exactly what we will inherit.[8]

Rather than set our hearts on things of the world, we should use our resources to build up the kingdom of God.

The possession of riches does not necessarily constitute sin. But sin may arise in the acquisition and use of wealth. . . .

Book of Mormon history eloquently reveals the corrosive effect of the passion for wealth. Each time the people became righteous, they prospered. Then followed the transition from prosperity to wealth, wealth to the love of wealth, then to the love of ease and luxury. They moved then into spiritual inactivity, then to gross sin and wickedness, then on to near destruction by their enemies. . . . Had the people used their wealth for good purposes they could have enjoyed a continuing prosperity.[9]

The Lord has blessed us as a people with a prosperity unequaled in times past. The resources that have been placed in our power are good, and necessary to our work here on the earth. But I am afraid that many of us have been surfeited with flocks and herds and acres and barns and wealth and have begun to worship them as false gods, and they have power over us. . . . Forgotten is the fact that our assignment is to use these many resources in our families and quorums to build up the kingdom of God—to further the missionary effort and the genealogical and temple work; to raise our children up as fruitful servants unto the Lord; to bless others in every way, that they may also be fruitful. Instead, we expend these blessings on our own desires, and as Moroni said, "Ye adorn yourselves with that which hath no life, and yet suffer the hungry, and the needy, and the naked, and the sick and the afflicted to pass by you, and notice them not." (Morm. 8:39.)

As the Lord himself said in our day, "They seek not the Lord to establish his righteousness, but every man walketh in his own way, and after the image of his own God, whose image is in the likeness of the world, and *whose substance is that of an idol,* which waxeth old and shall perish in Babylon, even Babylon the great, which shall fall." (D&C 1:16; italics added.)[10]

The Lord has said, ". . . seek ye first the kingdom of God, and his righteousness; and all these things shall be added unto you." (Matt. 6:33.) Too often, though, we want the "things" first.[11]

Perhaps the sin is not in "things" but in our attitude toward and worship of "things." Unless an acquisitive person can positively accumulate and hold wealth while still giving full allegiance to God and his program—unless the rich man can keep the Sabbath, keep his mind and body and spirit uncontaminated, and give unstinted service to his fellowmen through God's appointed way—unless the affluent man has total control and can hold all his possessions in trust, subject to the call of the Lord through his authorized servants, then that man, for the good of his soul, should certainly "go and sell that thou hast and give to the poor, . . . and come and follow me." (Matthew 19:21.)

"Our assignment is to use [our] resources in our families and quorums to build up the kingdom of God."

"For where your treasure is, there will your heart be also." (Matthew 6:21.)[12]

Blessings we receive from serving the Lord far exceed the rewards offered by the world.

One man I know of was called to a position of service in the Church, but he felt that he couldn't accept because his investments required more attention and more of his time than he could spare for the Lord's work. He left the service of the Lord in search of Mammon, and he is a millionaire today.

But I recently learned an interesting fact: If a man owns a million dollars worth of gold at today's prices, he possesses approximately one 27-billionth of all the gold that is present in the earth's thin crust alone. This is an amount so small in proportion as to be inconceivable to the mind of man. But there is more to this: The Lord who created and has power over all the earth created many other earths as well, even "worlds without number" (Moses 1:33); and when this man received the oath and covenant of the priesthood (D&C 84:33–44), he received a promise from the Lord of "all that my Father hath" (v. 38). To set aside all these great promises in favor of a chest of gold and a sense of carnal security is a mistake in perspective of colossal proportions. To think that he has settled for so little is a saddening and pitiful prospect indeed; the souls of men are far more precious than this.

One young man, when called on a mission, replied that he didn't have much talent for that kind of thing. What he was good at was keeping his powerful new automobile in top condition. He enjoyed the sense of power and acceleration, and when he was driving, the continual motion gave him the illusion that he was really getting somewhere.

All along, his father had been content with saying, "He likes to do things with his hands. That's good enough for him."

Good enough for a son of God? This young man didn't realize that the power of his automobile is infinitesimally small in comparison with the power of the sea, or of the sun; and there are many suns, all controlled by law and by priesthood, ultimately— a priesthood power that he could have been developing in the service of the Lord. He settled for a pitiful god, a composite of steel and rubber and shiny chrome.

An older couple retired from the world of work and also, in effect, from the Church. They purchased a pickup truck and camper and, separating themselves from all obligations, set out to see the world and simply enjoy what little they had accumulated the rest of their days. They had no time for the temple, were too busy for genealogical research and for missionary service. He lost contact with his high priests quorum and was not home enough to work on his personal history. Their experience and leadership were sorely needed in their branch, but, unable to "endure to the end," they were not available.[13]

We should love and follow the Lord with all our hearts.

It is not enough for us to acknowledge the Lord as supreme and refrain from worshipping idols; we should love the Lord with all our heart, might, mind, and strength. We should honor him and follow him into the work of eternal life. What joy he has in the righteousness of his children![14]

Our assignment is affirmative: to forsake the things of the world as ends in themselves; to leave off idolatry and press forward in faith; to carry the gospel to our enemies, that they might no longer be our enemies.

We must leave off the worship of modern-day idols and a reliance on the "arm of flesh," for the Lord has said to all the world in our day, "I will not spare any that remain in Babylon." (D&C 64:24.)

When Peter preached such a message as this to the people on the day of Pentecost, many of them "were pricked in their heart, and said unto Peter and to the rest of the apostles, Men and brethren, what shall we do?" (Acts 2:37.)

And Peter answered: "Repent, and be baptized every one of you in the name of Jesus Christ for the remission of sins, and . . . receive the Holy Ghost." (V. 38.)

. . . Our message is the same as that which Peter gave. And further, that which the Lord himself gave "unto the ends of the earth, that all that will hear may hear:

"Prepare ye, prepare ye for that which is to come, for the Lord is nigh." (D&C 1:11–12.)

We believe that the way for each person and each family to prepare as the Lord has directed is to begin to exercise greater faith, to repent, and to enter into the work of his kingdom on earth, which is The Church of Jesus Christ of Latter-day Saints. It may seem a little difficult at first, but when a person begins to catch a vision of the true work, when he begins to see something of eternity in its true perspective, the blessings begin to far outweigh the cost of leaving "the world" behind.[15]

Suggestions for Study and Teaching

Consider these ideas as you study the chapter or as you prepare to teach. For additional help, see pages v–ix.

- Why do you think "Thou shalt have no other gods before me" is the first of the Ten Commandments?

- Ponder this statement: "Whatever thing a man sets his heart and his trust in most is his god" (page 146). What are some false gods in the world today? (See examples on pages 146–47.)

- What can we learn from the story about monkey traps? (See pages 147–48.) What do we risk if we take too firm a hold on the things of this world?

- Review pages 148–50. What are some dangers of being wealthy? In what ways can we make righteous use of the resources the Lord gives us?

- Review the stories on pages 150–51. Why do you think some people willingly forfeit the blessings of serving in the Lord's kingdom? What should be our motivation when we serve?

- What do you think it means to "love the Lord with all our heart, might, mind, and strength"? (page 151). What can parents do to help their children love the Lord?

Related Scriptures: Exodus 20:3–6; Matthew 6:24; 22:36–38; Colossians 3:1–5; 2 Nephi 9:30, 37; D&C 133:14

Notes

1. *The Miracle of Forgiveness* (1969), 40.
2. Andrew Kimball, in Edward L. Kimball and Andrew E. Kimball Jr., *Spencer W. Kimball* (1977), 20.
3. See Edward L. Kimball, "Spencer W. Kimball," in *The Presidents of the Church*, ed. Leonard J. Arrington (1986), 381.
4. In *Spencer W. Kimball*, 205.
5. "The False Gods We Worship," *Ensign*, June 1976, 4.
6. *The Miracle of Forgiveness*, 40, 41–42.
7. *Ensign*, June 1976, 6.
8. *Ensign*, June 1976, 5–6.
9. *The Miracle of Forgiveness*, 47.
10. *Ensign*, June 1976, 4–5.
11. In Conference Report, Apr. 1972, 28; or *Ensign*, July 1972, 38.
12. *The Teachings of Spencer W. Kimball*, ed. Edward L. Kimball (1982), 358.
13. *Ensign*, June 1976, 5.
14. *The Teachings of Spencer W. Kimball*, 243.
15. *Ensign*, June 1976, 6.

Celestial room in the Mount Timpanogos Utah Temple. President Kimball taught that the temple "should be a place of reverence."

We Should Be a Reverent People

*More than just a behavior, reverence is a virtue
that should be part of our way of life.*

From the Life of Spencer W. Kimball

In 1955 President David O. McKay dedicated the first temple in Europe, the Bern Switzerland Temple. Elder Spencer W. Kimball, then a member of the Quorum of the Twelve Apostles, was scheduled to speak at the afternoon session on the first day of the dedication. He spent an hour alone in the temple that day "preparing mind and heart for the afternoon, unhurried, quiet, respectful and reverential."[1] During his address he said: "As I awakened this morning and began to attain consciousness after the night, I saw the dawn advancing, and my thought first came to the holy temple which was to be dedicated this day. I thought, 'No food today. Shoes must be shined, clothes pressed, and I must have a clean mind.' All the way to Zollikofen I desired to say no word, and when I came into this room and sat by [President McKay] and all he said was in sacred whispers, I knew then that I had been feeling some of the feeling he has felt. 'Holiness to the Lord, Holiness becometh the Saints of the Lord.' "[2]

President Kimball did not reserve his reverence only for occasions such as temple dedications. He spoke of reverence as a way of life, and he exemplified this teaching even in small, day-to-day activities. For example, once when he visited a meetinghouse, he quietly entered a restroom, threw away paper towels that were on the floor, and cleaned the sink. A local Church leader noticed this simple expression of respect. Inspired by President Kimball's example, he taught others to show greater reverence for sacred places and things.[3]

Teachings of Spencer W. Kimball

Reverence is not a temporary behavior adopted on Sunday but an ongoing attitude of devotion to God.

Reverence has been defined as a "feeling or attitude of deep respect, love, and awe, as for something sacred." To describe it as devotion to God is another way to express the meaning of reverence.

Many of our leaders have expressed regard for reverence as one of the highest qualities of the soul, indicating it involves true faith in God and in his righteousness, high culture, and a love for the finer things in life. . . .

As with the other principles of the gospel, reverence leads to increased joy.

We must remember that reverence is not a somber, temporary behavior that we adopt on Sunday. True reverence involves happiness, as well as love, respect, gratitude, and godly fear. It is a virtue that should be part of our way of life. In fact, Latter-day Saints should be the most reverent people in all the earth.[4]

We should have reverence for the Father and the Son and for Their holy names.

Reverence toward the Father and the Son is an essential qualification or characteristic of those who attain the celestial kingdom. In section 76 of the Doctrine and Covenants, known as "The Vision," given to Joseph Smith and Sidney Rigdon in February 1832, we find:

"And thus we saw the glory of the celestial, which excels in all things—where God, even the Father, reigns upon his throne forever and ever;

"Before whose throne all things bow in humble reverence, and give him glory forever and ever.

"They who dwell in his presence are the church of the Firstborn; and they see as they are seen, and know as they are known, having received of his fulness and of his grace.

"And he makes them equal in power, and in might, and in dominion." (D&C 76:92–95.)

Another modern revelation directs us to hold in reverence even the very name of Deity; we are told not to profane the name of the Father, and even to avoid too frequent use of it. (D&C 107:2–4.) . . .

It would appear that reverence for God and his name is one of the most important qualities we can develop.[5]

In the hospital one day I was wheeled out of the operating room by an attendant who stumbled, and there issued from his angry lips vicious cursing with a combination of the names of the Savior. Even half-conscious, I recoiled and implored: "Please! Please! That is my Lord whose names you revile."

There was a deathly silence, then a subdued voice whispered, "I am sorry." He had forgotten for the moment that the Lord had forcefully commanded all his people, "Thou shalt not take the name of the Lord thy God in vain; for the Lord will not hold him guiltless that taketh his name in vain" (Exod. 20:7). . . .

On the stage, on the telephone, sensitive ears and eyes are outraged daily by the unwarranted and blasphemous use of the names of the Lord our God. In the club, on the farm, in social circles, in business, and in every walk of life the names of the Redeemer are used presumptuously and sinfully. We who are thoughtless and careless, and we who are vicious and defiant, should remember that we cannot take the name of the Lord in vain with impunity. Are we not inviting eventual destruction as we desecrate all things holy and sacred, even to the common and irreverent use in our daily talk of the names of Deity? . . .

It is a terrible thing for any human being to use the names of Deity in disrespect. And this includes the use of the name of the Lord without authority, and there are many people who claim revelations and claim authority who do not have it directly from the Lord.

Through the ages, the prophets have never ceased to rebuke this grave sin. The prophet Isaiah called to accounting and repentance those "which swear by the name of the Lord, and make mention of the God of Israel, but not in truth, nor in righteousness" (Isa. 48:1). . . .

Speaking the Lord's name with reverence must simply be part of our lives as members of the Church. For example, we, as good Latter-day Saints, do not smoke. We do not drink. We do not use tea and coffee. By the same token, we do not use foul language. We do not curse or defame. We do not use the Lord's name in vain. It is not difficult to become perfect in avoiding a swearing habit, for if one locks his mouth against all words of cursing, he is en route to perfection in that matter.

But our responsibility does not end there. That would merely be to refrain from committing sin. To perform righteousness, we must speak our Lord's name with reverence and holiness in our prayers, our discourses, and our discussions. . . .

Jesus perfected his life and became our Christ. Priceless blood of a god was shed, and he became our Savior; his perfected life was given, and he became our Redeemer; his atonement for us made possible our return to our Heavenly Father, and yet how thoughtless, how unappreciative are most beneficiaries! Ingratitude is a sin of the ages.

Great numbers profess belief in him and his works, and yet relatively few honor him. Millions of us call ourselves Christians, yet seldom kneel in gratitude for his supreme gift, his life.

Let us rededicate ourselves to reverential attitudes, toward an expression of gratitude to our Lord for his incomparable sacrifice. Let us remember the modern command, "Wherefore, let all men beware how they take my name in their lips" (D&C 63:61).[6]

Temples, meetinghouses, and homes should be places of reverence.

In yet another area of extreme importance, the Lord has directed by modern revelation that we should have proper reverence for his holy house. In the important revelation given to Joseph Smith known as the dedicatory prayer for the Kirtland Temple, a directive was given that this, as with all other sacred

President Kimball taught that "faith is born, rekindled, and sanctified" in Latter-day Saint chapels.

temples erected unto the Lord, should be a place of reverence to Him. (See D&C 109:13, 16–21.)

In a very real sense, what is said of the sacred temples of the Church is applicable to every "house of the Lord," whether it be a meetinghouse or any place where the Saints worship, or in fact, any Latter-day Saint home.[7]

To Latter-day Saints the chapel is not a recess or a cell in a cathedral, not a place with altars of gold and precious stones. It is a place without ostentation or show, without statues and mostly without pictures, decorated simply and plainly, clean and light and worshipful. It is a place where the people are seated comfortably, in true brotherhood, where lessons are taught, choirs sing, members pray and preach, and where all gain knowledge and inspiration—and where old and young receive the sacrament. Here habits of thought and action are conceived and introduced into lives, and here faith is born, rekindled, and sanctified.

The chapel is not dedicated to pharisaical piety where are found long faces, stiff formalities, or cold and barren silences, yet reverence for holy places, sacred purposes, and divine personages should always be found there.[8]

Are we a reverent people? Do our actions in the home and at church show reverence for our Creator?

Sometimes we wonder. We attend sacrament meetings and conferences where children wander unrestrained in the aisles. During the service, we notice adults talking with their neighbors, people dozing, and young people gathering in the foyers. We see families coming late and filing noisily to their seats, and groups engaged in loud conversation in the chapel after the meeting.

Our thoughts turn to investigators, friends, and those whose testimonies are fragile and developing. Are our meetings the powerful missionary tools they can be, where the Spirit of the Lord reigns and penetrates hearts? Or to sense the Spirit must we first block out many needless distractions?[9]

A great person is reverent. He will be deferential in a house of worship even though he be the only soul therein. No congregation was assembled when the Lord commanded Moses: "Put off thy shoes from off thy feet, for the place whereon thou standest is holy ground!" [See Exodus 3:5.] Presiding officers should plan so carefully that no whispering would be heard or seen on the stand. Parents should train and discipline their children and sit with them (except where class groups are supervised). Ushers should be trained to quietly care for seating with a minimum of disturbance. Attenders should arrive early, do their friendly greeting in subdued tones, slow their step, find seats toward the front, and sit in quiet contemplative mood. All should participate as fully as possible—singing with the singers, praying with him who prays, partaking of the sacrament with a grateful heart and a reconsecration to covenants previously made. An opportunity is given to follow sympathetically lessons that are taught, the sermons that are preached and the testimonies that are borne, judging not by eloquence but by sincerity. Here is a chance to drink deeply from fountain heads, for the humblest teacher or speaker will contribute thought which can be developed. As we quietly enter the door of the chapel we may leave behind us outside all criticisms, worries, and cares—all occupational, political, social, and recreational plans—and calmly give ourselves to contemplation and to worship. We may bathe in the spiritual atmosphere. We may devote ourselves to learning, repenting, forgiving, testifying, appreciating, and loving.[10]

Reverence begins at home.

Where, then, does reverence begin, and how can we develop it?

The home is the key to reverence, as it is to every other god-like virtue.

Let me emphasize the importance of teaching children to pray. It is during personal and family prayers that little ones learn to bow their heads, fold their arms, and close their eyes while our Father in heaven is being addressed. Behavior learned at home determines behavior in Church meetings. A child who has learned to pray at home soon understands that he must be quiet and still during prayers in worship services.

Likewise, when family home evenings are part of home life, children know that there are special times, not only at church but at home, when we learn about our Heavenly Father and when everyone needs to be on his best behavior.

Music is a special delight for children. Hymns that are frequently sung at church can become familiar in the home too. Small children especially could benefit if parents helped them learn simple hymns at home. In this way, children would eagerly anticipate singing at sacrament and other meetings.

Of course, parents should attend Sunday meetings with their children.

The father and mother should work together to make sure that preparation for meetings is a pleasant family experience. The last minute rush to gather the children, dress, and hurry to meeting is destructive to reverence.

When families fall into this pattern they are frequently late to church, there are often cross words and hurt feelings, and the children are often upset and restless during the service. How much more reverent is the family that prepares well ahead of time for meetings, that arrives at the chapel well before the

161

"Behavior learned at home determines behavior in Church meetings."

meeting begins, and that sits together to listen to the prelude music and put worldly concerns out of their minds.

Parents with small children sometimes have a difficult time helping their youngsters appreciate meetings and keeping them from creating disturbances. Perseverance, firmness, and preparation in the home are essential ingredients for success. If they are perplexed about how to handle their children at church, young parents might seek the advice of a more experienced couple in the ward.

Often, before and after meetings, members of the Church cluster in the chapel to exchange greetings. Some seeming irreverence is due innocently to the fact that we are a friendly people and that the Sabbath is a convenient time to visit, to fellowship, and to meet new people. Parents should set an example for their families by doing their visiting in the foyers or other areas outside of the chapel before or after meetings. After a meeting, parents can help to carry the spirit of the service into the home by discussing at home a thought, a musical number, or some other positive aspect of the meeting with their children.[11]

Our example of reverence can have a powerful impact on others.

We have discussed the importance of reverence and examined some of its meanings. We have also offered several suggestions about promoting reverence at home and at church. The real improvement in actions of the people, however, will come as local leaders and families combine their efforts to overcome their specific reverence problems. We envision an effort throughout the Church to improve reverence. . . .

True reverence is a vital quality, but one that is fast disappearing in the world as the forces of evil broaden their influences. We cannot fully comprehend the power for good we can wield if the millions of members of Christ's true church will serve as models of reverent behavior. We cannot imagine the additional numbers of lives we could touch. Perhaps even more important, we cannot foresee the great spiritual impact on our own families if we become the reverent people we know we should be.[12]

Suggestions for Study and Teaching

Consider these ideas as you study the chapter or as you prepare to teach. For additional help, see pages v–ix.

- Review the examples of reverence on page 155. What do these two stories suggest about what it means to be reverent? What examples of reverence have you noticed in your life? What have you learned from these experiences?

- Review the first four paragraphs on page 156, looking for President Kimball's teachings about what reverence is and what reverence is not. Why should Latter-day Saints be "the most reverent people in all the earth"?

- How do you think we should respond when we hear someone take the Lord's name in vain? What do you learn from President Kimball's example? (See page 157.) What can we do to honor the Lord's name?

- Review pages 158–61, looking for reverent actions and attitudes and irreverent actions and attitudes. In what ways might such actions and attitudes influence us personally? How might they influence our families and others? Consider what you and your family can do to be reverent at church.

- What do you think parents can do at home to help their children want to be reverent in sacrament meeting? in other Church meetings and activities? (See the examples on pages 161–62.)

- Study the final two paragraphs in the chapter (page 163). In what ways might our improved reverence influence our families? our communities?

Related Scriptures: 1 Kings 6:1, 7; Matthew 21:12–14; Alma 37:14–16; D&C 63:61–62, 64

Notes

1. See Francis M. Gibbons, *Spencer W. Kimball: Resolute Disciple, Prophet of God* (1995), 192.
2. *The Teachings of Spencer W. Kimball,* ed. Edward L. Kimball (1982), 534.
3. See Gibbons, *Spencer W. Kimball: Resolute Disciple, Prophet of God,* xi.
4. *We Should Be a Reverent People* (pamphlet, 1976), 1, 2.
5. *We Should Be a Reverent People,* 1–2.
6. "President Kimball Speaks Out on Profanity," *Ensign,* Feb. 1981, 3, 4–5.
7. *We Should Be a Reverent People,* 2.
8. *The Teachings of Spencer W. Kimball,* 222.
9. *We Should Be a Reverent People,* 1.
10. *The Teachings of Spencer W. Kimball,* 222–23.
11. *We Should Be a Reverent People,* 2–3.
12. *We Should Be a Reverent People,* 4.

The Sabbath—A Delight

The Sabbath is a day for active, joyful worship.

From the Life of Spencer W. Kimball

As President Spencer W. Kimball traveled throughout the Church, he was pleased when he found the Saints honoring the Sabbath day. He told of meeting two men in particular who had been blessed for their efforts to keep the Sabbath day holy:

"In a stake recently I interviewed a man for an important position in the stake reorganization. And I said to him, 'What is your occupation?' And he said, 'I operate a service station.' And I asked, 'Do you operate on the Sabbath?' His answer was, 'No, I do not.' 'Well, how can you get along? Most service station operators seem to think they must open on the Sabbath.' 'I get along well,' he said. 'The Lord is good to me.' 'Do you not have stiff competition?' I asked. 'Yes, indeed,' he replied. 'Across the street is a man who keeps open all day Sunday.' 'And you never open?' I asked. 'No, sir,' he said, 'and I am grateful, and the Lord is kind, and I have sufficient for my needs.'

"I was in another stake, also in a reorganization program, and another brother was considered for one of the highest positions; and when we asked him of his occupation, he said he was a grocer by trade. 'Well, most of the stores keep open on the Sabbath. Do you?' 'We lock our store on Sunday,' he said. 'But how can you compete with these people who are open seven days a week?' 'We compete. At least we get along very well,' was his reply. 'But would not the Sabbath be your biggest day?' 'Yes,' he answered, 'we would probably sell twice as much on the Sabbath as we would on an average day, but we get along without it, and the Lord has been kind; he has been gracious; he has been good.' . . . And I could not refrain from saying, 'God bless you, my faithful brother. The Lord will not be unmindful of these

165

"Call the sabbath a delight, the holy of the Lord" (Isaiah 58:13).

seeming sacrifices. Your dollars are clean. They will surely not hinder you in finding your way into the kingdom of God.'"[1]

President Kimball saw the Sabbath as a day for active, joyful worship—a time to leave behind the things of the world and fill the day with righteous activity. Quoting scriptures, he encouraged the Saints to make the Sabbath "a delight" and to approach the day with "cheerful hearts and countenances" (Isaiah 58:13; D&C 59:15).[2]

Teachings of Spencer W. Kimball

The Lord has always commanded His people to honor the Sabbath day.

Moses came down from the quaking, smoking Mount Sinai and brought to the wandering children of Israel the Ten Commandments, fundamental rules for the conduct of life. These commandments were, however, not new. They had been known to Adam and his posterity, who had been commanded to live them from the beginning, and were merely reiterated by the Lord to Moses. And the commandments even antedated earth life and were part of the test for mortals established in the council in heaven.

The first of the Ten Commandments requires that men worship the Lord; the fourth designates a Sabbath day especially for such worship:

"Thou shalt have no other gods before me. [. . .]

"Remember the sabbath day, to keep it holy.

"Six days shalt thou labour, and do all thy work:

"But the seventh day is the sabbath of the Lord thy God: in it thou shalt not do any work, thou, nor thy son, nor thy daughter, thy manservant, nor thy maidservant, nor thy cattle, nor thy stranger that is within thy gates:

"For in six days the Lord made heaven and earth, the sea, and all that in them is, and rested the seventh day: wherefore the Lord blessed the sabbath day, and hallowed it." (Exodus 20:3, 8–11.)

To many, Sabbath-breaking is a matter of little moment, but to our Heavenly Father it is disobedience to one of the principal commandments. It is evidence of man's failure to meet the individual test set for each of us before the creation of the world, "to see if they will do all things whatsoever the Lord their God shall command them." (Abraham 3:25.) . . .

The solemn command brought down from the thundering of Mount Sinai was "Remember the sabbath day, to keep it holy." That commandment has never been rescinded nor modified. Instead, it has been reinforced in modern times:

"But remember that on this, the Lord's day, thou shalt offer thine oblations and thy sacraments unto the Most High, confessing thy sins unto thy brethren, and before the Lord.

"And on this day thou shalt do none other thing, only let thy food be prepared with singleness of heart that . . . thy joy may be full." (D&C 59:12–13.)[3]

The Sabbath is not a day for business or recreation.

I . . . would urge upon all Saints everywhere a more strict observance of the Sabbath day. The Lord's holy day is fast losing its sacred significance throughout the world. . . . More and more, man destroys the Sabbath's sacred purposes in pursuit of wealth, pleasure, recreation, and the worship of false and material gods. We continue to urge all Saints and God-fearing people everywhere to observe the Sabbath day and keep it holy. Businesses will not be open on the Sabbath if they are not patronized on that holy day. The same is true of resorts, sporting events, and recreation areas of all kinds. Pursuit of the almighty dollar is winning, it seems, over the Lord's commandment, "Keep my sabbaths, and reverence my sanctuary" (Lev. 19:30).[4]

We note that in our Christian world in many places we still have business establishments open for business on the sacred Sabbath. We are sure the cure of this lies in ourselves, the buying public. Certainly the stores and business houses would not remain open if we, the people, failed to purchase from them. Will you all please reconsider this matter. Take it to your home evenings and discuss it with your children. It would be wonderful if every family determined that henceforth no Sabbath purchase would be made.[5]

We have become largely a world of Sabbath breakers. On the Sabbath the lakes are full of boats, the beaches are crowded, the shows have their best attendance, the golf links are dotted with players. The Sabbath is the preferred day for rodeos, conventions, family picnics; even ball games are played on the sacred day. "Business as usual" is the slogan for many, and our holy day has become a holiday. And because so many people treat the day as a holiday, numerous others cater to the wants of the fun-lovers and money-makers. . . .

To hunt and fish on the Lord's day is not keeping it holy. To plant or cultivate or harvest crops on the Sabbath is not keeping holy the Lord's day. To go into the canyons for picnics, to attend games or rodeos or races or shows or other amusements on that day is not to keep it in holy remembrance.

Strange as it may seem, some Latter-day Saints, faithful in all other respects, justify themselves in missing their church meetings on occasion for recreational purposes, feeling that the best fishing will be missed if one is not on the stream on opening day or that the vacation will not be long enough if one does not set off on Sunday or that one will miss a movie he wanted to see if he does not go on the Sabbath. And in their breach of the Sabbath they often take their families with them. . . .

There is no criticism of legitimate recreation—sports, picnics, plays, and motion pictures. All have potential for revitalizing life, and the Church as an organization actively sponsors such activities. But there is a proper time and place for all worthwhile things—a time for work, a time for play, a time for worship. . . .

It is true that some people must work on the Sabbath. And, in fact, some of the work that is truly necessary—caring for the sick, for example—may actually serve to hallow the Sabbath. However, in such activities our motives are a most important consideration.[6]

Sometimes Sabbath observance is characterized as a matter of sacrifice and self-denial, but it is not so. It is merely a matter of shifting times and choosing seasons. There is time enough, particularly in our era of the world's history, during the six days of the week in which to do our work and play. Much can be done to organize and encourage weekday activities, avoiding the Sabbath.[7]

The Sabbath is a day for us to be spiritually enriched through worship and worthy actions.

The Sabbath is a holy day in which to do worthy and holy things. Abstinence from work and recreation is important, but insufficient. The Sabbath calls for constructive thoughts and acts, and if one merely lounges about doing nothing on the Sabbath, he is breaking it. To observe it, one will be on his knees in prayer, preparing lessons, studying the gospel, meditating, visiting the ill and distressed, writing letters to missionaries, taking a nap, reading wholesome material, and attending all the meetings of that day at which he is expected.[8]

Take time [on the Sabbath] to be together as families to converse with one another, to study the scriptures, to visit friends, relatives, and the sick and lonely. This is also an excellent time to work on your journals and genealogy.[9]

In Hebrew the term *Sabbath* means "rest." It contemplates quiet tranquility, peace of mind and spirit. It is a day to get rid of selfish interests and absorbing activities.

The Sabbath day is given throughout the generations of man for a perpetual covenant [see Exodus 31:16]. It is a sign between the Lord and his children forever [see Exodus 31:17]. It is a day in which to worship and to express our gratitude and appreciation to the Lord. It is a day on which to surrender every worldly interest and to praise the Lord humbly, for humility is the beginning of exaltation. It is a day not for affliction and burden but for rest and righteous enjoyment. It is a day not for lavish banqueting, but a day of simple meals and spiritual feasting. . . . It is a day graciously given us by our Heavenly Father. It is a day when animals may be turned out to graze and rest; when the plow may be stored in the barn and other machinery cooled down; a day when employer and employee, master and servant may be free from plowing, digging, toiling. It is a day when the office may be

*The Sabbath "is a day in which to worship
and to express our gratitude and appreciation to the Lord."*

locked and business postponed, and troubles forgotten; a day when man may be temporarily released from that first injunction, "In the sweat of thy face shalt thou eat bread, until thou return unto the ground. . . ." [See Genesis 3:19.] It is a day when bodies may rest, minds relax, and spirits grow. It is a day when songs may be sung, prayers offered, sermons preached, and testimonies borne, and when man may climb high, almost annihilating time, space, and distance between himself and his Creator.

The Sabbath is a day on which to take inventory—to analyze our weaknesses, to confess our sins to our associates and our Lord. It is a day on which to fast in "sackcloth and ashes." It is a day on which to read good books, a day to contemplate and ponder, a day to study lessons for priesthood and auxiliary organizations, a day to study the scriptures and to prepare sermons, a day to nap and rest and relax, a day to visit the sick, a day to preach the gospel, a day to proselyte, a day to visit quietly with the family and get acquainted with our children, a day for proper courting, a day to do good, a day to drink at the fountain of knowledge and of instruction, a day to seek forgiveness of our sins, a day for the enrichment of our spirit and our soul, a day to

171

restore us to our spiritual stature, a day to partake of the emblems of [the Lord's] sacrifice and atonement, a day to contemplate the glories of the gospel and of the eternal realms, a day to climb high on the upward path toward our Heavenly Father.[10]

We hope . . . that either before or after your series of Sunday meetings, depending upon your particular . . . meeting schedule, you will do what the Savior asked the Nephite disciples to do: After he taught them, he asked them to go to their homes and to ponder and to pray over what was said (see 3 Ne. 17:3). Let us keep that pattern in mind.[11]

A full and abundant Sabbath includes attending Church meetings and partaking of the sacrament.

It seems the Lord's idea of a full and abundant Sabbath is the worship and the learning of him and partaking of his sacrament. He would have us fill the day with useful and spiritual activities. He would have us do these things with thanksgiving and cheerful hearts and countenances, and not with much laughter. He would have our men and boys attend their priesthood meeting having prepared their lessons and with a glad heart. He would have his people attend the Sunday School and there learn his plan of salvation. He would have his people attend the sacrament meeting to sing with the Saints and to pray in spirit with him who is mouth, and to partake of the sacrament emblems, repledging total allegiance, unconditional surrender, undeviating works, a constant remembrance of him.[12]

Who should attend sacrament meetings? The commandment was addressed through the Prophet to those "whose feet stand upon the land of Zion," the membership of his church [see D&C 59:3, 9]. The requirement is not confined to adults but includes young and old alike. . . . What could parents do to better help in solidifying the family than for the entire family, large and small, to go in a body to the meetinghouse to the sacrament meetings? There the children will learn the habit of regular attendance, will be kept from breaking the Sabbath, and even though very young, will absorb of the teachings and testimonies, and of the spirit there. Stake and ward and quorum leaders should be exemplary in this respect to the people.[13]

When I was a very small boy, I was taught the habit of going to sacrament meetings. Mother always took me with her. Those warm afternoons I soon became drowsy and leaned over on her lap to sleep. I may not have learned much from the sermons, but I learned the habit of "going to meeting." The habit stayed with me through my life.[14]

No little child absorbs knowingly the sunlight; but unconsciously the light brings power to his little body. No child knows the value of his mother's milk nor of the food from opened cans which gives him nourishment. Yet, that is where he gets his strength and his power to grow and to become a man eventually. . . .

And every child, without realizing the full portent, can absorb much from a sacrament meeting. They will absorb something every time.[15]

Wouldn't it be a loss of a great deal of time and effort if every Sunday morning we had to stop and say, "Shall I or shall I not go to priesthood meeting? Shall I or shall I not go to sacrament meeting today? Shall we or shall we not go?" What a lot of wasted effort. . . . Settle it once and for all.[16]

A man of my acquaintance remained home each Sabbath and justified himself by saying that he could benefit more by reading a good book at home than by attending the sacrament meeting and listening to a poor sermon. But the home, sacred as it should be, is not the house of prayer. In it no sacrament is administered; in it is not found the fellowship with members, nor the confession of sins to the brethren. The mountains may be termed the temples of God and the forests and streams his handiwork, but only in the meetinghouse, or house of prayer, can be fulfilled all the requirements of the Lord. And so he has impressed upon us that: "It is expedient that the church meet together often to partake of bread and wine in the remembrance of the Lord Jesus." (D&C 20:75.)[17]

We do not go to Sabbath meetings to be entertained or even solely to be instructed. We go to worship the Lord. It is an individual responsibility, and regardless of what is said from the pulpit, if one wishes to worship the Lord in spirit and in truth, he may do so by attending his meetings, partaking of the sacrament, and contemplating the beauties of the gospel. If the service is a failure to you, you have failed. No one can worship for you; you must do your own waiting upon the Lord.[18]

The Lord has promised blessings to those who faithfully observe the Sabbath.

The purpose of the commandment [to keep the Sabbath day holy] is not to deprive man of something. Every commandment that God has given to his servants is for the benefit of those who receive and obey it. It is man who profits by the careful and strict observance; it is man who suffers by the breaking of the laws of God. . . .

In my travels I find faithful people who forego Sabbath day profits and the handling of forbidden things. I have found cattlemen who have no roundup on the Sabbath; fruit stands along the roadside, generally open day and night through the fruit season, closed on the Sabbath; drug stores, eating houses, and wayside stands closed on the Lord's day—and the owners seem to get along, at the same time taking genuine satisfaction in abiding by the law. And every time I see good folk foregoing these kinds of earnings, I rejoice and feel within my heart to bless them for their faith and steadfastness.[19]

I know that men will never suffer, ultimately, for any seeming financial sacrifices that might be made, for [God] has commanded us to live his laws and then has challenged us:

". . . prove me now herewith, saith the Lord of hosts, if I will not open you the windows of heaven, and pour you out a blessing, that there shall not be room enough to receive it." (Malachi 3:10.)[20]

With respect to this commandment, among the others, let us follow the prophet Joshua: "Now therefore fear the Lord, and serve him in sincerity and in truth: . . . choose you this day whom ye will serve; . . . but as for me and my house, we will serve the Lord." (Josh. 24:14–15.)

174

President Kimball taught that the Sabbath is a day
"to visit quietly with the family."

Then we can hope for the blessings promised the children of Israel: "Ye shall keep my sabbaths, and reverence my sanctuary: I am the Lord.

"If ye walk in my statutes, and keep my commandments, and do them;

"Then I will give you rain in due season, and the land shall yield her increase, and the trees of the field shall yield their fruit.

"And your threshing shall reach unto the vintage, and the vintage shall reach unto the sowing time: and ye shall eat your bread to the full, and dwell in your land safely.

"And I will give peace in the land, and ye shall lie down, and none shall make you afraid." (Lev. 26:2–6.)[21]

If we love the Lord, we will observe the Sabbath day and keep it holy.

It would appear that the reason the Sabbath day is so hard to live for so many people is that it is still written on tablets of stone rather than being written in their hearts. . . .

175

. . . In our own day it would seem that [the Lord] recognized the intelligence of his people, and assumed that they would catch the total spirit of worship and of the Sabbath observance when he said to them:

"Thou shalt offer a sacrifice unto the Lord thy God in righteousness, even that of a broken heart and a contrite spirit." (D&C 59:8.)

. . . He gave us the first and great commandment:

"Thou shalt love the Lord thy God with all thy heart, and with all thy soul, and with all thy mind." (Matt. 22:37.)

It is unthinkable that one who loves the Lord with all his heart and with all his soul and who with a broken heart and contrite spirit recognizes the limitless gifts which the Lord had given him would fail to spend one day in seven in gratitude and thankfulness, and carrying forward the good works of the Lord. The observance of the Sabbath is an indication of the measure of our love for our Heavenly Father.[22]

People frequently wonder where to draw the line: what is worthy and what is unworthy to do upon the Sabbath. But if one loves the Lord with all his heart, might, mind, and strength; if one can put away selfishness and curb desire; if one can measure each Sabbath activity by the yardstick of worshipfulness; if one is honest with his Lord and with himself; if one offers a "broken heart and a contrite spirit," it is quite unlikely that there will be Sabbath breaking in that person's life.[23]

Suggestions for Study and Teaching

Consider these ideas as you study the chapter or as you prepare to teach. For additional help, see pages v–ix.

- Review pages 167–68. Think about the importance the Lord has given to the Sabbath and why the Sabbath is different from the other days of the week. What makes the Sabbath "a delight"?

- Review pages 168–69, looking for things we should not do on the Sabbath. Why are these activities inappropriate on the Sabbath? On pages 170–74, President Kimball gives examples of "useful and spiritual activities" for the Sabbath. What have you and your family done to enrich your observance of the Sabbath?

• President Kimball said that "motives are a most important consideration" for those who are required to work on the Sabbath (page 169). What can people do to maintain the spirit of Sabbath-day worship when they are required to work?

• What do we mean when we say that the Sabbath is a day of rest? (For some examples, see pages 170–72.) Why is it wrong to merely lounge about, doing nothing on the Sabbath?

• Review the purposes for attending Church meetings on pages 172–74. When have you recently felt worshipful at a Church meeting and why? How can you make your Church attendance and worship more meaningful?

• President Kimball testified of blessings we receive when we keep the Sabbath day holy (pages 174–75; see also the stories on pages 165, 167). What are some blessings you have received as you have kept this commandment?

• In a family home evening or family council, consider what your family can do to help each other keep the Sabbath day holy.

Related Scriptures: Genesis 2:1–3; Mark 2:23–28; 3:1–5; Mosiah 13:16–19; D&C 68:29

Notes

1. In Conference Report, Oct. 1953, 55.
2. See "The Sabbath—A Delight," *Ensign,* Jan. 1978, 4–5.
3. *Faith Precedes the Miracle* (1972), 267–69.
4. In Conference Report, Oct. 1978, 5; or *Ensign,* Nov. 1978, 5.
5. In Conference Report, Oct. 1975, 6; or *Ensign,* Nov. 1975, 6.
6. *Ensign,* Jan. 1978, 2, 4, 5.
7. *Ensign,* Jan. 1978, 4.
8. *Ensign,* Jan. 1978, 4.
9. In Conference Report, Apr. 1981, 62; or *Ensign,* May 1981, 45.
10. "The Fourth Commandment," in *M Man–Gleaner Manual 1963–1964* (leader's manual), 277–78.
11. In Conference Report, Apr. 1980, 5; or *Ensign,* May 1980, 4.
12. "The Fourth Commandment," 279–80.
13. *The Teachings of Spencer W. Kimball,* ed. Edward L. Kimball (1982), 221.
14. In Conference Report, Oct. 1944, 43.
15. *The Teachings of Spencer W. Kimball,* 517.
16. *The Teachings of Spencer W. Kimball,* 517.
17. *The Teachings of Spencer W. Kimball,* 220.
18. *Ensign,* Jan. 1978, 4–5.
19. *Ensign,* Jan. 1978, 4, 5.
20. In Conference Report, Oct. 1953, 56.
21. *Ensign,* Jan. 1978, 5.
22. "The Fourth Commandment," 275–76.
23. "The Fourth Commandment," 280.

"Marriage is for time and eternity. . . . Marriage gives life."

The Law of Chastity

The Lord has only one standard of morality—
total chastity for both men and women before marriage
and complete fidelity afterward.

From the Life of Spencer W. Kimball

In counseling Church members about dating, courtship, and marriage, President Spencer W. Kimball emphasized the importance of living by the Lord's law of chastity and fidelity. He also warned against Satan's attempts to make the violation of this law seem justified or harmless. He told of a young couple who had fallen prey to this deception of the adversary:

"The boy said, 'Yes, we yielded to each other, but we do not think it wrong because we love one another.' I thought I had misunderstood him. Since the world began, there have been countless immoralities, but to hear them justified by Latter-day Saint youth shocked me. He repeated, 'No, it is not wrong, because we love one another.'

"They had repeated this abominable heresy so often that they had convinced themselves, and a wall of resistance had been built, and behind this wall they stubbornly, almost defiantly, stood."

To their rationalization, President Kimball responded, "No, my beloved young people, you did not love one another. Rather, you lusted for one another. . . . If one really loves another, one would rather die for that person than injure him. At the hour of indulgence, pure love is pushed out one door while lust sneaks in the other."[1]

President Kimball also testified that joy and peace come from obeying the law of chastity. He saw these blessings in the lives of faithful members, as in this experience he had in the temple:

"Here were peace and harmony and eager anticipation. A well-groomed young man and an exquisitely gowned young woman, lovely beyond description, knelt [at] the altar. Authoritatively, I pronounced the heavenly ceremony which married and sealed them for eternity on earth and in the celestial worlds. The pure in heart were there. Heaven was there."[2]

Teachings of Spencer W. Kimball

The law of chastity prohibits
all sexual relations outside marriage.

That the Church's stand on morality may be understood, we declare firmly and unalterably it is not an outworn garment, faded, old-fashioned, and threadbare. God is the same yesterday, today, and forever, and his covenants and doctrines are immutable; and when the sun grows cold and the stars no longer shine, the law of chastity will still be basic in God's world and in the Lord's church. Old values are upheld by the Church not because they are old, but rather because they are right.[3]

Total chastity before marriage and total fidelity after are still the standard from which there can be no deviation without sin, misery, and unhappiness.[4]

Those who seem to flout the institution of marriage, and who regard chastity before marriage with fidelity after as old-fashioned, seem determined to establish a new fashion on their own and impose it upon others. Can they not see the gross selfishness that will lead finally to deep loneliness? Can they not see that, pushed by pleasure, they will become more and more distant from joy? Can they not see that their kind of fulfillment will produce a hollowness and an emptiness from which no fleeting pleasure can finally rescue them? The law of the harvest has not been repealed [see Galatians 6:7].[5]

The early apostles and prophets mention numerous sins that were reprehensible to them. Many of them were sexual sins—adultery, being without natural affection, lustfulness, infidelity, incontinence, filthy communications, impurity, inordinate affection, fornication. They included all sexual relations outside marriage—petting, sex perversion, masturbation, and pre-occupation with sex in one's thoughts and talking. Included are every hidden and secret sin and all unholy and impure thoughts and practices. One of the worst of these is incest.[6]

If one has [homosexual] desires and tendencies, he overcomes them the same as if he had the urge toward petting or fornication or adultery. The Lord condemns and forbids this practice with a vigor equal to his condemnation of adultery and other such sex acts. . . . Again, contrary to the belief and statement of many people, this [practice], like fornication, is overcomable and forgivable, but again, only upon a deep and abiding repentance, which means total abandonment and complete transformation of thought and act. The fact that some governments and some churches and numerous corrupted individuals have tried to reduce such behavior from criminal offense to personal privilege does not change the nature nor the seriousness of the practice. Good men, wise men, God-fearing men everywhere still denounce the practice as being unworthy of sons and daughters of God; and Christ's church denounces it and condemns it. . . . This heinous homosexual sin is of the ages. Many cities and civilizations have gone out of existence because of it.[7]

Pure sex life in proper marriage is approved. There is a time and an appropriateness for all things that have value. But sexual encounters outside of legalized marriage render the individual a thing to be used, a thing to be exploited, and make him or her exchangeable, exploitable, expendable. . . .

Illicit sex is a selfish act, a betrayal, and is dishonest. To be unwilling to accept responsibility is cowardly, disloyal. Marriage is for time and eternity. Fornication and all other deviations are for today, for the hour, for the "now." Marriage gives life. Fornication leads to death.[8]

Love is wholesome and selfless, but lust is corrupt and selfish.

The young man is untrue to his manhood who promises popularity, good times, security, fun, and even love, when all he can give is passion and its diabolical fruits—guilt complexes, disgust, hatred, abhorrence, eventual loathing, and possible pregnancy without legitimacy and honor. He pleads his case in love and all he gives is lust. Likewise, the young lady sells herself cheap. The result is damage to life and canker to the soul. . . .

And still these young people talk of love. What a corruption of the most beautiful term! The fruit is bitter because the tree is corrupt. Their lips say, "I love you." Their bodies say, "I want you." Love is kind and wholesome. To love is to give, not to take. To love is to serve, not to exploit. . . .

What is love? Many people think of it as mere physical attraction and they casually speak of "falling in love" and "love at first sight.". . . One might become immediately attracted to another individual, but love is far more than physical attraction. It is deep, inclusive, and comprehensive. Physical attraction is only one of the many elements; there must be faith and confidence and understanding and partnership. There must be common ideals and standards. There must be great devotion and companionship. Love is cleanliness and progress and sacrifice and selflessness. This kind of love never tires or wanes, but lives through sickness and sorrow, poverty and privation, accomplishment and disappointment, time and eternity. For the love to continue, there must be an increase constantly of confidence and understanding, of frequent and sincere expression of appreciation and affection. There must be a forgetting of self and a constant concern for the other. Interests, hopes, objectives must be constantly focused into a single channel. . . .

The young man who protects his sweetheart against all use or abuse, against insult and infamy from himself or others, could be expressing true love. But the young man who uses his companion as a biological toy to give himself temporary satisfaction— that is lust.

A young woman who conducts herself to be attractive spiritually, mentally, and physically but will not by word or dress or act stir or stimulate to physical reactions the companion beside her could be expressing true love. That young woman who must touch and stir and fondle and tempt and use exhibits lust and exploitation. . . .

Beware of the devil's trick of making evil seem good by giving it a label that conceals its character. Just such a device is the rationalization that lust is love.[9]

Even though sex can be an important and satisfactory part of married life, we must remember that life is not designed just for sex.[10]

The union of the sexes, husband and wife (and *only* husband and wife), was for the principal purpose of bringing children into the world. Sexual experiences were never intended by the Lord to be a mere plaything or merely to satisfy passions and lusts. We know of no directive from the Lord that proper sexual experience between husbands and wives need be limited totally to the procreation of children, but we find much evidence from Adam until now that no provision was ever made by the Lord for indiscriminate sex.[11]

We must shun pornography and other forms of immorality.

We are the spiritual children of God, and . . . we are his supreme creation. In each of us there is the potentiality to become a God—pure, holy, true, influential, powerful, independent of earthly forces. We learn from the scriptures that we each have eternal existence, that we were in the beginning with God (see Abr. 3:22). That understanding gives to us a unique sense of man's dignity.

But there are false teachers everywhere, using speech and pornographic literature, magazines, radio, TV, street talk—spreading damnable heresies which break down moral standards, and this to gratify the lust of the flesh.[12]

We abhor pornography that seems to be flooding the land. Legislation makes an effort to curb it, but the best way to stop it is to have men and women, with their families, build barriers against it. We ask you, "Do you good people of your community want this ugly vice to corrupt your families and your neighbors?"[13]

When we see the depravity of numerous people of our own society in their determination to force upon people vulgar presentations, filthy communications, unnatural practices, we wonder, has Satan reached forth with his wicked, evil hand to pull into his forces the people of this earth? Do we not have enough good people left to stamp out the evil which threatens our world? Why do we continue to compromise with evil and why do we continue to tolerate sin?[14]

We hope that our parents and leaders will not tolerate pornography. It is really garbage, but today is peddled as normal and satisfactory food. . . . There is a link between pornography and the low, sexual drives and perversions.[15]

Sins spawned by pornography unfortunately perpetuate other serious transgressions, including abortion.[16]

It is ridiculous to imply that pornography has no effect. There is a definite relationship to crime. Murder, robbery, rape, prostitution, and commercialized vice are fed on this immorality. Sex crime statistics seem to reflect a relationship between crime and pornography.

It is utterly without redeeming social value. We urge our families to protect their children in every way possible. We live in a permissive world, but we must make certain we do not become a part of that permissive world, that degenerate world.[17]

Members of the Church everywhere are urged to not only resist the widespread plague of pornography, but as citizens to become actively and relentlessly engaged in the fight against this insidious enemy of humanity around the world. . . .

. . . Teach your children to avoid smut as the plague it is. As citizens, join in the fight against obscenity in your communities. Do not be lulled into inaction by the pornographic profiteers who say that to remove obscenity is to deny people the rights of free choice. Do not let them masquerade licentiousness as liberty.

Precious souls are at stake—souls that are near and dear to each of us.[18]

President Kimball gave clear guidelines for young people who date.

Parents and leaders should safeguard children and youth against immoral influences.

Your children will learn from you early in their lives that they must never involve themselves in immoral practices of any kind. This cannot be told to them just once. But before they are married they should be told hundreds of times, and they should know that not only their family and their parents expect this great service, but the Lord in heaven, Jesus Christ, expects them to keep clean and free from immorality.[19]

Unchastity is the great demon of the day. Like an octopus, it fastens its tentacles upon one. There are many paths that lead youth to these defilements. May I mention some approaches that break down moral structures.

Some become casual in their church activity and estrange themselves from the refining and protective influences of the Church. The gospel seems to take second place to their personal interests. They miss their meetings, permitting school work, social life, or business or professions to crowd out the important church activities and the gospel until their feelings toward the Church and its standards are somewhat anesthetized.

Another of the many things that lead to unchastity is immodesty. Today many young women and young men are smug in their knowledge of the facts of life. They think they know all the answers. They talk about sex as freely as they talk about cars and shows and clothes. And a spirit of immodesty has developed until nothing seems to be sacred.[20]

There is no reason why women need to wear a low-cut or otherwise revealing gown just because it is the worldly style. We can create a style of our own. . . .

Neither is there excuse for young men to bare and expose their bodies. The fellows could show courage and good judgment if they encouraged their young women friends to wear modest clothing. If a young man would not date a young woman who is improperly clothed, the style would change very soon. . . .

The Lord has promised to the valiant, "All that I have is thine." To reach these lofty heights and limitless blessings, you must take no chances. Keep your lives sweet and clean and pure, so that there will never be any forfeiture. To do this, you will do well to avoid "the very appearance of evil" and "the very approach toward evil."[21]

We cannot overemphasize immodesty as one of the pitfalls to be avoided if we would shun temptation and keep ourselves clean.[22]

I suggest . . . the following standard. Any dating or pairing off in social contacts should be postponed until at least the age of 16 or older, and even then there should still be much judgment used in selections and in the seriousness. Young people should still limit the close contacts for several years, since the boy will be going on his mission when he is 19 years old.

Dating and especially steady dating in the early teens is most hazardous. It distorts the whole picture of life. It deprives you of worthwhile and rich experiences; it limits friendships; it reduces the acquaintances which can be so valuable in selecting a partner for time and eternity.

There is definitely a time for the dance, for travel, for associations, for the date, and even for the steady date that will culminate in the romance which will take young people to the holy temple for eternal marriage. But it is the timing that is so vital. It is wrong to do even the right things at the wrong time in the wrong place under the wrong circumstances.[23]

Keep your life clean and free from all unholy and impure thoughts and actions. Avoid all associations which degrade and lower the high, righteous standards set up for us. Then your life will sail smoothly and peace and joy will surround you.[24]

Suggestions for Study and Teaching

Consider these ideas as you study the chapter or as you prepare to teach. For additional help, see pages v–ix.

- Compare the couple President Kimball describes on page 179 with the couple he refers to in the first paragraph on page 180. What could have led these Latter-day Saint couples to such different attitudes and actions?

- Read the second paragraph on page 180. What would you say to someone who claims that chastity is old-fashioned? (For some examples, see pages 180–81.) What are some of the consequences of disregarding the law of chastity? What are some of the blessings of obeying it?

- Think about how you would complete these sentences: To love is _____. To lust is _____. (For some examples, see pages 181–83.) How should our understanding of love influence our thoughts and actions?

- Why do you think President Kimball and many Church leaders since him have warned against pornography? (See pages 183–84.) In what ways can we fight the spread and influence of pornography? What can we do in our families to "build barriers against it"?

- Review the standards on pages 185–87. Why should parents and leaders begin teaching the law of chastity early in a child's life? What can parents and leaders do to help youth stay true to the Church and its standards? What resources does the Church provide to help youth understand and keep Church standards?

- How are modesty and chastity related?

- What does it mean to be modest in the way we dress? In what ways can we "create a style of our own"? (page 186). What does it mean to be modest in our language and behavior? How can we help youth understand the need for modesty in all aspects of their lives?

Related Scriptures: 1 Corinthians 6:9, 18–20; Jacob 2:7; Alma 39:3–5, 9; 3 Nephi 12:27–30; D&C 42:22–23, 40–41; 59:6

Notes

1. *Faith Precedes the Miracle* (1972), 151–52, 153, 154.
2. In Conference Report, Oct. 1971, 153; or *Ensign*, Dec. 1971, 36.
3. *Faith Precedes the Miracle,* 155.
4. In Conference Report, Oct. 1980, 4; or *Ensign*, Nov. 1980, 4.
5. In Conference Report, Apr. 1978, 117; or *Ensign*, May 1978, 78.
6. "President Kimball Speaks Out on Morality," *Ensign*, Nov. 1980, 95.
7. *Ensign,* Nov. 1980, 97.
8. *Faith Precedes the Miracle,* 155, 156–57.
9. *Faith Precedes the Miracle,* 157–59.
10. *The Miracle of Forgiveness* (1969), 73.
11. "The Lord's Plan for Men and Women," *Ensign*, Oct. 1975, 4.
12. *Ensign,* Nov. 1980, 94.
13. In Conference Report, Apr. 1975, 8–9; or *Ensign*, May 1975, 7.
14. In Conference Report, Apr. 1975, 162; or *Ensign*, May 1975, 109.
15. In Conference Report, Oct. 1974, 7; or *Ensign*, Nov. 1974, 7.
16. "A Report and a Challenge," *Ensign*, Nov. 1976, 6.
17. In Conference Report, Oct. 1974, 7; or *Ensign*, Nov. 1974, 7.
18. *Ensign,* Nov. 1976, 5, 6.
19. In Conference Report, La Paz Bolivia Area Conference 1977, 22–23.
20. *Faith Precedes the Miracle,* 162–63.
21. *Faith Precedes the Miracle,* 166, 167, 168.
22. *The Miracle of Forgiveness,* 227.
23. *Ensign,* Nov. 1980, 96.
24. *Ensign,* Nov. 1980, 98.

Honorable, Happy, Successful Marriage

Married couples enjoy a harmonious and
eternal relationship when they remain true
to the Lord and to each other.

From the Life of Spencer W. Kimball

Before his call to the Quorum of the Twelve Apostles, Spencer W. Kimball was part-owner of an insurance and realty company in Safford, Arizona. One of his employees, Carmen Richardson Smith, recalled the faithfulness of Spencer and Camilla Kimball when their son Edward was stricken with polio in the early 1930s:

"The relationship between Brother Kimball and his wife was something I admired very much. When Eddie was in California, receiving extended treatment, Sister Kimball stayed with him and President Kimball traveled there at critical times. During periods of recuperation following Eddie's surgery, Brother Kimball would return home to take care of the rest of the family, while his wife stayed with Eddie.

"I believe he wrote to her every single day. Not just a short 50-word letter, either. Sometimes when he was particularly pressed for time he would dictate a letter to me, and I remember how I felt: it was almost a sacred honor.

"Theirs was a good, happy marriage, and they seemed to have great regard for each other. It seemed that their worlds revolved very much around each other."[1]

Spencer and Camilla Kimball's love for one another, which was so evident when they were young, grew stronger and deeper as they grew older. President Kimball often expressed gratitude for the relationship he and his wife shared: "Camilla has been by my

189

"Camilla has been by my side in every experience."

side in every experience. We have buried our parents and other loved ones, and have given up our own little children prematurely born. We have been in the depths and soared to the heights. . . . We have wept together and we have laughed together. . . . Our life has been full of fun in spite of all the sad and serious things. We have danced; we have sung; we have entertained; we have loved and been loved. With a wife like Camilla Eyring, life becomes inclusive, full, and abundant."[2]

Having experienced a long and happy marriage, he observed: "We need an unspoiled companion who will not count our wrinkles, remember our stupidities nor remember our weaknesses; . . . we need a loving companion with whom we have suffered and wept and prayed and worshipped; one with whom we have suffered sorrow and disappointments, one who loves us for what we are or intend to be rather than what we appear to be in our gilded shell."[3]

Teachings of Spencer W. Kimball

Eternal marriage is ordained of God, and the family is essential in Heavenly Father's plan for us.

Marriage, *honorable* marriage, is ordained of God. He decreed that the basic unit of society should be the home and the family, and we must be warned that the false culture of the day is turning away from this God-ordained plan. . . .

There seems to be a growing trend against marriage from degenerate areas of the world and a very strong trend toward marriage without children. Naturally the next question is, "Why marry?" And the "antimarriage revolution" comes into focus. Arguments are given that children are a burden, a tie, a responsibility. Many have convinced themselves that education, freedom from restraint and responsibility—that is the life. And unfortunately this benighted and destructive idea is taking hold of some of our own people.[4]

To offset and neutralize the evil teachings in the media and on the cameras and in the show and on the street, we must teach marriage, proper marriage, eternal marriage.[5]

A basic reason for eternal marriage is that life is eternal; and marriage, to be in harmony with eternal purposes, must be consistent with life in duration. Marriage by civil officers, or by Church officers outside of the temples, is made for time only, "till death do you part" or "so long as you both shall live." It terminates with death. . . . Eternal marriage is performed by the prophet of the Lord or by one of the very few to whom he has delegated the authority. It is performed in holy temples erected and dedicated for that purpose. Only such marriage transcends the grave and perpetuates the husband-wife and parent-child relationships into and through eternity.[6]

Honorable, happy, and successful marriage is surely the principal goal of every normal person. Marriage is designed of the Lord to make strong and happy homes and posterity. Anyone who would purposely avoid marriage is not only not normal, but is frustrating his own program.

I defend the term *normal* because the Lord set the norm himself by bringing together Adam and Eve, his first male and first female on this earth, and performing a holy marriage ceremony to make them husband and wife. They were quite different in their makeup, with different roles to play. Hardly had he performed the ceremony than he said to them: "Multiply, and replenish the earth, and subdue it: and have dominion" (Gen. 1:28).

It is normal to marry and normal and proper to bear children. Every person should want and plan to be married because that is what God in heaven planned for us. That is the way he worked it out.[7]

The [Lord's] whole program was intelligently organized to bring children into the world with love and filial interdependence. Had the superficial ideas of many mortals of today prevailed, the world, the human race, and all proper things would long ago have come to an end. . . .

. . . The Lord has said that in order to obtain the highest of the three heavens or degrees of glory in the celestial kingdom, "a man must enter into this order of the priesthood [meaning the new and everlasting covenant of marriage];

"And if he does not, he cannot obtain it." (D&C 131:2–3.)

This is the proper way.

There are some men who fail to marry through their own choice. They deprive themselves. There may be many women who also deprive themselves of blessings. There are others who have never married because they have had no opportunity. We know, of course, that the Lord will make ample provision and that no one will ever be condemned for something he or she could not have helped. . . .

But, concerning marriage and the roles of man and woman, let no man defy God. . . .

I sincerely hope that our Latter-day Saint girls and women, and men and boys, will drink deeply of the water of life and conform their lives to the beautiful and comprehensive roles the Lord assigned to them.

I hope we shall not attempt to perfect an already perfect plan, but seek with all our might, mind, and strength to perfect ourselves in the comprehensive program given to us. Because some of us have failed, certainly it would be unfair to place the blame upon the program. Let us control our attitudes, our activities, our total lives, that we may be heir to the rich and numerous blessings promised to us.[8]

Eternal marriage requires careful preparation.

Marriage is perhaps the most vital of all the decisions and has the most far-reaching effects, for it has to do not only with immediate happiness, but also with eternal joys. It affects not only the two people involved, but also their families and particularly their children and their children's children down through the many generations.

In selecting a companion for life and for eternity, certainly the most careful planning and thinking and praying and fasting should be done to be sure that of all the decisions, this one must not be wrong. In true marriage there must be a union of minds as well as of hearts. Emotions must not wholly determine decisions, but the mind and the heart, strengthened by fasting and prayer and serious consideration, will give one a maximum

"Almost any good man and any good woman can have happiness and a successful marriage if both are willing to pay the price."

chance of marital happiness. It brings with it sacrifice, sharing, and a demand for great selflessness. . . .

. . . "Soul mates" are fiction and an illusion; and while every young man and young woman will seek with all diligence and prayerfulness to find a mate with whom life can be most compatible and beautiful, yet it is certain that almost any good man and any good woman can have happiness and a successful marriage if both are willing to pay the price. . . .

Two individuals approaching the marriage altar must realize that to attain the happy marriage which they hope for they must know that marriage is not a legal coverall, but it means sacrifice, sharing, and even a reduction of some personal liberties. It means long, hard economizing. It means children who bring with them financial burdens, service burdens, care and worry burdens; but also it means the deepest and sweetest emotions of all.[9]

Delayed marriage . . . is not fully acceptable. All normal people should plan their lives to include a proper temple marriage in their early life and to multiply and have their families in the years of their early maturity.[10]

Those young people who chart their course to a marriage in the temple have already established a pattern of thought which will make them amenable to mutual planning with the chosen partner once he or she is found. Even before their marriage is solemnized in the holy place they will be planning their life together, and will continue the process as bride and groom when they sit down to chart their way through a happy, successful and spiritual life to exaltation in the kingdom of God.[11]

Any of you would go around the world for the sealing ordinance if you knew its importance, if you realized how great it is. No distance, no shortage of funds, no situation would ever keep you from being married in the holy temple of the Lord.[12]

There will be a new spirit in Zion when the young women will say to their boyfriends, "If you cannot get a temple recommend, then I am not about to tie my life to you, even for mortality." And the young returned missionary boys will say to their girlfriends, "I am sorry, but as much as I love you, I will not marry out of the holy temple." . . .

. . . We wonder why, with all these blessings and promises, that people will fail to marry correctly and thus waste their lives in a frozen wilderness that may never thaw. Why will any young person ever give a single thought to a marriage out of the temple and jeopardize those glories that are available?[13]

Married couples can follow a never-failing formula to find happiness together.

Almost all marriages could be beautiful, harmonious, happy, and eternal ones, if the two people primarily involved would determine that it should be, that it must be, that it will be.[14]

The mere performance of a ceremony does not bring happiness and a successful marriage. Happiness does not come by pressing a button, as does the electric light; happiness is a state of mind and comes from within. It must be earned. It cannot be purchased with money; it cannot be taken for nothing.

Some think of happiness as a glamorous life of ease, luxury, and constant thrills; but true marriage is based on a happiness which is more than that, one which comes from giving, serving, sharing, sacrificing, and selflessness.

Two people coming from different backgrounds learn soon after the ceremony is performed that stark reality must be faced. There is no longer a life of fantasy or of make-believe; we must come out of the clouds and put our feet firmly on the earth. Responsibility must be assumed and new duties must be accepted. Some personal freedoms must be relinquished, and many adjustments, unselfish adjustments, must be made.

One comes to realize very soon after marriage that the spouse has weaknesses not previously revealed or discovered. The virtues which were constantly magnified during courtship now grow relatively smaller, and the weaknesses which seemed so small and insignificant during courtship now grow to sizable proportions. The hour has come for understanding hearts, for self-appraisal, and for good common sense, reasoning, and planning. . . .

There is a never-failing formula which will guarantee to every couple a happy and eternal marriage; but like all formulas, the principal ingredients must not be left out, reduced, or limited. The selection before courting and then the continued courting after the marriage process are equally important, but not more important than the marriage itself, the success of which depends upon the two individuals—not upon one, but upon two.

In a marriage commenced and based upon reasonable standards . . . , there are not combinations of power which can destroy it except the power within either or both of the spouses themselves; and they must assume the responsibility generally. Other people and agencies may influence for good or bad. Financial, social, political, and other situations may seem to have a bearing; but the marriage depends first and always on the two spouses who can always make their marriage successful and happy if they are determined, unselfish, and righteous.

The formula is simple; the ingredients are few, though there are many amplifications of each.

First, there must be the proper approach toward marriage, which contemplates the selection of a spouse who reaches as nearly as possible the pinnacle of perfection in all the matters which are of importance to the individuals. And then those two parties must come to the altar in the temple realizing that they must work hard toward this successful joint living.

Second, there must be a great unselfishness, forgetting self and directing all of the family life and all pertaining thereunto to the good of the family, subjugating self.

Third, there must be continued courting and expressions of affection, kindness, and consideration to keep love alive and growing.

Fourth, there must be a complete living of the commandments of the Lord as defined in the gospel of Jesus Christ.

With these ingredients properly mixed and continually kept functioning, it is quite impossible for unhappiness to come, misunderstandings to continue, or breaks to occur. Divorce attorneys would need to transfer to other fields and divorce courts would be padlocked.[15]

Unselfishness and observance of the commandments lead to success in marriage.

Sweethearts should realize before they take the vows that each must accept literally and fully that the good of the little new family must always be superior to the good of either spouse. Each party must eliminate the "I" and the "my" and substitute . . . "we" and "our." Every decision must take into consideration that there are two or more affected by it. As she approaches major decisions now, the wife will be concerned as to the effect they will have upon the parents, the children, the home, and their spiritual lives. The husband's choice of occupation, his social life, his friends, his every interest must now be considered in the light that he is only a part of a family, that the totalness of the group must be considered.[16]

For two people to work out their marriage together, they need a carefully worked out budget, made by both husband and wife, and then careful adherence to the same. Many marriages are defeated in the marketplace when unscheduled purchases are made. Remember that marriage is a partnership and is not likely to be successful otherwise.[17]

A marriage may not always be even and incidentless, but it can be one of great peace. A couple may have poverty, illness, disappointment, failures, and even death in the family, but even these will not rob them of their peace. The marriage can be a successful one so long as selfishness does not enter in. Troubles and problems will draw parents together into unbreakable unions if there is total unselfishness there. . . .

Love is like a flower, and, like the body, it needs constant feeding. The mortal body would soon be emaciated and die if there were not frequent feedings. The tender flower would wither and die without food and water. And so love, also, cannot be expected to last forever unless it is continually fed with portions of love, the manifestation of esteem and admiration, the expressions of gratitude, and the consideration of unselfishness.

Total unselfishness is sure to accomplish another factor in successful marriage. If one is forever seeking the interests, comforts, and happiness of the other, the love found in courtship and cemented in marriage will grow into mighty proportions. Many couples permit their marriages to become stale and their love to grow cold like old bread or worn-out jokes or cold gravy. Certainly the foods most vital for love are consideration, kindness, thoughtfulness, concern, expressions of affection, embraces of appreciation, admiration, pride, companionship, confidence, faith, partnership, equality, and interdependence.

To be really happy in marriage, one must have a continued faithful observance of the commandments of the Lord. No one, single or married, was ever sublimely happy unless he was righteous. There are temporary satisfactions and camouflaged situations for the moment, but permanent, total happiness can come only through cleanliness and worthiness. . . .

. . . If two people love the Lord more than their own lives and then love each other more than their own lives, working together in total harmony with the gospel program as their basic structure, they are sure to have this great happiness. When a husband and wife go together frequently to the holy temple, kneel in prayer together in their home with their family, go hand in hand to their religious meetings, keep their lives wholly chaste—mentally and physically—so that their whole thoughts and desires and loves are all centered in the one being, their companion, and both work together for the upbuilding of the kingdom of God, then happiness is at its pinnacle.[18]

Marriage requires total allegiance and total fidelity.

There are those married people who permit their eyes to wander and their hearts to become vagrant, who think it is not improper to flirt a little, to share their hearts and have desire for someone other than the wife or the husband. The Lord says in no uncertain terms: "Thou shalt love thy wife with all thy heart, and shalt cleave unto her and none else." (D&C 42:22.)

And, when the Lord says *all* thy heart, it allows for no sharing nor dividing nor depriving. And, to the woman it is paraphrased: "Thou shalt love thy husband with *all* thy heart and shalt cleave unto him and none else."

The words *none else* eliminate everyone and everything. The spouse then becomes preeminent in the life of the husband or wife, and neither social life nor occupational life nor political life nor any other interest nor person nor thing shall ever take precedence over the companion spouse. We sometimes find women who absorb and hover over the children at the expense of the husband, sometimes even estranging them from him.

The Lord says to them: "Thou shalt cleave unto *him* and none else."[19]

Frequently, people continue to cleave unto their mothers and their fathers and their chums. Sometimes mothers will not relinquish the hold they have had upon their children, and husbands as well as wives return to their mothers and fathers to obtain advice and counsel and to confide, whereas cleaving should be to the wife in most things, and all intimacies should be kept in great secrecy and privacy from others.[20]

Marriage presupposes total allegiance and total fidelity. Each spouse takes the partner with the understanding that he or she gives totally to the spouse all the heart, strength, loyalty, honor, and affection, with all dignity. Any divergence is sin; any sharing of the heart is transgression. As we should have "an eye single to the glory of God," so should we have an eye, an ear, a heart single to the marriage and the spouse and family.[21]

I plead with all those bound by marriage vows and covenants to make that marriage holy, keep it fresh, express affection meaningfully and sincerely and often.

Husbands, come home—body, spirit, mind, loyalties, interests, and affections—and love your companion in an holy and unbreakable relationship.

Wives, come home with all your interests, fidelity, yearnings, loyalties, and affections—working together to make your home a blessed heaven. Thus would you greatly please your Lord and Master and guarantee yourselves happiness supreme.[22]

Suggestions for Study and Teaching

Consider these ideas as you study the chapter or as you prepare to teach. For additional help, see pages v–ix.

- What do you think are some evidences that a marriage is honorable? happy? successful? Which of these evidences do you see reflected in President Kimball's relationship with his wife, Camilla? (See pages 189, 191.)

- Review the section that begins on page 191. What are some influences in the world today that you consider antimarriage? What effects are such attacks having? What can we do to "offset and neutralize" them, particularly in our homes?

- Which teachings of President Kimball about preparing for eternal marriage impress you the most and why? (See pages 193–95.) Which teachings might help those who are already married?

- President Kimball spoke of a "never-failing formula" for marriage (pages 196–97). If any one of the ingredients is missing, how might a marriage be influenced?

- President Kimball taught that spouses should "cleave" to each other and none else (pages 199–200). What can married couples do to ensure that outside commitments and interests do not interfere with their allegiance to each other?

Related Scriptures: Genesis 2:18, 21–24; 1 Corinthians 11:11; Ephesians 5:22–25; D&C 132:7–21

Notes

1. In "President Spencer W. Kimball: On the Occasion of His 80th Birthday," *Ensign,* Mar. 1975, 6, 8.

2. In Caroline Eyring Miner and Edward L. Kimball, *Camilla: A Biography of Camilla Eyring Kimball* (1980), viii.

3. *The Teachings of Spencer W. Kimball,* ed. Edward L. Kimball (1982), 310.

4. In Conference Report, Apr. 1979, 5–6, 7; or *Ensign,* May 1979, 6.

5. "Marriage Is Honorable," in *Speeches of the Year, 1973* (1974), 266.

6. *The Miracle of Forgiveness* (1969), 243.

7. "The Importance of Celestial Marriage," *Ensign,* Oct. 1979, 5.

8. "The Lord's Plan for Men and Women," *Ensign,* Oct. 1975, 4–5.

9. "Oneness in Marriage," *Ensign,* Mar. 1977, 3, 4.

10. In Conference Report, Stockholm Sweden Area Conference 1974, 10.

11. *The Miracle of Forgiveness,* 249.

12. *Ensign,* Oct. 1979, 4–5.

13. "The Marriage Decision," *Ensign,* Feb. 1975, 6.

14. "Marriage Is Honorable," 257.

15. *Ensign,* Mar. 1977, 3, 4.

16. *Ensign,* Mar. 1977, 4.

17. In Conference Report, Oct. 1975, 6; or *Ensign,* Nov. 1975, 6.

18. *Ensign,* Mar. 1977, 4, 5.

19. *Faith Precedes the Miracle* (1972), 142–43.

20. *Ensign,* Mar. 1977, 5.

21. *Faith Precedes the Miracle,* 143.

22. *Faith Precedes the Miracle,* 148.

President and Sister Kimball with members of their family.

Strengthening Our Families

We need to strengthen and protect our families
by teaching and living the gospel in our homes.

From the Life of Spencer W. Kimball

President Spencer W. Kimball often emphasized the need to strengthen families through gospel living in the home. Describing his own experiences, he said: "As a youth, and with my wife and children in our own home, I remember our beloved family activities. Heaven was in our home. When each person did something, whether it was sing a song, lead a game, recite an article of faith, tell a story, share a talent, or perform an assignment, there was growth and good feeling."[1]

President Kimball and his wife, Camilla, strengthened their children by teaching and encouraging them and then letting them take responsibility for their own choices. Their daughter, Olive Beth, recalled that they "guided rather than pushed us into the paths that they wanted us to go."[2]

President and Sister Kimball showed great love for each of their children. One son, Edward, said: "My father was always very affectionate. I knew he loved me." Edward recalled an experience he had when he attended a solemn assembly in the Salt Lake Temple: "There were thousands of men there. As the meeting ended, [my father] spotted me where I was singing in a chorus. On his way out, he came over, embraced and kissed me."[3]

Teachings of Spencer W. Kimball

The family is central to our Father's plan and is the foundation of society.

Family life is the best method for achieving happiness in this world, and it is a clear pattern given to us from the Lord about what is to be in the next world.[4]

The Lord organized the whole program in the beginning with a father who procreates, provides, and loves and directs, and a mother who conceives and bears and nurtures and feeds and trains. The Lord could have organized it otherwise but chose to have a unit with responsibility and purposeful associations where children train and discipline each other and come to love, honor, and appreciate each other. The family is the great plan of life as conceived and organized by our Father in heaven.[5]

The family is the basic unit of the kingdom of God on earth. The Church can be no healthier than its families.[6]

From the beginning, The Church of Jesus Christ of Latter-day Saints has emphasized family life. We have always understood that the foundations of the family, as an eternal unit, were laid even before this earth was created! Society without basic family life is without foundation and will disintegrate into nothingness. . . .

We of all people . . . should not be taken in by the specious arguments that the family unit is somehow tied to a particular phase of development a mortal society is going through. We are free to resist those moves which downplay the significance of the family and which play up the significance of selfish individualism. We know the family to be eternal. We know that when things go wrong in the family, things go wrong in every other institution in society. . . .

Our political institutions . . . cannot rescue us if our basic institution, the family, is not intact. Peace treaties cannot save us when there is hostility instead of love in the home. Unemployment programs cannot rescue us when many are no longer taught how to work or do not have the opportunity to work or the inclination, in some cases, to do so. Law enforcement cannot safeguard us if too many people are unwilling to discipline themselves or be disciplined.[7]

We have no choice . . . but to continue to hold up the ideal of the Latter-day Saint family. The fact that some do not now have the privilege of living in such a family is not reason enough to stop talking about it. We do discuss family life with sensitivity, however, realizing that many . . . do not presently have the privilege of belonging or contributing to such a family. But we cannot set aside this standard, because so many other things depend upon it.[8]

Parents need to build reservoirs of spiritual strength to sustain their children through life's experiences.

There are in our lives reservoirs of many kinds. Some reservoirs are to store water. Some are to store food, as we do in our family welfare program and as Joseph did in the land of Egypt during the seven years of plenty. There should also be reservoirs of knowledge to meet the future needs; reservoirs of courage to overcome the floods of fear that put uncertainty in lives; reservoirs of physical strength to help us meet the frequent burdens of work and illness; reservoirs of goodness; reservoirs of stamina; reservoirs of faith. Yes, especially reservoirs of faith so that when the world presses in upon us, we stand firm and strong; when the temptations of a decaying world about us draw on our energies, sap our spiritual vitality, and seek to pull us down, we need a storage of faith that can carry youth and later adults over the dull, the difficult, the terrifying moments, disappointments, disillusionments, and years of adversity, want, confusion, and frustration. . . .

I am grateful to my parents, for they made reservoirs for my brothers, my sisters, and me. The reservoirs were filled with prayer habits, study, activities, positive services, and truth and righteousness. Every morning and every night we knelt at our chairs by the table and prayed, taking turns. When I was married, the habit persisted, and our new family continued the practice.[9]

Home life, proper teaching in the home, parental guidance and leadership—these are the panacea for the ailments of the

*"Home life, proper teaching in the home, parental guidance and leadership—
these are the panacea for the ailments of the world and its children."*

world and its children. They are the cure for spiritual and emotional diseases and the remedy for its problems. Parents should not leave the training of children to others.

There seems to be a growing tendency to shift this responsibility from the home to outside influences such as the school and the church, and of greater concern, to various child-care agencies and institutions. Important as these outward influences may be, they never can adequately take the place of the influence of the mother and the father. Constant training, constant vigilance, companionship, and being watchmen of our own children are necessary in order to keep our homes intact and to bless our children in the Lord's own way.[10]

The Church auxiliaries are very important, and we should all partake of the blessings they offer. But we should never, never allow them to replace parents, to relieve parents of the responsibility to teach their children the gospel of Jesus Christ.[11]

Auxiliary leaders and teachers of youth should ask, how can I help these young people to love and obey their parents, honor them, and be supportive of their family responsibilities? How can we schedule meetings, practices, and activities to avoid disrupting home relationships and responsibilities, and to allow time for family activities?

Our commitment to home-centered gospel living should become the clear message of every priesthood and auxiliary program, reducing, where necessary, some of the optional activities that may detract from proper focus on the family and the home.[12]

Only by properly planning and charting our family life can we guide our children and keep them free from the pitfalls that lead to sin and destruction, and put them on the pathway to happiness and exaltation. In this, nothing is more powerful than the example of their own parents and the influence of their home life. Our children's lives will be much the same as they see in their own homes as they are growing to manhood and womanhood. We should therefore chart our course along the pathway which we would want our children to follow.[13]

The child will carry into his own life much that he sees in his family home life. If he sees his parents going to the temple frequently, he will begin to plan a temple life. If he is taught to pray for the missionaries, he will gradually gravitate toward the missionary program. Now, this is very simple, but it is the way of life. And we promise you that your children will bring you honor and glory as you give them proper example and training.[14]

I have sometimes seen children of good families rebel, resist, stray, sin, and even actually fight God. In this they bring sorrow to their parents, who have done their best . . . to teach and live as examples. But I have repeatedly seen many of these same children, after years of wandering, mellow, realize what they have been missing, repent, and make great contribution to the spiritual life of their community. The reason I believe this can take place is that, despite all the adverse winds to which these people have been subjected, they have been influenced still more, and much more than they realized, by the current of life in the homes in which they were reared. When, in later years, they feel a longing to recreate in their own families the same atmosphere they enjoyed as children, they are likely to turn to the faith that gave meaning to their parents' lives.[15]

Fathers and mothers, your foremost responsibility is your family. By working together you can have the kind of home the Lord expects you to have. By showing love and consideration for one another and for your children, you can build a reservoir of spiritual strength that will never run dry.[16]

We need to fortify our families against the evils around us.

The time will come when only those who believe deeply and actively in the family will be able to preserve their families in the midst of the gathering evil around us.[17]

The evil one knows where to attack. He is going to attack the home. He is going to destroy the family. That's what he wants to do. . . . Let us make up our minds he will not do it in our families.[18]

We need continually to fortify our homes and families and defend them against the onslaught of evils such as divorce, broken families, brutality, and abuse, especially of wives and children. We need to constantly guard against immorality, pornography, and sexual permissiveness that would destroy the purity of the family members, young and old. . . .

. . . We find these evil forces almost everywhere we go. Exposure is almost constant. We track them into the home from the school, from the playground, from the theater, the office, and the marketplace. There are but few places we go in our everyday world where we can escape them.

What then must be our service? What must we do? We must be constantly alert to their evil presence in our homes and destroy them as we would the germs and filth of disease. We must hunt them from the closets of our minds, freeing ourselves of such worldliness, quenching the embers of wickedness before they become destructive flames. How do we do this?

If we would escape those deadly thrusts of the evil one and keep our homes and families free and solidly fortified against all destructive influences so rampant about us, we must have the

Through "regular, earnest prayer," the home becomes
"a place where reliance on the Lord is a matter of common experience."

help of the very founder and organizer of this family plan—the Creator himself. There is only one sure way and that is through the gospel of the Lord Jesus Christ and being obedient to its profound and inspired teachings. Surely we must be made to realize that the purchase price of a family hearth free of such evil influences is the keeping of the commandments of God.[19]

As parents read the newspapers and magazines and see what the world is trying to teach their children, they should become all the more determined that their children not be damaged by such sin and error. Parents should then provide the home life, the discipline, and the training that will offset and neutralize the evil that is being done in the world. As children learn of the ugly things in the world, they must also learn of the good things in the world and the proper responses and proper attitudes.[20]

Some years ago we visited a country where strange ideologies were taught and "pernicious doctrines" were promulgated every day in the schools and in the captive press. Every day the children listened to the doctrines, philosophies, and ideals their teachers related.

Someone said that "constant dripping will wear away the hardest stone." This I knew, so I asked about the children: "Do they retain their faith? Are they not overcome by the constant pressure of their teachers? How can you be sure they will not leave the simple faith in God?"

The answer amounted to saying "We mend the damaged reservoir each night. We teach our children positive righteousness so that the false philosophies do not take hold. Our children are growing up in faith and righteousness in spite of the almost overwhelming pressures from outside."

Even cracked dams can be mended and saved, and sandbags can hold back the flood. And reiterated truth, renewed prayer, gospel teachings, expression of love, and parental interest can save the child and keep him on the right path.[21]

Home is where spirituality should be taught and nurtured.

A true Latter-day Saint home is a haven against the storms and struggles of life. Spirituality is born and nurtured by daily prayer, scripture study, home gospel discussions and related activities, home evenings, family councils, working and playing together, serving each other, and sharing the gospel with those around us. Spirituality is also nurtured in our actions of patience, kindness, and forgiveness toward each other and in our applying gospel principles in the family circle. Home is where we become experts and scholars in gospel righteousness, learning and living gospel truths together.[22]

The home should be a place where reliance on the Lord is a matter of common experience, not reserved for special occasions. One way of establishing that is by regular, earnest prayer. It is not enough just to pray. It is essential that we really speak to the Lord, having faith that he will reveal to us as parents what we need to know and do for the welfare of our families.[23]

Scripture study as individuals and as a family is most fundamental to learning the gospel. Daily reading of the scriptures and discussing them together has long been suggested as a powerful tool against ignorance and the temptations of Satan. This practice will produce great happiness and will help family members love the Lord and his goodness.

Concerning the governing of our families, we have been correctly taught that the family council is the most basic council of the Church. Under the direction of the father and mother, who should also counsel together, family councils may discuss family matters, discuss family finances, make plans, and support and strengthen family members.[24]

Regarding our home evenings, an evening home with the family or an evening out to some place of interest with your family only partly solves the need of the home evening. Basically important is the teaching of the children the way of life that is vitally important. Merely going to a show or a party together, or fishing, only half satisfies the real need, but to stay home and teach the children the gospel, the scriptures, and love for each other and love for their parents is most important.[25]

By committing ourselves to having the regular and inspirational family home evening and by carefully planning the content of that evening, we are sending a signal to our children which they will remember forevermore. When thus we give our children of our own time, we are giving of our presence, a gift that is always noticed.[26]

I like to compare the home evening, family prayer, and other associated activities of the Church for the saving of the family, when they are conscientiously carried out, with an umbrella. If the umbrella is not opened up, it is little more than a cane and can give little protection from the storms of nature. Likewise, God-given plans are of little value unless they are used.

The umbrella spread out makes the silken material taut. When the rain falls, it runs off; when the snow falls, it slides off; when the hail comes, it bounces off; when the wind blows, it is diverted around the umbrella. And in like manner, this spiritual umbrella wards off the foes of ignorance, superstition, skepticism, apostasy, immorality, and other forms of godlessness.

It is my prayer that we shall all spread our spiritual umbrellas for protection of our families.[27]

We should love our children as God loves us.

God is our Father. He loves us. He spends much energy trying to train us, and we should follow His example and love intensely our own children and rear them in righteousness.[28]

How long has it been since you took your children, whatever their size, in your arms and told them that you love them and are glad that they can be yours forever?[29]

Oh, brothers and sisters, *families can be forever!* Do not let the lures of the moment draw you away from them! *Divinity, eternity,* and *family*—they go together, hand in hand, and so must we![30]

Suggestions for Study and Teaching

Consider these ideas as you study the chapter or as you prepare to teach. For additional help, see pages v–ix.

- Referring to his own family life, President Kimball recalled, "Heaven was in our home" (page 203). How can we create a heavenly atmosphere in our homes? In what ways can home life prepare us for eternal life?

- What are some of the most important things parents can do to provide reservoirs of spiritual strength for their children? (For some examples, see pages 205–11.)

- What are the risks of parents leaving the training of children to others? What Church resources are there to help parents teach children? In what ways can Church leaders and teachers support parents? (For some examples, see pages 206–7.)

- Consider President Kimball's counsel on pages 210–12. What evidence have you seen that family prayer, family scripture study, family councils, and family home evening really make a difference?

• Read the last paragraph on page 203. Then ponder President Kimball's question on page 212: "How long has it been since you took your children, whatever their size, in your arms and told them that you love them and are glad that they can be yours forever?"

Related Scriptures: Deuteronomy 6:3–7; 2 Nephi 25:26; Mosiah 4:14–15; D&C 68:25–28

Notes

1. "Therefore I Was Taught," *Ensign,* Jan. 1982, 3.
2. Olive Beth Mack, "How a Daughter Sees Her Father, the Prophet," devotional address, Salt Lake Institute of Religion, Apr. 9, 1976, 8.
3. In Gerry Avant, "As Father, Prophet Made Time Count," *Church News,* June 11, 1977, 5.
4. "Privileges and Responsibilities of Sisters," *Ensign,* Nov. 1978, 103.
5. In Conference Report, Apr. 1973, 151; or *Ensign,* July 1973, 15.
6. In Conference Report, Apr. 1978, 67; or *Ensign,* May 1978, 45.
7. In Conference Report, Oct. 1980, 3, 4; or *Ensign,* Nov. 1980, 4, 5.
8. *Ensign,* Nov. 1978, 103.
9. *Faith Precedes the Miracle* (1972), 110–11.
10. In Conference Report, Apr. 1979, 4–5; or *Ensign,* May 1979, 5.
11. "The Example of Abraham," *Ensign,* June 1975, 5.
12. "Living the Gospel in the Home," *Ensign,* May 1978, 101.
13. *The Miracle of Forgiveness* (1969), 258–59.
14. In Conference Report, Seoul Korea Area Conference 1975, 35.
15. In Conference Report, Oct. 1974, 160; or *Ensign,* Nov. 1974, 111.
16. *Ensign,* June 1975, 5.
17. In Conference Report, Oct. 1980, 3; or *Ensign,* Nov. 1980, 4.
18. In Conference Report, Oct. 1975, 165; or *Ensign,* Nov. 1975, 111.
19. In Conference Report, Apr. 1979, 5; or *Ensign,* May 1979, 5, 6.
20. "Train Up a Child," *Ensign,* Apr. 1978, 4.
21. *Faith Precedes the Miracle,* 113–14.
22. *Ensign,* Jan. 1982, 3.
23. In Conference Report, Oct. 1974, 161–62; or *Ensign,* Nov. 1974, 113.
24. *Ensign,* Jan. 1982, 4.
25. In Conference Report, Oct. 1977, 4; or *Ensign,* Nov. 1977, 4.
26. In Conference Report, Apr. 1978, 5; or *Ensign,* May 1978, 5.
27. In Conference Report, Oct. 1969, 23; or *Improvement Era,* Dec. 1969, 50–51.
28. *Ensign,* Apr. 1978, 5.
29. In Conference Report, Oct. 1974, 161; or *Ensign,* Nov. 1974, 112–13.
30. In Conference Report, Oct. 1980, 5; or *Ensign,* Nov. 1980, 5.

The Women of the Church

Righteous women who fulfill the tremendous responsibilities given to them by God are a great blessing to their families, to the Church, and to the world.

From the Life of Spencer W. Kimball

"I marvel at the faithfulness of so many of our sisters and their unswerving devotion to the cause of righteousness," wrote President Spencer W. Kimball. He then related the following:

"My own wonderful mother's journal records a lifetime of being grateful for the opportunity to serve and sorry only that she couldn't do more. I smiled when I recently read one entry dated January 16, 1900. She was serving as first counselor in our Relief Society in Thatcher, Arizona, and the presidency went to a sister's home where a sick baby had prevented the mother from doing her sewing. Mother took her machine, a picnic lunch, her baby, and a high chair, and they began work. She wrote that night, we 'made four aprons, four pairs of pants and started a shirt for one of the boys.' They had to stop at 4 P.M. to go to a funeral, so we 'did not get any more than that done.' I would have been impressed by such achievement, rather than thinking, 'Well, that's not much.'

"Then two days later, the Relief Society met in our home for a work meeting. 'We had quite a turnout,' wrote my mother, and 'accomplished considerable.' Then after that work meeting, she went uncomplainingly to a board meeting.

"That's the kind of home I was born in, one conducted by a woman who breathed service in all her actions. That is the kind of home my wife has made. That is the kind of home that thousands of wonderful women all over the Church make."[1]

President Kimball taught the importance that all righteous women have in Heavenly Father's plan for His children. He said: "Someday, when the whole story of this and previous dispensations is told, it will be filled with courageous stories of our women, of their wisdom and their devotion, their courage, for one senses that perhaps, just as women were the first at the sepulchre of the Lord Jesus Christ after his resurrection, our righteous women have so often been instinctively sensitive to things of eternal consequence."[2]

Teachings of Spencer W. Kimball

Having been given different responsibilities, women and men are to work together in a partnership of equality and respect.

The scriptures and the prophets have taught us clearly that God, who is perfect in his attribute of justice, "is no respecter of persons" (Acts 10:34). . . . We had full equality as his spirit children. We have equality as recipients of God's perfected love for each of us. The late Elder John A. Widtsoe wrote:

"The place of woman in the Church is to walk beside the man, not in front of him nor behind him. In the Church there is full equality between man and woman. The gospel . . . was devised by the Lord for men and women alike" (*Improvement Era,* Mar. 1942, p. 161).

Within those great assurances, however, our roles and assignments differ. These are eternal differences—with women being given many tremendous responsibilities of motherhood and sisterhood and men being given the tremendous responsibilities of fatherhood and the priesthood—but the man is not without the woman nor the woman without the man in the Lord (see 1 Cor. 11:11). Both a righteous man and a righteous woman are a blessing to all those their lives touch.

Remember, in the world before we came here, faithful women were given certain assignments while faithful men were foreordained to certain priesthood tasks. While we do not now

President Spencer W. Kimball and his wife, Camilla.

remember the particulars, this does not alter the glorious reality of what we once agreed to.[3]

Sometimes we hear disturbing reports about how sisters are treated. Perhaps when this happens, it is a result of insensitivity and thoughtlessness, but it should not be, brethren. The women of this Church have work to do which, though different, is equally as important as the work that we do. Their work is, in fact, the same basic work that we are asked to do—even though our roles and assignments differ. . . .

Our sisters do not wish to be indulged or to be treated condescendingly; they desire to be respected and revered as our sisters and our equals. I mention all these things, my brethren, not because the doctrines or the teachings of the Church regarding women are in any doubt, but because in some situations our behavior is of doubtful quality.[4]

The Relief Society is the Lord's organization for women. It complements the priesthood training given to the brethren. There is a power in this organization that has not yet been fully exercised to strengthen the homes of Zion and build the Kingdom of God. . . .

. . . In his wisdom and mercy, our Father made men and women dependent on each other for the full flowering of their potential. Because their natures are somewhat different, they can complement each other; because they are in many ways alike, they can understand each other. Let neither envy the other for their differences; let both discern what is superficial and what is beautifully basic in those differences, and act accordingly. And may the brotherhood of the priesthood and the sisterhood of the Relief Society be a blessing in the lives of all the members of this great Church, as we help each other along the path to perfection.[5]

God has called women to help enrich, protect, and guard the home and family.

To be a righteous woman is a glorious thing in any age. To be a righteous woman during the winding up scenes on this earth, before the second coming of our Savior, is an especially noble calling. The righteous woman's strength and influence today can be tenfold what it might be in more tranquil times. She has been placed here to help to enrich, to protect, and to guard the home— which is society's basic and most noble institution. Other institutions in society may falter and even fail, but the righteous woman can help to save the home, which may be the last and only sanctuary some mortals know in the midst of storm and strife.[6]

You read the papers, you watch television, you hear the radio, you read books and magazines, and much that comes to your consciousness is designed to lead you astray. . . . Some of the things they are telling you these days are: it is not necessary to marry; it is not necessary to marry to have children; it is not necessary to have children; you may have all the worldly pleasures without these obligations and responsibilities. . . . There are [many] ways to give you this loosely held, so-called freedom. They are telling you that you are manacled [chained] to your homes, to your husbands, to your children, to your housework. They are talking and writing to you about a freedom they know nothing about. . . .

Eve, so recently from the eternal throne, seemed to understand the way of life, for she was happy—happy!—that they had eaten the forbidden fruit. . . . Our beloved mother Eve began the human race with gladness, wanting children, glad for the joy that they would bring to her, willing to assume the problems connected with a family, but also the joys. . . .

Mothers have a sacred role. They are partners with God, as well as with their own husbands, first in giving birth to the Lord's spirit children and then in rearing those children so they will serve the Lord and keep his commandments. . . . Motherhood is a holy calling, a sacred dedication for carrying out the Lord's work, a consecration and devotion to the rearing and fostering, the nurturing of body, mind, and spirit of those who kept their first estate and who came to this earth for their second estate to learn and be tested and to work toward godhood.[7]

Too many women spend their time in socializing, in politicking, in public services when they should be home to teach and train and receive and love their children into security.[8]

No greater honor could be given to a woman than to assist in [God's] divine plan. I wish to say without equivocation that a woman will find no greater satisfaction and joy and peace and make no greater contribution to mankind than in being a wise and worthy woman and raising good children.[9]

"Motherhood is a holy calling, a sacred dedication for carrying out the Lord's work."

The Lord has promised the blessings of eternal family life to all faithful women.

Some of you have lost your husbands through death, others through divorce. Some of you have not yet had the great privilege of marriage. But, on the scale of eternity, the missing of these blessings "shall be but a small moment" (see D&C 121:7). . . .

Remember, too, as we focus on the glories and importance of family life here, that all of us belong to the eternal family of our Father in Heaven.

Be assured, too, that all faithful sisters, who, through no fault of their own, do not have the privilege during their second estate of being sealed to a worthy man, will have that blessing in eternity. On occasions when you ache for that acceptance and affection which belong to family life on earth, please know that our Father in Heaven is aware of your anguish, and that one day he will bless you beyond your capacity to express.

Sometimes to be tested and proved requires that we be temporarily deprived—but righteous women and men will one day receive *all*—think of it, sisters—*all* that our Father has! It is not only worth waiting for; it is worth living for!

Meanwhile, one does not need to be married or a mother in order to keep the first and second great commandments—those of loving God and our fellowmen—on which Jesus said hang all the law and all the prophets.[10]

Those of you who do not now experience the traditional woman's role, not by choice, but for reasons beyond control, can still do so much to help others.[11]

Each woman should seek to fulfill her divine potential.

We delight and marvel in the appropriate development and expressions of our sisters' many talents.[12]

We encourage all our sisters to take advantage of their opportunities to receive light and knowledge in school, in personal study, and in Relief Society.[13]

You can set your goals, young women, to make you reach and strain. Keep striving for them. Be prayerful and humble in seeking wisdom and knowledge. You are in the time of your life for studying and preparing. Learn all you can. Growth comes from setting your goals high and reaching for the stars.[14]

Every girl, and I say every girl, should prepare herself for marriage and for domestic responsibilities. You are not reading that in the magazines today, but it's true nevertheless. She should be encouraged to be proud to prepare for true womanly service. She should become skilled in things that are useful and enriching to her family life. She should develop her talents, strengthen her knowledge and testimony of the gospel, and be eager to serve others. Some girls may be called on full-time missions, and all will have the opportunity to be highly useful in the kingdom of God if they prepare themselves. . . . We want our women to be well educated, for children may not recover from the ignorance of their mothers.[15]

We wish you to pursue and to achieve that education . . . which will fit you for eternity *as well as* for full service in mortality. In addition to those basic and vital skills which go with homemaking, there are other skills which can be appropriately cultivated and which will increase your effectiveness in the home, in the Church, and in the community.

Again, you must be wise in the choices that you make, but we do not desire the women of the Church to be uninformed or ineffective. You will be better mothers and wives, both in this life and in eternity, if you sharpen the skills you have been given and use the talents with which God has blessed you.[16]

We are interested in our sisters having everything that is good. We believe in having all these blessings—culture, refinement, education, knowledge, perfection—so that the mothers of our children may be able to rear and train them in righteousness.[17]

I stress again the deep need each woman has to study the scriptures. We want our homes to be blessed with sister scriptorians—whether you are single or married, young or old, widowed or living in a family.

Regardless of your particular circumstances, as you become more and more familiar with the truths of the scriptures, you will be more and more effective in keeping the second great commandment, to love your neighbor as yourself. Become scholars of the scriptures—not to put others down, but to lift them up! After all, who has any greater need to "treasure up" the truths of the gospel (on which they may call in their moments of need) than do women and mothers who do so much nurturing and teaching?

Seek excellence in all your righteous endeavors, and in all aspects of your lives.

Bear in mind, dear sisters, that the eternal blessings which are yours through membership in The Church of Jesus Christ of Latter-day Saints are far, far greater than any other blessings you could possibly receive. No greater recognition can come to you in this world than to be known as a woman of God. No greater status can be conferred upon you than being a daughter of God who experiences true sisterhood, wifehood, and motherhood, or other tasks which influence lives for good. . . .

. . . All of you need to drink in deeply the gospel truths about the eternal nature of your individual identity and the uniqueness of your personality. You need, more and more, to feel the perfect love which our Father in Heaven has for you and to sense the value he places upon you as an individual. Ponder upon these great truths, especially in those moments when (in the stillness of such anxiety as you may experience as an individual) you might otherwise wonder and be perplexed. . . .

There is no greater and more glorious set of promises given to women than those which come through the gospel and the Church of Jesus Christ. Where else can you learn who you really are? Where else can you be given the necessary explanations and assurances about the nature of life? From what other source can you learn about your own uniqueness and identity? From whom else could you learn of our Father in Heaven's glorious plan of happiness?[18]

Righteous women can be great contributors to the world and to the kingdom of God.

There has never been a time in the world when the role of woman has been more confused. There has never been a time in the Church when women are able to do more to show what their true role in the world can and ought to be. The impact and influence of women and mothers on our world is most important. The thought that "the hand that rocks the cradle rules the world" is more viable today than ever before.[19]

How special it is for Latter-day Saint women to be given the lofty assignments they have been given by our Father in Heaven, especially those of you who have been privileged to be born in this part of this last dispensation. Let other women pursue heedlessly . . . their selfish interests. You can be a much needed force for love and truth and righteousness on this planet. . . .

. . . My dear sisters, may I suggest to you something that has not been said before or at least in quite this way. Much of the

"There is no greater and more glorious set of promises given to women than those which come through the gospel and the Church of Jesus Christ."

major growth that is coming to the Church in the last days will come because many of the good women of the world (in whom there is often such an inner sense of spirituality) will be drawn to the Church in large numbers. This will happen to the degree that the women of the Church reflect righteousness and articulateness in their lives and to the degree that the women of the Church are seen as distinct and different—in happy ways—from the women of the world. . . . Thus it will be that female exemplars of the Church will be a significant force in both the numerical and the spiritual growth of the Church in the last days. . . .

We love you sisters. We have confidence in you. We rejoice in your devotion. We are greatly heartened by your presence . . . in this portion of this dispensation wherein your talents and spiritual strength are so desperately needed.[20]

Suggestions for Study and Teaching

Consider these ideas as you study the chapter or as you prepare to teach. For additional help, see pages v–ix.

- Review the story on page 214 and the first paragraph on page 215. What inspiring stories come to mind concerning women in your family and in the Church?

- Study the third full paragraph on page 217. In light of their different natures and responsibilities, how can men and women help each other? How should they work in partnership in the family? in the Church?

- Why is being a righteous woman today an especially important and "noble calling"? (page 217). In what ways is the world trying to divert women from this calling? How can we help young men and young women appreciate this noble calling?

- As you read page 219 and the first three paragraphs on page 220, ponder what these teachings say about Heavenly Father's love for all His children.

- What are some ways in which women of the Church can fulfill their divine potential? (See pages 220–22.) How can the men of the Church support the efforts of the women of the Church? (See pages 216–17.)

- Ponder the paragraph that begins at the bottom of page 222. What impresses you about this statement? How is this prophecy about the growth of the Church being fulfilled today?

Related Scriptures: Proverbs 31:10–31; Ephesians 5:22–29; Alma 56:41–48; D&C 25:1, 5–10; Moses 3:18, 21–25

Notes

1. "Relief Society—Its Promise and Potential," *Ensign,* Mar. 1976, 2, 4.
2. In Conference Report, Apr. 1978, 6; or *Ensign,* May 1978, 5.
3. "The Role of Righteous Women," *Ensign,* Nov. 1979, 102.
4. In Conference Report, Oct. 1979, 71–72; or *Ensign,* Nov. 1979, 49.
5. "Relief Society—Its Promise and Potential," *Ensign,* Mar. 1976, 4, 5.
6. "Privileges and Responsibilities of Sisters," *Ensign,* Nov. 1978, 103.
7. "The Blessings and Responsibilities of Womanhood," *Ensign,* Mar. 1976, 71, 72–73.
8. *The Teachings of Spencer W. Kimball,* ed. Edward L. Kimball (1982), 319.
9. "Sisters, Seek Everything That Is Good," *Ensign,* Mar. 1979, 4.
10. *Ensign,* Nov. 1979, 102–3.

11. *My Beloved Sisters* (1979), 11.
12. In Conference Report, Apr. 1978, 6; or *Ensign,* May 1978, 6.
13. "Relief Society—Its Promise and Potential," *Ensign,* Mar. 1976, 4.
14. *Ensign,* Nov. 1978, 103.
15. *Men of Example* (pamphlet, 1975), 9, 10.
16. *Ensign,* Nov. 1979, 103.
17. *Ensign,* Mar. 1979, 4.
18. *Ensign,* Nov. 1979, 102, 103.
19. Introduction to *Woman* (1979), 1.
20. *Ensign,* Nov. 1979, 103–4.

"That morning in the grove in New York when the Father and Son came to [Joseph Smith] was perhaps the greatest revelation ever given to the world."

The Prophet Joseph Smith

Joseph Smith was an instrument in the Lord's hands in restoring all that had been lost during centuries of spiritual darkness.

From the Life of Spencer W. Kimball

During the 1970s, President Spencer W. Kimball traveled with other Church leaders all over the world to meet with members in area conferences. At one of these conferences, he expressed gratitude for the legacy of the Prophet Joseph Smith:

"Because a boy fourteen years old went out in the woods to pray in New York, all of these hundreds of thousands of people come to area conferences. Because the fourteen-year-old boy went out in the woods to pray, having read in the scriptures, 'If any of you lack wisdom, let him ask of God' (James 1:5), because he did live the revelations from on high, we have The Church of Jesus Christ of Latter-day Saints. We have all of the blessings that can make us the happiest people in the whole world, because a boy of fourteen went out into the woods to pray. I am grateful that Joseph found his way into the woods, and I am grateful that he knew what he was doing and that he was serious-minded enough that he could take the word of the Lord as it came to him and enlarge upon it and build this kingdom."[1]

On another occasion, President Kimball described feelings he had when viewing a portrait of the Prophet Joseph Smith found in a room of the Salt Lake Temple: "I look over on the front wall, and there is Joseph Smith, and I think what a great, great prophet Joseph Smith was. He was no common man. . . . I think of all of his persecutions and the suffering that he went through. I think of all the revelations that came from heaven to him which he gave to us. And then I gain new strength again."[2]

Teachings of Spencer W. Kimball

Joseph Smith was called as a prophet according to the foreknowledge and wisdom of God.

Joseph Smith was prepared for centuries before he was born. He was even named Joseph before he was ever born [see 2 Nephi 3:14–15]. His mission was to come to the earth at the proper time in these last days to open the doors to the great world, to give the gospel to them, to give the priesthood to them, and to give hope to them as they look forward to eternal life.[3]

Joseph Smith, the prophet of the Lord, was set apart, called before he was born, called long ages ago, to come forth at this time and to . . . open the world to the preaching of the true and living gospel.

. . . Joseph Smith came into this world that was crying for help; for hundreds of years it had been helpless. . . . It had been hundreds and hundreds of years since there had been a prophet. . . . And so it was time.[4]

Surely God our Father and his Son Jesus Christ, who appeared to an Aaronic Priesthood-age youth, Joseph Smith, to give that lad instructions for all mankind, did not simply make a random appearance to a person on this planet. Rather, the Lord says that this appearance, which was precisely planned, occurred because ". . . I the Lord, knowing the calamity which should come upon the inhabitants of the earth, called upon my servant Joseph Smith, Jun., and spake unto him from heaven, and gave him commandments." (D&C 1:17.)

God does nothing by chance, but always by design as a loving father.[5]

Joseph Smith's First Vision opened a new dispensation of divine revelation.

Under special need, at special times, under proper circumstances, God reveals himself to men who are prepared for such manifestations. And since God is the same yesterday, today, and forever, the heavens cannot be closed except as men lock them against themselves with disbelief.

In our own dispensation came [such a] grand experience. The need was imperative; an apostasy had covered the earth and gross darkness the people, and the minds of men were clouded and light had been obscured in darkness [see Isaiah 60:2]. The time had come. Religious liberty would protect the seed until it could germinate and grow. And the individual was prepared in the person of a youth, clean and open minded, who had such implicit faith in the response of God that the heavens could not remain as iron and the earth as brass as they had been for many centuries [see Leviticus 26:19].

This budding prophet had no preconceived false notions and beliefs. He was not steeped in the traditions and legends and superstitions and fables of the centuries. He had nothing to unlearn. He prayed for knowledge and direction. The powers of darkness preceded the light. When he knelt in solitude in the silent forest, his earnest prayer brought on a battle royal that threatened his destruction. For centuries, Lucifer with unlimited dominion had fettered men's minds and could ill-afford to lose his satanic hold. This threatened his unlimited dominion. Let Joseph Smith tell his own story:

". . . I was seized upon by some power which entirely overcame me . . . to bind my tongue. . . . Thick darkness gathered around me, and it seemed to me for a time as if I were doomed to sudden destruction.

". . . at the very moment when I was ready to . . . abandon myself to destruction—not to an imaginary ruin, but to the power of some actual being from the unseen world . . . I saw a pillar of light exactly over my head, above the brightness of the sun. . . .

". . . I found myself delivered from the enemy which held me bound. When the light rested upon me I saw two Personages, whose brightness and glory defy all description, standing above me in the air. One of them spake unto me, calling me by name and said, pointing to the other—*This is My Beloved Son. Hear Him!*" [Joseph Smith—History 1:15–17.][6]

The heavens which had been closed in large measure for many centuries were now opened. The voices that had been still and subdued and unheard through many centuries now began to speak. The revelation that had been well-nigh obliterated and reasoned out of existence was again available. . . .

A new truth, a concept not understood by the myriads of people on the earth, burst forth, and in that moment there was only one man on the face of the whole earth who knew with absolute assurance that God was a personal being, that the Father and Son were separate individuals with [glorified] bodies of flesh and bones [and that he] had been created in their image. As the Son was in the image of his Father, the Father God was the same kind of image as the Son.[7]

Nothing short of this total vision to Joseph could have served the purpose to clear away the mists of the centuries. Merely an impression, a hidden voice, a dream could [not] have dispelled the old vagaries and misconceptions.[8]

This young boy was entrusted with the greatest block of knowledge known to men. Remember, that spring morning not one of all the people in the world had absolute knowledge of God. There were many good people, but they had all walked in spiritual darkness these many centuries. But here was a boy who knew. . . .

Joseph knew, as no other soul living, these absolutes:

He knew that God lives, that He is a [glorified] person with flesh and bones and personality, like us or we like Him, in His image.

He knew that the long-heralded trinity of three Gods in one was a myth, a deception. He knew that the Father and the Son were two distinct beings with form, voices, and . . . personalities.

He knew that the gospel was not on the earth, for by the Deities he had learned it, and the true Church was absent from the earth, for the God of heaven and earth had so informed him.[9]

That morning in the grove in New York when the Father and Son came to him was perhaps the greatest revelation ever given to the world.[10]

As part of the Restoration, the Prophet Joseph Smith and Oliver Cowdery received the Aaronic Priesthood from the resurrected John the Baptist.

Joseph Smith was the Lord's instrument in restoring the gospel.

The young prophet was advised that he would be an instrument in the hands of the Lord in restoring the eternal gospel with all that was lost in early centuries. Then these visions and revelations continued on through years in which the voice of Jehovah was heard again and again, restoring to the earth through this young prophet the truths of the gospel, the priesthood of God, the apostleship, the authorities and powers, the organization of the Church, so that again the revelations and the everlasting truths are upon the earth and available to all men who will accept them.[11]

The prophet Moroni appeared unto Joseph and spent long hours explaining the peopling of the American continents by the Lehites and also the Book of Mormon, which would be unearthed and translated. . . . This record, the Book of Mormon, would help to establish the divinity of the Lord Jesus Christ.[12]

Through the gift and power of God, [Joseph] translated that record, now known as the Book of Mormon.[13]

The gospel was revealed, line upon line and precept upon precept, and truths were restored, and power was given and authority was revealed, and gradually enough light and enough people were there for the organization of this kingdom of God which Daniel saw two and a half millennia ago [see Daniel 2:44–45].[14]

After long centuries of spiritual darkness, the light began to shine when revelation opened up this dispensation. The Prophet Joseph Smith received the revelations from the Lord bringing back to the earth that which was lost—the priesthood of God—the authority, the power, the right to administer ordinances, and the continuation of the revelations of the Lord to his people here on the earth.[15]

The power was given to Joseph Smith, whereby he could seal on earth and it would be sealed in heaven. Those keys have been handed down from president to president.[16]

Joseph Smith sealed his testimony with his blood.

The details of the life of Joseph Smith are familiar to us. He announced at once his glorious vision of the Father and the Son and was immediately oppressed and persecuted. Modern scribes and Pharisees have published libelous books and articles by the hundreds, imprisoned him . . . , tarred and feathered him, shot at him, and done everything in their power to destroy him. In spite of their every effort to take his life, he survived through more than a score of years of bitter and violent persecution to fill his mission until his hour should come.

Twenty-four years of hell he suffered, but also twenty-four years of ecstasy he enjoyed in converse with God and other immortals! His mission was accomplished—heaven and earth were linked again; the Church was organized; Brigham Young and other great leaders were trained to carry on; and he had conferred upon the heads of the Twelve every key and power belonging to the apostleship which he himself held, and he had said to them: "I have laid the foundations and you must build thereon, for upon your shoulders the kingdom rests."

The martyrdom of Joseph Smith, who was killed with his brother Hyrum in 1844, "is another of the infallible proofs of the divinity of the gospel of Jesus Christ."

And his hour had come to seal with his blood his testimony, so often borne to multitudes of friends and foes. . . .

. . . Though he hoped and prayed that the cup could pass, he knew it was inevitable. He said: "I am going like a lamb to the slaughter." [See D&C 135:4.] . . .

And a slaughter it was! The shots rang out! And freely flowed the blood of martyrs, for Hyrum, his older brother, had chosen to remain with him. This precious blood soaked into the earth, sealing an undying and unanswerable testimony which continued to ring in minds and hearts.[17]

Jesus sealed his testimony with his blood. Stephen did. Joseph Smith has now sealed his testimony with blood and died as a young man to say unto all the world that the plates from which the Book of Mormon came forth were found on a hill near Palmyra in the state of New York. And thus, through understanding of this book and the Holy Bible, the gospel of Jesus Christ, through administration of his angels, was again restored to the earth.[18]

Joseph was protected and his life saved in every instance of persecution until his work was finished and he had done his part in the restoration of the gospel and the priesthood and all other keys of the dispensation, and until the organization of the kingdom was effected. He could not be killed before that time, though all hell raged against him. He wanted to live. Life was sweet to him. It held promise of sweet associations with his family, his brethren, and the satisfaction of seeing the work blossom into a full-blown flower. But his work was done; other strong leaders could now carry on; he was needed in other fields. Only in his thirties, a very young man, he died, and commenced his work in other realms.[19]

"Mormonism will fail if we kill their prophet," they said . . . as they murdered Joseph Smith in cold blood. Undoubtedly their fiendish grins of satisfaction at such a foul deed changed to perturbed grimaces when they came to realize that they had been but kicking against sharp points, injuring only themselves. Mormonism was not destroyed by the cruel martyrdom, but here was its vitality. The bullet-torn flesh fertilized the soil; the blood they shed moistened the seed; and the spirits they sent heavenward will testify against them throughout eternities. The cause persists and grows.[20]

[Joseph Smith's] work was not lost. His testimony goes steadily forward, on to infinity.[21]

Today a great people hailed for their education, practicality, and virtue, stand to bear witness that the martyrdom of Joseph Smith, like that of the martyrs before him, is another of the infallible proofs of the divinity of the gospel of Jesus Christ, restored in its fulness through that humble prophet.[22]

Suggestions for Study and Teaching

Consider these ideas as you study the chapter or as you prepare to teach. For additional help, see pages v–ix.

- What do you think are some of the greatest things the Lord revealed through the Prophet Joseph Smith? (For some examples, see pages 228–32.) When someone who is not a member of the Church asks you about Joseph Smith, what do you say?

- What was God's role and what was Joseph Smith's role in opening the heavens for the Restoration of the gospel? (See pages 227, 228–30.) In what ways was Joseph Smith prepared to receive revelation?

- What did Joseph Smith know after the First Vision that he did not know before? (For some examples, see pages 229–30.) How do you think his feelings about God and himself changed? How have you been influenced by your testimony of the First Vision?

- In what ways was Joseph Smith an instrument of the Lord in linking heaven and earth? (See pages 231–32.) What do you think it means to be an instrument in the hands of the Lord?

- President Kimball said that the mob hoped to destroy Mormonism by killing Joseph Smith (page 234). What thoughts and feelings do you have as you consider what has happened in the Church since the death of Joseph Smith?

Related Scriptures: Isaiah 29:11–14; D&C 135; 136:37–39

Notes

1. In Conference Report, Melbourne Australia Area Conference 1976, 23.

2. In Conference Report, Guatemala City Guatemala Area Conference 1977, 22.

3. In Conference Report, Manila Philippines Area Conference 1975, 6.

4. In Conference Report, Temple View New Zealand Area Conference 1976, 51.

5. "Small Acts of Service," *Ensign,* Dec. 1974, 4–5.

6. *Faith Precedes the Miracle* (1972), 92–93.

7. *The Teachings of Spencer W. Kimball,* ed. Edward L. Kimball (1982), 429.

8. *The Teachings of Spencer W. Kimball,* 430.

9. "The Prophet Joseph Smith and the First Vision," Annual Joseph Smith Memorial Sermon, Utah State University, Dec. 13, 1970, 7.

10. In Conference Report, Taipei Taiwan Area Conference 1975, 14.

11. In Conference Report, Apr. 1974, 67–68; or *Ensign,* May 1974, 47.

12. In Conference Report, Apr. 1976, 11, 12; or *Ensign,* May 1976, 9.

13. In Conference Report, Apr. 1980, 74; or *Ensign,* May 1980, 51.

14. In Conference Report, Apr. 1976, 12; or *Ensign,* May 1976, 9.

15. In Conference Report, London England Area Conference 1976, 35.

16. In Conference Report, São Paulo Brazil Area Conference 1975, 72.

17. *The Teachings of Spencer W. Kimball,* 179–80.

18. *The Teachings of Spencer W. Kimball,* 143.

19. In Conference Report, Apr. 1945, 59.

20. In Conference Report, Apr. 1955, 96.

21. In Conference Report, Apr. 1946, 50.

22. *The Teachings of Spencer W. Kimball,* 181–82.

"Every night and morning I kneel and pray with deep sincerity that the Lord will inspire me and reveal to me the direction I should go and what I should tell the people of this Church."

Revelation: "A Continuous Melody and a Thunderous Appeal"

Continuing revelation is the lifeblood of the gospel of Jesus Christ.

From the Life of Spencer W. Kimball

President Spencer W. Kimball once spoke at a press conference held at the Arizona Temple Visitors' Center. A news reporter asked him: "You were introduced as the president of The Church of Jesus Christ of Latter-day Saints and also as a prophet. My question is: Does God speak to you? And if so, how?" President Kimball responded: "Yes. God speaks to his prophets today, just as he spoke to his prophets yesterday and just as he will speak to them tomorrow. You will remember that Amos wrote, 'Surely the Lord God will do nothing, but he revealeth his secret unto his servants the prophets.' (Amos 3:7.) Sometimes he speaks with an audible voice. Sometimes he sends his angels, as he did to Joseph, the stepfather of Jesus. Usually it is by the still small voice of God to the spirit within. Yes. Have I answered your question, young man?"[1]

President Kimball trusted in the principle of continuing revelation, declaring that it was "the very lifeblood of the gospel of the living Lord and Savior, Jesus Christ."[2] This trust, said Elder Neal A. Maxwell of the Quorum of the Twelve Apostles, "was clearly a part of the makeup of this very special man."[3] President Kimball took his responsibility as President of the Church seriously, knowing that he was the only person on the earth who was authorized to receive revelation for the Church. He testified: "I know that the Lord called me to this position. I know that there are greater prophets, perhaps, than I, but I wish to do all I can to carry forward the work of the Lord as he wants it done. Every night and morning I kneel and pray with deep sincerity that the Lord will inspire me and reveal to me the direction I should go and what I should tell the people of this Church."[4]

Throughout his service as President of the Church, he received revelations to guide the Saints. The most well known of all these revelations came in June 1978, when the Lord revealed to him and also to his brethren in the First Presidency and the Quorum of the Twelve Apostles that the blessings of the priesthood, which had been restricted to some, could now be available to all worthy members of the Church (see Doctrine and Covenants, Official Declaration 2). This revelation came after a period of years in which other Presidents of the Church had pondered and prayed about the matter.

Publicly, President Kimball did not speak at length about this revelation. But he did provide glimpses of his personal preparation to receive it, and he occasionally shared his feelings about it:

"I knew that something was before us that was extremely important to many of the children of God. I knew that we could receive the revelations of the Lord only by being worthy and ready for them and ready to accept them and put them into place. Day after day I went alone and with great solemnity and seriousness in the upper rooms of the temple, and there I offered my soul and offered my efforts to go forward with the program. I wanted to do what he wanted. I talked about it to him and said, 'Lord, I want only what is right. We are not making any plans to be spectacularly moving. We want only the thing that thou dost want, and we want it when you want it and not until.'"[5]

"Those of us today who are sustained by you as prophets, seers, and revelators came to feel in the spring of 1978 much as the early brethren did when the revelation came to the effect 'that the Gentiles should be fellowheirs . . . and partakers of his promise in Christ by the gospel' (Eph. 3:6). This was a thing, Paul said, 'which in other ages was not made known unto the sons of men, as it is now revealed unto the holy apostles and prophets by the Spirit' (Eph. 3:5).

"We had the glorious experience of having the Lord indicate clearly that the time had come when all worthy men and women everywhere can be fellowheirs and partakers of the full blessings of the gospel. I want you to know, as a special witness of the Savior, how close I have felt to him and to our Heavenly Father as I have made numerous visits to the upper rooms in the temple, going on some days several times by myself. The Lord made it very clear to me what was to be done. We do not expect the people of the world to understand such things, for they will always be quick to assign their own reasons or to discount the divine process of revelation."[6]

In addition to testifying that revelation guides the decisions of Church leaders, President Kimball taught that we can all receive revelation to guide our lives and strengthen us in our responsibilities. He said, "The blessing of revelation is one that all should seek for."[7]

Teachings of Spencer W. Kimball

God the Father and Jesus Christ are eager to communicate with mankind.

Someone has said that we live in a day in which God, if there be a God, chooses to be silent, but The Church of Jesus Christ of Latter-day Saints proclaims to the world that neither the Father nor the Son is silent. They are vocal and commune as proper and necessary, and constantly express a willingness, indeed an eagerness, to maintain communication with men.[8]

One theologian indicated it was impossible for man to find God or know God. This is like saying: "I have never climbed Mt. Ararat—no one can climb Ararat; or, I have never bathed in the clear warm waters of the Adriatic—there is no Adriatic Sea; or, I have never seen the wild life in Kruger Park—there is no Kruger Park; or, I have always had health—therefore, the pain which people claim, must be a figment of their imaginations. I have never astronauted into space; therefore, no one can speed through space."

How different then is it to say I have never heard nor seen God—therefore, no man has ever seen nor heard God nor walked with Him. How presumptuous and arrogant for any man to say God is unapproachable, unknowable, unseeable, unhearable because that one himself has not prepared himself for the experience.[9]

It should be kept in mind that God cannot be found through research alone, nor his gospel understood and appreciated by study only, for no one may know the Father or the Son but "he to whom the Son will reveal him." (Luke 10:22.) The skeptic will some day either in time or eternity learn to his sorrow that his egotism has robbed him of much joy and growth.[10]

We are happy in our knowledge that the God of this universe is a God of revelation. Our Lord communicates his mind and will to his children on earth. If we seek it, he will reveal himself more and more and in greater and greater fulness, and we shall comprehend him as well as it is possible for mortal man to comprehend God. We cannot worship a being of our own creation or of the imaginations of our minds. We worship a being who lives, who has created, who communicates to us his character and his attributes and the greatness of his being.[11]

Neither the Father Elohim nor the Son Jehovah would alienate himself from the children of men. It is they, the men, who cut themselves off if there be estrangement. Both the Father and the Son would gladly commune and associate with men. . . .

. . . In spite of all the gods which men make for themselves and the confusion incident thereto, the Living and True God is in his heaven and is available to his children.[12]

While some revelations are spectacular, most come as deep impressions to the mind and heart.

In our day, as in times past, many people expect that if there be revelation it will come with awe-inspiring, earth-shaking display. For many it is hard to accept as revelation those numerous ones in Moses' time, in Joseph's time, and in our own year—those revelations which come to prophets as deep, unassailable impressions settling down on the prophet's mind and heart as dew from heaven or as the dawn dissipates the darkness of night.

Expecting the spectacular, one may not be fully alerted to the constant flow of revealed communication. I say, in the deepest of humility, but also by the power and force of a burning testimony in my soul, that from the prophet of the Restoration to the prophet of our own year, the communication line is unbroken, the authority is continuous, a light, brilliant and penetrating, continues to shine. The sound of the voice of the Lord is a continuous melody and a thunderous appeal.[13]

Revelation does not always mean "walking with God," nor "face-to-face," nor "lips-to-ear." There are many kinds of revelation—some more and some less spectacular.[14]

Some revelations come by dreams. Most of our dreams are flighty and have no meaning, but the Lord does use dreams for enlightening his people. . . . Nebuchadnezzar had a dream. (See Daniel 2.) It was a powerful one which he forgot, but Daniel came along and recalled to the king his dream and gave the interpretation. The Lord made it known to Daniel for a specific reason.

There was Peter's dream in which he saw a sheet come down from heaven filled with all kinds of animals and beasts, and it had a very specific meaning. (See Acts 10:9–35.) . . .

Paul in his great experience had the same kind of a revelation through a dream. "And a vision appeared to Paul in the night." And he received instructions that were necessary for him and for the kingdom. (Acts 16:9.) . . .

There are other spectacular revelations mentioned. There was the coming of Moroni, an individual, a resurrected being, to bring back the great record of the ancients of America and the restoration of the gospel. . . .

Then came John the Baptist who had been beheaded by the king in a moment of weakness . . . [then] Peter, James and John. . . . So there came, step by step, a restoration of everything, and it all came by revelation, by vision, by dreams, or by deep impression.

Now, all of the revelations in the holy scriptures did not come by spectacular manifestations. As you read the Old Testament,

*Like Enos, we will find that revelation often comes quietly,
without spectacular manifestations.*

you will find the Lord speaks. He spoke to Isaiah, to Jeremiah,
and others, but those were not always personal appearances. It
was much like Enos's experience, for as you read in the book of
Enos in the Book of Mormon, he had been fasting and praying
and was reaching and asking for information and for a forgiveness of his sins particularly: "And while I was thus struggling in
the spirit, behold, the voice of the Lord came into my mind
again, saying: . . ." (Enos 1:10.) In that manner, many, many of
the revelations have come.

So revelation came: sometimes with actual personal appearance of heavenly beings. . . . But most of the revelations of the
Prophet Joseph Smith in this holy record, the Doctrine and

Covenants, did not come in that manner. They came as deep impressions.[15]

Most recorded revelations in the Doctrine and Covenants and in the Bible were deep feelings and an impressive consciousness of direction from above. This is the sort of revelation individuals often have for their own needs.[16]

Sometimes we don't recognize [revelations] when they come. We pray and pray and pray for wisdom and judgment and then we feel somewhat like we ought to go this particular direction. There was revelation there. The Lord answers these questions that you propose.[17]

What will be the language the Lord will use? Through the Prophet Joseph Smith, the Lord counseled Oliver Cowdery, who wondered about an answer to his prayers:

"Verily, verily, I say unto you, if you desire a further witness, cast your mind upon the night that you cried unto me in your heart, that you might know concerning the truth of these things.

"Did I not speak peace to your mind concerning the matter? What greater witness can you have than from God?" (D&C 6:22–23.)[18]

Through living prophets, the Lord reveals His will for the Church.

Of all things, that for which we should be most grateful today is that the heavens are indeed open and that the restored church of Jesus Christ is founded upon the rock of revelation. Continuous revelation is indeed the very lifeblood of the gospel of the living Lord and Savior, Jesus Christ.[19]

Vital and priceless records of ancient America, with teachings of Christ, another testimony of his divinity, form the Book of Mormon, which we declare to be divine scripture, contemporary with and sustaining the Bible.

Since [Joseph Smith's First Vision] in 1820, additional scripture has continued to come, including the numerous and vital revelations flowing in a never-ending stream from God to his prophets on the earth. Many of these revelations are recorded in another scripture called the Doctrine and Covenants. Completing our Latter-day Saint scriptures is the Pearl of Great Price, another record of revelation and translated writings of both ancient and modern prophets.

There are those who would assume that with the printing and binding of these sacred records, that would be the "end of the prophets." But again we testify to the world that revelation continues and that the vaults and files of the Church contain these revelations which come month to month and day to day. We testify also that there is, since 1830 when The Church of Jesus Christ of Latter-day Saints was organized, and will continue to be, so long as time shall last, a prophet, recognized of God and his people, who will continue to interpret the mind and will of the Lord.[20]

When . . . , after prayer and fasting, important decisions are made [by Church leaders], new missions and new stakes are created, new patterns and policies initiated, the news is taken for granted and possibly thought of as mere human calculations. But to those who sit in the intimate circles and hear the prayers of the prophet and the testimony of the man of God; to those who see the astuteness of his deliberations and the sagacity of his decisions and pronouncements, to them he is verily a prophet. To hear him conclude important new developments with such solemn expressions as "the Lord is pleased"; "that move is right"; "our Heavenly Father has spoken," is to know positively.[21]

Revelation has not ceased and will not cease. This kingdom of God has been set up for the rest of time, never to be torn down nor given to another people. It is a continuous program and will grow instead of diminish. Its doctrines are well established, but because of growth and expansion, improved ways are afforded to teach the gospel all over the world. Additional servants are called to the increasing work for a bigger world. Revelation and other miracles will never cease unless faith ceases. Where there is adequate faith, these things will continue.

The prophet Mormon warned: "Yea, wo unto him that shall deny the revelations of the Lord, and that shall say the Lord no longer worketh by revelation, or by prophecy, or by gifts, or by tongues, or by healings, or by the power of the Holy Ghost!" (3 Ne. 29:6.)[22]

I bear witness that the Church moves on through the revelations of God to its divinely called leaders. The Almighty is with this people.[23]

When we keep the commandments, exercise faith, and pray sincerely, we qualify ourselves to receive personal revelation.

The blessing of revelation is one that all should seek for. Righteous men and women find that they have the spirit of revelation to direct their families and to aid them in their other responsibilities. But . . . we must seek to qualify for such revelation by setting our lives in order and by becoming acquainted with the Lord through frequent and regular conversations with him.[24]

The Lord will not force himself upon people; and if they do not believe, they will receive no visitation. If they are content to depend upon their own limited calculations and interpretations, then, of course, the Lord will leave them to their chosen fate. . . .

. . . The same revelations, visions, healings, and tongues are all available today as in any other day, providing there is the necessary faith.[25]

The Almighty is with this people. We shall have all the revelations that we shall need if we will do our duty and keep the commandments of God. . . .

Remember:

If there be eyes to see, there will be visions to inspire.

If there be ears to hear, there will be revelations to experience.

If there be hearts which can understand, know this: that the exalting truths of Christ's gospel will no longer be hidden and mysterious, and all earnest seekers may know God and his program.[26]

Having given them their free agency, their Heavenly Father persuades and directs his children, but waits for their upreaching, their prayers, their sincere approach to him. . . .

*"The Lord will give you answer to your questions
and to your prayers if you are listening."*

The Lord is eager to see their first awakening desires and their beginning efforts to penetrate the darkness. Having granted freedom of decision, he must permit man to grope his way until he reaches for the light. But when man begins to hunger, when his arms begin to reach, when his knees begin to bend and his voice becomes articulate, then and not till then does our Lord push back the horizons, draw back the veil, and make it possible for men to emerge from dim uncertain stumbling to sureness, in heavenly light.[27]

If one rises from his knees having merely said words, he should fall back on his knees and remain there until he has established communication with the Lord who is very anxious to bless, but having given man his free agency, will not force himself upon that man.[28]

Do you want guidance? Have you prayed to the Lord for inspiration? Do you want to do right or do you want to do what you want to do whether or not it is right? Do you want to do what is best for you in the long run or what seems more desirable for the moment? Have you prayed? How much have you prayed? How did you pray? Have you prayed as did the Savior of the world in Gethsemane or did you ask for what you want regardless of its being proper? Do you say in your prayers: "Thy will be done"? Did you say, "Heavenly Father, if you will inspire and impress me with the right, I will do that right"? Or, did you pray, "Give me what I want or I will take it anyway"? Did you say: "Father in Heaven, I love you, I believe in you, I know you are omniscient. I am honest. I am sincerely desirous of doing right. I know you can see the end from the beginning. You can see the future. You can discern if under this situation I present, I will have peace or turmoil, happiness or sorrow, success or failure. Tell me, please, loved Heavenly Father, and I promise to do what you tell me to do." Have you prayed that way? Don't you think it might be wise? Are you courageous enough to pray that prayer?[29]

The Lord will give you answer to your questions and to your prayers if you are listening. It doesn't have to all come through the prophet. . . . But all people, if they are worthy enough and close enough to the Lord, can have revelations.[30]

Suggestions for Study and Teaching

Consider these ideas as you study the chapter or as you prepare to teach. For additional help, see pages v–ix.

- Review the account of President Kimball receiving the 1978 revelation on the priesthood (pages 238–39). While some aspects of President Kimball's experience were unique to that revelation, what aspects of his experience are common to all our efforts to receive revelation? How can we follow his example?

- Review the section that begins on page 239. What would you say to a friend who claims that God is silent? What scriptures or experiences could you share to help your friend?

- What are some ways in which revelation can come? (For some examples, see pages 240–43.) President Kimball taught that most revelations come as deep impressions rather than spectacular manifestations. How can we recognize whether a thought or feeling is from the Lord? (See page 243.)

- Why do we need living prophets in addition to the scriptures? (For some examples, see pages 243–45.) How have you been blessed through revelations to the President of the Church?

- What advice would you give someone who is seeking guidance from the Lord? (See pages 245–47.)

Related Scriptures: 1 Kings 19:9–12; Moroni 10:3–5; D&C 1:38; 8:2–3; 43:1–4; 76:5–10

Notes

1. In Oscar W. McConkie, *Aaronic Priesthood* (1977), 13.
2. In Conference Report, Apr. 1977, 113; or *Ensign,* May 1977, 76.
3. "Spencer, the Beloved: Leader-Servant," *Ensign,* Dec. 1985, 17.
4. In Conference Report, Guatemala City Guatemala Area Conference 1977, 24.
5. *The Teachings of Spencer W. Kimball,* ed. Edward L. Kimball (1982), 451.
6. "The Savior: The Center of Our Lives," *New Era,* Apr. 1980, 36.
7. "The Example of Abraham," *Ensign,* June 1975, 4.
8. *Faith Precedes the Miracle* (1972), 65–66.
9. Commencement address, Brigham Young University, May 27, 1966, as printed in *Church News,* June 4, 1966, 12.
10. In Conference Report, Oct. 1944, 44.
11. *The Teachings of Spencer W. Kimball,* 7–8.
12. In Conference Report, Apr. 1964, 93, 94; or *Improvement Era,* June 1964, 496.
13. In Conference Report, Apr. 1977, 115; or *Ensign,* May 1977, 78.
14. In Conference Report, Oct. 1966, 23; or *Improvement Era,* Dec. 1966, 1106.
15. *The Teachings of Spencer W. Kimball,* 455–56.
16. *Faith Precedes the Miracle,* 30.
17. *The Teachings of Spencer W. Kimball,* 454.
18. "Pray Always," *Ensign,* Oct. 1981, 5.
19. In Conference Report, Apr. 1977, 113; or *Ensign,* May 1977, 76.
20. In Conference Report, Apr. 1977, 115; or *Ensign,* May 1977, 77–78.
21. ". . . To His Servants the Prophets," *Instructor,* Aug. 1960, 257.
22. "Gospel Forum: Continuing Revelation," *Ensign,* Feb. 1971, 21.
23. *Faith Precedes the Miracle,* 46.
24. *Ensign,* June 1975, 4–5.
25. In Conference Report, Oct. 1966, 22, 23; or *Improvement Era,* Dec. 1966, 1106.
26. In Conference Report, Oct. 1966, 26; or *Improvement Era,* Dec. 1966, 1108.
27. In Conference Report, Munich Germany Area Conference 1973, 74–75.
28. *The Teachings of Spencer W. Kimball,* 124.
29. *The Teachings of Spencer W. Kimball,* 123–24.
30. *The Teachings of Spencer W. Kimball,* 455.

Shepherds of the Flock

There is safety in sustaining and following the prophet and other Church leaders.

From the Life of Spencer W. Kimball

President Spencer W. Kimball frequently taught the importance of sustaining local and general Church leaders. During the priesthood session of general conference in April 1978, he recalled feelings he had as a youth regarding each man who served as his bishop: "We always had a good bishop. We always loved him. There was Bishop Zundel and Bishop Moody and Bishop Tyler and Bishop Wilkins. I loved all my bishops. I hope all my young brethren love their bishops as I did."[1]

In another address he said: "I remember coming to this tabernacle [the Salt Lake Tabernacle] as a boy from Arizona, with my father, to attend general conference. I was thrilled to hear all the Brethren speak. . . . I was thrilled at their utterances and took their warnings seriously, even as a young man. These men are among the prophets of God, just as were the prophets of the Book of Mormon and of the Bible."[2]

President Kimball often expressed appreciation to members for their willingness to sustain him and other Church leaders: "Everywhere I go, there is a great outpouring of love and kindness, and for that I am humbly thankful. It is manna to my soul. Your prayers and your love sustain me. The Lord hears your prayers and blesses me and my Brethren with health and strength and directs us in the affairs of his kingdom here upon the earth. For this all of us are deeply grateful."[3] He also spoke of the love he and other Church leaders felt for the Saints: "We love you people and wish for you total progress and joy and happiness, which we know can come only through following the admonitions of God as proclaimed through his prophets and leaders."[4]

President Kimball greets people as he enters the Salt Lake Tabernacle for general conference.

Teachings of Spencer W. Kimball

The Lord directs His Church through divinely appointed leaders.

The Master and Savior, the Lord Jesus Christ himself, stands at the head of this Church in all his majesty and glory. He directs his affairs through his divinely appointed and sustained prophets and apostles.[5]

The affairs of the Church of Jesus Christ are administered by the Presidency of the Church and the Twelve Apostles, with numerous other General Authorities assisting, and also through the stake and mission presidents and the bishops. These men are the shepherds of the flock. The Lord has placed these men to lead his kingdom on earth, and upon them he has placed authority and responsibility, each in his particular sphere. He has given these men the Melchizedek Priesthood, which is his own power and authority delegated to men. He recognizes and ratifies the acts of these chosen and anointed servants.[6]

It is my testimony to you that the leaders in this the Church of Jesus Christ are divinely called and set apart to lead through the spirit of prophecy as in other dispensations.[7]

To every member of this Church, the Lord has given leaders on three levels: the Bishop or Branch President, the Stake President or the Mission President, and the General Authorities. These leaders are dependable. One of them may be limited in knowledge, education or training, but he is entitled to the revelations of the Lord for his people and he has the channel open to God himself.[8]

Since the crucifixion, there have been tens of thousands of men called by the Savior to fill positions of responsibility, not one of whom has been perfect, and yet all are called of the Lord and must be upheld and sustained by those who would be disciples of the Lord. That is the true spirit of the gospel.[9]

Chosen, approved, ordained leaders will protect us against "the sleight of men, and cunning craftiness." [Ephesians 4:14.] One can never be deceived if he protects himself against the blind or vicious guide by following the Spirit and the proper leaders of the Church.[10]

No one is more anxious than the Brethren who stand at the head of this Church to receive such guidance as the Lord would give them for the benefit of mankind and for the people of the Church.[11]

I know that the Lord has contact with his prophets, and that he reveals the truth today to his servants as he did in the days of Adam and Abraham and Moses and Peter and Joseph and the numerous others throughout time. God's messages of light and truth are as surely given to man today as in any other dispensation.[12]

Prophets teach similar messages.

Some may wonder why General Authorities speak of the same things from conference to conference. As I study the utterances of the prophets through the centuries, their pattern is very clear. We seek, in the words of Alma, to teach people "an everlasting hatred against sin and iniquity." We preach "repentance, and faith on the Lord Jesus Christ." (Alma 37:32, 33.) We praise humility. We seek to teach people "to withstand every temptation of the devil, with their faith on the Lord Jesus Christ." (Alma 37:33.) We teach our people "to never be weary of good works." (Alma 37:34.)

Prophets say the same things because we face basically the same problems. Brothers and sisters, the solutions to these problems have not changed. It would be a poor lighthouse that gave off a different signal to guide every ship entering a harbor. It would be a poor mountain guide who, knowing the safe route up a mountainside, took his trusting charges up unpredictable and perilous paths from which no traveler returns.[13]

Church leaders are not able, each time we teach you, to offer a new or more glamorous route that will lead back to the presence of our Heavenly Father. The route remains the same. Hence, encouragement must often be given concerning the same things and warnings must be repeated. Just because a truth is repeated does not make that truth any less important or true. Indeed, the opposite is true.[14]

I can imagine that if the Lord himself were standing on the Mount of Olives and if he were instructing the people, he would say much the same things that have been said and will be said [in our conferences]. I can imagine that if he were standing on the Sea of Galilee with the boats in the water and the people standing around him, that he would say very much the same things: to live the commandments of God, to keep ourselves unspotted from the world, and to live every commandment that God has given us. That is what he would say, and so today he is saying these things through his servants.[15]

Prophets have often been dismissed or rejected in their own time.

When the world has followed prophets, it has moved forward; when it has ignored them, the results have been stagnation, servitude, death.[16]

Even in the Church many are prone to garnish the sepulchres of yesterday's prophets and mentally stone the living ones [see Matthew 23:29–30, 34].[17]

Let us not make the error of the ancients. Numerous modern sectarians believe in the Abrahams, the Moseses, and the Pauls, but resist believing in today's prophets. The ancients also could accept the prophets of an earlier day, but denounced and cursed the ones who were their contemporaries.[18]

Various excuses have been used over the centuries to dismiss these divine messengers [living prophets]. There has been denial because the prophet came from an obscure place. "Can there any good thing come out of Nazareth?" (John 1:46.) Jesus was also met with the question, "Is not this the carpenter's son?" (Matthew 13:55.) By one means or another, the swiftest method of rejection of the holy prophets has been to find a pretext, however false or absurd, to dismiss the man so that his message could also be dismissed. Prophets who were not glib, but slow of speech, were esteemed as naught. Instead of responding to Paul's message, some saw his bodily presence as weak and

"Instead of responding to Paul's message, some saw his bodily presence as weak and regarded his speech as contemptible."

regarded his speech as contemptible [see 2 Corinthians 10:10]. Perhaps they judged Paul by the timbre of his voice or by his style of speech, not the truths uttered by him.

. . . The cares of the world are so many and so entangling, even very good people are diverted from following the truth because they care too much for the things of the world. . . .

Sometimes people let their hearts get so set upon things and the honors of this world that they cannot learn the lessons they most need to learn. Simple truths are often rejected in favor of the much less-demanding philosophies of men, and this is another cause for the rejection of the prophets. . . .

The holy prophets have not only refused to follow erroneous human trends, but have pointed out these errors. No wonder the response to the prophets has not always been one of indifference. So often the prophets have been rejected because they first rejected the wrong ways of their own society. . . .

Prophets have a way of jarring the carnal mind. Too often the holy prophets are wrongly perceived as harsh and as anxious to make a record in order to say, "I told you so." Those prophets I have known are the most loving of men. It is because of their love and integrity that they cannot modify the Lord's message merely to make people feel comfortable. They are too kind to be so cruel. I am so grateful that prophets do not crave popularity.[19]

Parents are to teach their children to sustain and follow Church leaders.

How do you teach your children to love the authorities of the Church? If you are constantly saying good things about the branch presidency, the district presidency, the mission presidency, and the Presidency of the Church, your children will grow up to love the brethren.[20]

We pray for the Church leaders. If children all their days in their turn at family prayers and in their secret prayers remember before the Lord the leaders of the Church, they are quite unlikely to ever fall into apostasy. . . .

The children who pray for the brethren will grow up loving them, speaking well of them, honoring and emulating them. Those who daily hear the leaders of the Church spoken of in prayer in deep affection will more likely believe the sermons and admonitions they will hear.

When boys speak to the Lord concerning their bishop, they are likely to take very seriously the interviews with the bishop in which priesthood advancements and mission and temple blessings are being discussed. And girls too will have a healthy respect for all church proceedings as they pray for the leaders of the Church.[21]

Those who follow the Church authorities find safety.

The membership of the Church will always be safe if they follow closely the instructions and admonitions and the leadership of the authorities of the Church.[22]

The authorities which the Lord has placed in his Church constitute for the people of the Church a harbor, a place of refuge, a hitching post, as it were. No one in this Church will ever go far astray who ties himself securely to the Church Authorities whom the Lord has placed in his Church. This Church will never go astray; the Quorum of the Twelve will never lead you into bypaths; it never has and never will. There could be individuals who would falter; there will never be a majority of the Council of the Twelve on the wrong side at any time. The Lord has chosen them; he has given them specific responsibilities. And those people who stand close to them will be safe. And, conversely, whenever one begins to go his own way in opposition to authority, he is in grave danger. I would not say that those leaders whom the Lord chooses are necessarily the most brilliant, nor the most highly trained, but they are the chosen, and when chosen of the Lord they are his recognized authority, and the people who stay close to them have safety.[23]

If we will live the gospel and follow the counsel of the leaders of the Church, we will be blessed to avoid many of the problems that plague the world.[24]

Let us harken to those we sustain as prophets and seers, as well as the other brethren, as if our eternal life depended upon it, because it does![25]

Suggestions for Study and Teaching

Consider these ideas as you study the chapter or as you prepare to teach. For additional help, see pages v–ix.

- Consider how your life has been blessed as you have sustained Church leaders on the three levels described by President Kimball (see page 251). As you do so, what experiences come to mind?

- Review the section that begins on page 252. What are some recurring messages you have noticed in recent general conferences?

- Review the third and fourth full paragraphs on page 253. Why do you think some people find it difficult to follow living prophets? What recent examples come to mind?

- What can we do to encourage children and others to respect and follow Church leaders? (For some examples, see page 255.)
- Review the last section of the chapter. Why is there safety in following the counsel of Church leaders?

Related Scriptures: Ephesians 2:19–20; 4:11–16; Helaman 13:24–29; D&C 1:14, 38; 21:4–6; 121:16–21

Notes

1. In Conference Report, Apr. 1978, 68; or *Ensign,* May 1978, 45.
2. In Conference Report, Apr. 1978, 115; or *Ensign,* May 1978, 76.
3. In Conference Report, Oct. 1978, 110–11; or *Ensign,* Nov. 1978, 73.
4. In Conference Report, Apr. 1974, 65; or *Ensign,* May 1974, 46.
5. In Conference Report, Apr. 1976, 7; or *Ensign,* May 1976, 6.
6. *The Miracle of Forgiveness* (1969), 325.
7. In Conference Report, Oct. 1958, 57.
8. *That You May Not Be Deceived,* Brigham Young University Speeches of the Year (Nov. 11, 1959), 12–13.
9. *The Miracle of Forgiveness,* 274.
10. *That You May Not Be Deceived,* 13.
11. "Second Century Address," *Brigham Young University Studies,* summer 1976, 447.
12. In Conference Report, Oct. 1976, 164; or *Ensign,* Nov. 1976, 111.
13. In Conference Report, Apr. 1976, 7; or *Ensign,* May 1976, 6.
14. *President Kimball Speaks Out* (1981), 89.
15. In Conference Report, Manila Philippines Area Conference 1975, 4.
16. In Conference Report, Apr. 1970, 121; or *Improvement Era,* June 1970, 94.
17. ". . . To His Servants the Prophets," *Instructor,* Aug. 1960, 257.
18. In Conference Report, Apr. 1977, 115; or *Ensign,* May 1977, 78.
19. In Conference Report, Apr. 1978, 115, 116; or *Ensign,* May 1978, 76–77.
20. *The Teachings of Spencer W. Kimball,* ed. Edward L. Kimball (1982), 460.
21. *The Teachings of Spencer W. Kimball,* 121.
22. *The Teachings of Spencer W. Kimball,* 461.
23. In Conference Report, Apr. 1951, 104.
24. In Conference Report, Apr. 1980, 128; or *Ensign,* May 1980, 92.
25. In Conference Report, Apr. 1978, 117; or *Ensign,* May 1978, 77.

Sharing the Gospel

We must lengthen our stride
in sharing the gospel with others.

From the Life of Spencer W. Kimball

During a trip to Quito, Ecuador, as a member of the Quorum of the Twelve Apostles, Elder Spencer W. Kimball was at a hotel restaurant with a group that included four young missionaries. "He commented to the others that their waiter was a fine-looking young man and would make a good missionary for the Church. Elder Kimball ordered bread and milk, then asked the waiter if he had any children at home. 'One son,' the waiter answered. 'Bread and milk will make him healthy,' Elder Kimball said, 'but he will be even healthier if you will feed him the food these young men have to give.' The waiter looked puzzled. Then Elder Kimball explained that the young men were missionaries who had the gospel of Jesus Christ to teach. The waiter expressed interest in having the missionaries teach him."[1]

President Kimball often referred to the Savior's charge that the gospel be taken to "all the world" (Mark 16:15). He asked for more full-time missionaries, particularly young men and older couples, and he reminded all members of the Church to participate in this divinely appointed work. "Our great need, and our great calling," he taught, "is to bring to the people of this world the candle of understanding to light their way out of obscurity and darkness and into the joy, peace, and truths of the gospel."[2]

Teachings of Spencer W. Kimball

The Lord promises us great blessings as we share the gospel.

There is a spiritual adventure in doing missionary work, in giving referrals, in accompanying the missionaries as they give the discussions. It is exciting and rewarding. The hours, the effort, the wondering, all are worth it when even one soul expresses repentance and faith and a desire to be baptized. Imagine how wonderful you would feel when they say, "When you are here, and we're talking about these things, it seems like I'm remembering things I knew before," or, "You can't leave here until you've told us all you know about the restored Church."[3]

Sharing the gospel brings peace and joy into our own lives, enlarges our own hearts and souls in behalf of others, increases our own faith, strengthens our own relationship with the Lord, and increases our own understanding of gospel truths.[4]

The Lord has promised great blessings to us in proportion to how well we share the gospel. We will receive help from the other side of the veil as the spiritual miracles occur. The Lord has told us that our sins will be forgiven more readily as we bring souls unto Christ and remain steadfast in bearing testimony to the world, and surely every one of us is looking for additional help in being forgiven of our sins. (See D&C 84:61.) In one of the greatest of missionary scriptures, section 4 of the Doctrine and Covenants, we are told that if we serve the Lord in missionary service "with all [our] heart, might, mind, and strength," then we may "stand blameless before God at the last day" (verse 2).

And, further, the Lord said:

"And if it so be that you should labor all your days in crying repentance unto this people, and bring, save it be one soul unto me, how great shall be your joy with him in the kingdom of my Father!

"And now, if your joy will be great with one soul that you have brought unto me into the kingdom of my Father, how great will be your joy if you should bring many souls unto me!" (D&C 18:15–16.)

Elder Spencer W. Kimball as a full-time missionary in the Central States Mission, June 1915. Elder Kimball is on the left, next to his companion L. M. Hawkes.

If one labors all his days and brings in save it be one soul! What joy! One soul! How precious! Oh, that God would give us that kind of love for souls![5]

The Lord has entrusted all members of the Church with a responsibility to serve as His messengers.

I wish we could more effectively and faithfully establish in the hearts of all members of the Church the understanding that if a person is old enough to be a member, he is old enough to be a missionary; and he doesn't need to be set apart especially for that calling. Every member has the obligation and the calling to take the gospel to those around him. We want every man, woman, and child to assume his rightful responsibility. It is very important. For this is the message of the gospel: We receive blessings from the gospel, and then we go out and share those blessings with others.

Now, we are a busy people; but the Lord did not say, "If it is convenient for you, would you consider preaching the gospel." He has said, "Let every man learn his duty" (D&C 107:99) and "Behold . . . it becometh every man who hath been warned to warn his neighbor." (D&C 88:81.)

We must remember that God is our ally in this. He is our help. He will open the way, for he gave the commandment.[6]

What a thrilling thing it is, my dear brothers and sisters who are fellow members of the kingdom of God, to be entrusted by the Lord to serve as messengers of His word to our brothers and sisters who are not members of the Church. Let us assume for a moment that the roles were reversed—that you were not a member of the Church but that your present nonmember neighbor was a Latter-day Saint. Would you want him or her to share the gospel with you? Would you then rejoice in the new truths you had learned? Would your love and respect increase for your neighbor who had shared these truths with you? Of course, the answer to all of these questions would be: Yes![7]

Brethren and sisters, I wonder if we are doing all we can. Are we complacent in our assignment to teach the gospel to others? Are we prepared to lengthen our stride? To enlarge our vision?[8]

The day for carrying the gospel to ever more places and people is here and now. We must come to think of our obligation to share the message rather than of our own convenience. Calls from the Lord are seldom convenient. The time is here when sacrifice must become an even more important element in the Church. We must increase our devotion so that we can do the work the Lord has for us to do. . . . The parting words of the Master to His Apostles just before His Ascension were, "Go ye into all the world, and preach the gospel to every creature.

"He that believeth and is baptized shall be saved; but he that believeth not shall be damned." (Mark 16:15–16.)

We must not falter nor weary in well-doing. We must lengthen our stride. Not only is our own eternal welfare at stake, but also the eternal welfare of many of our brothers and sisters who are not now members of this, the true Church. I thrill to the words of the Prophet Joseph Smith in a letter that he sent to the Church from Nauvoo on September 6, 1842: "Shall we not go on in so great a cause? Go forward. . . . Courage . . . and on, on to the victory!" (D&C 128:22.)[9]

Through our righteous influence and effort, we can help others receive the restored gospel.

Member-missionary work is the key to the future growth of the Church.[10]

I feel the Lord has placed, in a very natural way within our circles of friends and acquaintances, many persons who are ready to enter into his Church. We ask that you prayerfully identify those persons and then ask the Lord's assistance in helping you introduce them to the gospel.[11]

It should be clear to us that usually we must warm our neighbors before we can warn them properly. Our neighbors must experience our genuine friendship and fellowship. We want members to entreat neighbors, not to scold them or scare them.[12]

The gospel is true. By studying and living its principles and seeking the help of the Holy Ghost, any earnest seeker can know for himself that it is true. But how much easier it is to understand and accept if the seeker after truth can also see the principles of the gospel at work in the lives of other believers. No greater service can be given to the missionary calling of this Church than to be exemplary in positive Christian virtues in our lives.[13]

Righteous members, living the gospel by example, as well as by precept, are the Church's best advertisement.[14]

What every member ought to do, by good example and by bearing testimony, is to portray to nonmembers the joys of gospel living and understanding and thus help to bring them to the stage where they will accept more formal teaching.[15]

"The real goal for effective proselyting is that the members do the finding and the full-time missionaries do the teaching."

The real goal for effective proselyting is that the members do the finding and the full-time missionaries do the teaching. . . . When members do the finding they have a personal interest in fellowshipping, there are fewer investigators lost before baptism, and those who are baptized tend to remain active.[16]

Our goal should be to identify as soon as possible which of our Father's children are spiritually prepared to proceed all the way to baptism into the kingdom. One of the best ways to find out is to expose your friends, relatives, neighbors, and acquaintances to the full-time missionaries as soon as possible.[17]

Sometimes we forget that it is better to risk a little ruffling in the relationship of a friend than it is to deprive him of eternal life by keeping silent.[18]

Don't wait for long fellowshipping nor for the precise, perfect moment. What you need to do is find out if they are the elect. "[My] elect hear my voice and harden not their hearts." (D&C 29:7.) If they hear and have hearts open to the gospel, it will be evident immediately. If they won't listen and their hearts are hardened with skepticism or negative comments, they are not

263

ready. In this case, keep loving them and fellowshipping them and wait for the next opportunity to find out if they are ready. You will not lose their friendship. They will still respect you.

Of course, there are discouragements, but nothing is ever lost. No one ever loses a friend just because he doesn't want to continue with the visits from the missionaries. The member can continue the association with no threat to his friendship or special relationship with that family. Sometimes it takes more time for some to come into the Church than for others. The member should continue to fellowship and try again at a later date for conversion. Don't be discouraged just because of a temporary lack of progress. There are hundreds of stories about the value of perseverance in missionary service.[19]

Missionary work includes loving and persistent fellowshipping of new converts and less-active members.

When we baptize somebody it is a crime to let them just slide slowly back out of the Church and out of the gospel because of a lack of fellowship. Fellowshipping is an important responsibility. We should be able to fellowship everybody that comes in. That is the reason we want the members to do the missionary work as well as to get help from the missionaries. We want the people . . . to go out and do this work because they are still the neighbors after the person is baptized. They can still fellowship them; they can still call for them and take them to priesthood meeting; they can still encourage them and help them in their home evenings and so on.[20]

We cannot stress too strongly the need to do missionary work in the framework of priesthood correlation so that investigators are fellowshipped and tied into the programs of the Church in such a way that they promptly become active and faithful members. This, then, is another way in which all members of the Church can be actively and constantly engaged in missionary service—by fellowshipping, befriending, and encouraging the new members of the Church.[21]

It is imperative that those who are baptized as converts immediately be assigned home teachers who will fellowship them in a very personal and concerned manner. These home teachers, working with their priesthood officers, should see that each mature convert is given some challenging activity as well as an opportunity and encouragement to increase his knowledge of the gospel. He should be assisted in establishing social relationships with the members of the Church so that he will not feel alone as he begins his life as an active Latter-day Saint.[22]

It is an inspiration and joy to see . . . the Saints embrace and help and assist and pray for those who daily enter the kingdom of our Lord. Continue to reach out to each other—and the many more who will enter the Church. Welcome them and love and fellowship them.[23]

Our responsibility as brothers and sisters in the Church is to help those who may be lost to find their way, and to help those who have lost that which is precious to find their treasure again. The scriptures clearly teach us that every member has the obligation to strengthen his fellow members.

The Savior lovingly yet pointedly emphasized this when he said to Peter, "When thou art converted, strengthen thy brethren" (Luke 22:32). May I say the same to each of you: When you are converted, please strengthen your brethren and sisters. There are so many who hunger, sometimes without knowing the cause of their hunger. There are spiritual truths and principles that can be as bedrock to their lives, safety to their souls, peace to their hearts and minds if we would but turn our prayers and active concern to them. . . .

There may be someone who will say, "Well, we know a man or a woman who can never be touched." Of course he or she can be touched. He or she can always be blessed and helped! There is the promise of scripture. It reads, "Charity never faileth." (1 Cor. 13:8.) Never! Charity, applied long enough, never fails to work its miracle either in the individual, in us, in both of us, or in others around the individual.

. . . I believe there is none who cannot be converted—or I might say reactivated—if the right person makes the right approach at the right time in the right way with the right spirit. I know that the blessings of our Father in Heaven will attend our efforts if we prepare ourselves, and if we happily live gospel principles, and if we will seek our Heavenly Father's assistance. . . .

Let priesthood quorum home teachers, Relief Society visiting teachers, husbands and wives, parents and children, and members everywhere who love the Lord and desire to do his will, turn and under love and inspiration do the righteous labors required by helping those in need. Temporary flashes of interest and enthusiasm will not achieve the desired results. But our desired results can come, and will come more often than any of us imagines, if we will prayerfully enlarge our efforts. Not only will the choice blessings of the Lord come into your lives and the lives of others, but we will draw closer to the Lord and feel the presence of His love and His spirit.[24]

Parents should help their children prepare for full-time missionary service.

We need the missionary-age young men of the Church to step forward in even greater numbers than they are doing now so they can assume their rightful responsibility, privilege, and blessing as the Lord's servants in the missionary cause. How strengthened we and they would be if all young men readied themselves for the Lord's work![25]

When I ask for more missionaries, I am not asking for more testimony-barren or unworthy missionaries. I am asking that we start earlier and train our missionaries better in every branch and every ward in the world. That is another challenge—that the young people will understand that it is a great privilege to go on a mission and that they must be physically well, mentally well, spiritually well, and that "the Lord cannot look upon sin with the least degree of allowance." [Alma 45:16.]

I am asking for missionaries who have been carefully indoctrinated and trained through the family and the organizations of the Church, and who come to the mission with a great desire. I am asking . . . that we train prospective missionaries much better, much earlier, much longer, so that each anticipates his mission with great joy.[26]

"I hope that every family will hold home evening every Monday night without fail. Missionary work will be one of the strong points that will be brought before it."

We must think in larger numbers. We must prepare our missionaries better, not only with language but with scripture and above all with a testimony and a burning fire that puts power to their words.[27]

Send your boys on missions. The minute they come into your arms, you begin to teach them. They hear your prayers, night and morning. They hear you pray to the Lord to help to open the doors of all the nations. They hear about missionary work. They hear you pray for your bishops and your mission presidents and all others who are serving you, and it just grows into their consciousness gradually.[28]

Nearly every time I see a little boy, I say, "You will make a great missionary, won't you?" You plant into his mind a seed. It is just like plants and other vegetation. It grows and grows, and if a father and a mother talk to their little boys . . . about going on a mission—when they are infants, almost—that little seed will grow and grow.[29]

It is well for parents to start preparing their sons to save money early in their lives. Let them have the spirit of saving. Let them also have the spirit of studying and praying about the gospel, of seeing for themselves how the gospel works in their own lives and in the lives of those around them. Let them have the spirit of service throughout their growing years and the experience of helping others discuss the joys of the gospel message in their lives. Let them use their seminary and institute classes and experiences as a training ground for acquiring spiritual knowledge of great value to themselves and others. Let them prepare by keeping their lives clean and worthy and by wanting with all their heart to help the Lord take the gospel to those who are ready for it.[30]

I hope that every family will hold home evening every Monday night without fail. Missionary work will be one of the strong points that will be brought before it; and the father and the mother and the children in their turns will offer prayers which will be centered around this very important element—that the doors of the nations might be opened to us and then, secondly, that the missionaries, the young men and women of the Church, may be anxious to fill those missions and bring people into the Church.[31]

The Church needs couples to serve as missionaries.

If health and other conditions permit, parents can look to the day when they, too, may serve a mission.[32]

We have rather forgotten, we older people, who have been retired and who have found an easy place to go with our camping outfit and with our other opportunities. We have found an easy way to satisfy our own thoughts and our own consciences that the work must go on—we will send our boys, we say.

All of us have this responsibility. Not all of us are able, but many, many of us are.[33]

We could use hundreds of couples, older people like some of you folks, whose families are reared, who have retired in their business, who are able to go . . . to teach the gospel. We could use hundreds of couples. You just go and talk to your bishop—

that is all you need to do. Tell him, "We are ready to go, if you can use us." I think you will probably get a call.³⁴

This is the work of the Lord. We are on his errand. He has commanded us specifically, and yet we are unknown among many people of the world. It is time to gird up our loins and go forward with new dedication to this great work. We covenanted, you and I, to do it. May we all say with that young man, found in the temple by his anxious parents, sitting in the midst of the doctors, "I must be about my Father's business." [Luke 2:49.]³⁵

Suggestions for Study and Teaching

Consider these ideas as you study the chapter or as you prepare to teach. For additional help, see pages v–ix.

- In what ways is missionary work "a spiritual adventure"? (page 259). As we share the gospel, what "exciting and rewarding" experiences can we have? (For an example, see the story on page 258.)

- Review pages 259–60, looking for blessings we receive when we share the gospel. When have you experienced any of these blessings?

- Read the fourth full paragraph on page 261. What do you think it means to "lengthen our stride" and to "enlarge our vision"? How can we follow this counsel in missionary work?

- Review the section that begins on page 262. Think about or discuss the specific counsel you find about sharing the gospel with family and friends. For example: *(a)* What can we do to "warm our neighbors"? *(b)* In what ways might we be an "advertisement" for the Church? *(c)* What are some possible drawbacks of waiting for "the precise, perfect moment" to share the gospel? *(d)* How should we respond if our family members and friends do not accept our invitation to learn about the gospel?

- What are some of the needs of new members? of less-active members? What can we do to help them? (See pages 264–66.)

- What qualities do Church leaders seek in full-time missionaries? (For some examples, see pages 266–68.) What can parents and others do to help children develop these qualities? What are some ways parents and children can follow President Kimball's counsel to save money for missions?

- President Kimball urged older couples to serve missions (pages 268–69). What are some of the options and opportunities the Church gives to couple missionaries? What can couples do to prepare to serve? How are you doing missionary work in your current stage of life?

Related Scriptures: Mosiah 3:20; Alma 26:1–16; Helaman 6:3; Moroni 6:3–4; D&C 84:88

Notes

1. Edward L. Kimball and Andrew E. Kimball Jr., *Spencer W. Kimball* (1977), 354.
2. "Are We Doing All We Can?" *Ensign,* Feb. 1983, 5.
3. "It Becometh Every Man," *Ensign,* Oct. 1977, 7.
4. *Ensign,* Feb. 1983, 4.
5. "President Kimball Speaks Out on Being a Missionary," *New Era,* May 1981, 50.
6. *Ensign,* Feb. 1983, 3.
7. *Ensign,* Oct. 1977, 3.
8. "When the World Will Be Converted," *Ensign,* Apr. 1984, 4.
9. In Conference Report, Oct. 1982, 5; or *Ensign,* Nov. 1982, 5, 6.
10. Regional representatives' seminar, Oct. 3, 1980, Archives of The Church of Jesus Christ of Latter-day Saints, 2.
11. *Ensign,* Feb. 1983, 4.
12. Regional representatives' seminar, Sept. 30, 1976, Archives of The Church of Jesus Christ of Latter-day Saints, 2.
13. *The Teachings of Spencer W. Kimball,* ed. Edward L. Kimball (1982), 555.
14. Regional representatives' seminar, Oct. 3, 1980, 2.
15. "President Kimball Speaks Out on Service to Others," *New Era,* Mar. 1981, 48–49.
16. *Ensign,* Oct. 1977, 6.
17. *Ensign,* Oct. 1977, 6.
18. Regional representatives' seminar, Apr. 3, 1975, Archives of The Church of Jesus Christ of Latter-day Saints, 7.
19. *Ensign,* Oct. 1977, 6.
20. In Conference Report, Glasgow Scotland Area Conference 1976, 23.
21. *Ensign,* Oct. 1977, 7.
22. In Conference Report, Oct. 1977, 67; or *Ensign,* Nov. 1977, 45.
23. "Always a Convert Church: Some Lessons to Learn and Apply This Year," *Ensign,* Sept. 1975, 4.
24. "Helping Others Obtain the Promises of the Lord," *Ensign,* June 1983, 3, 5.
25. *Ensign,* Feb. 1983, 3.
26. "When the World Will Be Converted," *Ensign,* Oct. 1974, 7.
27. Regional representatives' seminar, Apr. 5, 1976, Archives of The Church of Jesus Christ of Latter-day Saints, 14.
28. In Conference Report, Glasgow Scotland Area Conference 1976, 6.
29. *The Teachings of Spencer W. Kimball,* 556.
30. *Ensign,* Feb. 1983, 5.
31. In Conference Report, Oct. 1978, 66; or *Ensign,* Nov. 1978, 46.
32. "Therefore I Was Taught," *Ensign,* Jan. 1982, 4.
33. *The Teachings of Spencer W. Kimball,* 551.
34. *The Teachings of Spencer W. Kimball,* 551.
35. *New Era,* May 1981, 50.

List of Visuals

Index

A

Abraham, exemplified obedience born of faith, 141

Adam and Eve, exemplified obedience born of faith, 140

Adversity. *See also* Death; Tragedies
agency and, 14, 15
can be for our learning and good, 15–18

Agency
allows choice between sin and righteousness, 110
and adversity, 14, 15
blessings of the Atonement obtained through, 29
use of, in reaching up to God for guidance, 245–46

Atonement of Jesus Christ. *See also* Jesus Christ
gives hope now and for the eternity ahead, 31–32
makes possible our return to Heavenly Father, 6, 158
receiving the full blessings of, 29–30
saves us from the effects of the Fall and from personal sins, 26–28, 37

B

Bangerter, William Grant, on address given by Spencer W. Kimball, xxvii

C

Camel, fable of traveler and, 107

Chastity. *See* Law of chastity

Children. *See also* Families; Parents
love for, 212
safeguarding, against immoral influences, 185–86
teaching integrity to, 129–30
teaching love for Church leaders to, 255

Church leaders. *See also* Prophets
blessings of following, 255–56
parents to teach children to sustain and follow, 255
the Lord directs the Church through, 243–45, 251–52

Church of Jesus Christ
carries the obedient to exaltation, 5
emphasizes family life, 204
future growth of, 222–23, 262
Jesus's saving mission is message of, 26
restored through Joseph Smith, 227, 231, 232
sole repository of the gospel, 5
stand of, on morality, 180–81
the Lord directs, through Church leaders, 243–45, 251–52
welfare assistance from, 116, 119–20

273

Sarah, exemplified obedience
born of faith, 141

Satan. *See also* Evil influences
a real being intent on our
destruction, 103–5
attachment to worldly things
makes us vulnerable to,
147–48
methods used by, 104–5

Scott, Richard G., motivated to
lifelong scripture study by
Spencer W. Kimball, 60–61

Scriptures. *See also* Scripture
study
a rare possession, 61–62
and story of King Josiah, 62–63
discovering and rediscovering,
62
examples of integrity in, 131–33
examples of obedience in,
140–42
publication of new editions of,
xxxi

Scripture study. *See also*
Scriptures
and return of spirituality, 67
commitment to Lord strengthened by, 62–64
in families, 211
lessons of life learned through,
64–66
love for God increased through,
67
spiritual knowledge gained
through, 66

Self-reliance. *See also*
Preparedness
economic, 120–21
need for, 116–17

Service
blessings of, exceed worldly
rewards, 150–51
following the Savior's example
of, 81
God meets others' needs
through our acts of, 81–82
leads to the abundant life,
85–87
use of talents and abilities in,
82–84
youth need opportunities to
render, 84–85

Shadrach, Meshach, and
Abednego, integrity of, 132–33

Simplification of Church programs, xxxii

Smith, George Albert, xxiv

Smith, Joseph
First Vision of, 228–30
foreordained, 228
martyrdom of, 232–34
the Lord's instrument in restoring the gospel, 231–32

Spirit. *See* Holy Ghost

T

Temple work, xxx

Temptations
avoiding, by making right decisions early, 108–9
not yielding to even smallest,
106–8

Testimony
a personal revelation, 70–71, 72
and testimony meetings, 75–76
available to everyone, 71–72
manner of bearing, 76
obtaining and maintaining,
72–75